A Garland Series

OUTSTANDING DISSERTATIONS IN THE

FINE ARTS

The Education
of
Le Corbusier

Paul Venable Turner

Garland Publishing, Inc., New York & London

1977

Library of Congress Cataloging in Publication Data

Turner, Paul V
    The education of Le Corbusier.

    (Outstanding dissertations in the fine arts)
    Thesis--Harvard, 1971.
    Bibliography: p.
    1. Jeanneret-Gris, Charles Edouard, 1887-1965--
Knowledge and learning. 2. Architects--Education--
France. I. Title.
NA1053.J4T87   720'.92'4 [B]   76-23658
ISBN 0-8240-2732-9

THE EDUCATION OF LE CORBUSIER

A Study of the Development of

Le Corbusier's Thought, 1900-1920

A thesis presented

by

Paul Venable Turner

to

The Department of Fine Arts

in partial fulfillment of the requirements

for the degree of

Doctor of Philosophy

in the subject of

Fine Arts

Harvard University

Cambridge, Massachusetts

April 1971

PREFACE

In 1969-70 I examined the personal library of Le Corbusier (housed at the Fondation Le Corbusier in Paris), looking for clues to the architect's early intellectual development. I discovered more than expected, especially after I found I could date quite precisely Le Corbusier's acquisition of most of his books, and that large numbers of them, often annotated, remained from his youth. My study of Le Corbusier's pre-1920 library, and other early influences on his thinking, formed the basis of this dissertation, which I wrote in late 1970.

The work is published here as originally presented, except for the deletion of superfluous illustrations, the correction of typographical errors, and the revision of a couple of pages in Chapter I. Since I completed this study, significant further research on Le Corbusier's youth has been conducted by several scholars, and important new discoveries continue to be made. As a result, if I were fully rewriting the dissertation now, I would make some additions and changes; but I believe these would not alter the main substance and arguments of the work.

I thank my dissertation advisors, Professors Eduard F. Sekler, James S. Ackerman, and John P. Coolidge--and also Professor Peter Collins of McGill University, who read and criticized part of the work while it was being written. I am also grateful to Professor H. Allen Brooks of the University of Toronto, who at various stages has given me suggestions and helped me penetrate the mysteries of Le Corbusier.

Paul Venable Turner
Stanford University
August 1976

ERRATA

P 26, line 20, "rate" should be "rare."

P 38, line 7, should read "A Pise, par exemple, où . . ."

P 48, the indented quotation should have footnote number 47.

P 57, line 9, "Superman" should be "Uebermensch."

P 68, line 2, "Jeannert" should be "Jeanneret."

P 94, line 18, "recented" should be "recently."

P 131, line 2, "common" should be "commun."

P 135, line 18, "achieved" should be "conceived."

P 175, line 18, "under" should be "around."

P 177, line 7, "it is" should be "is it."

P 182, line 10, "inefficiency" should be "efficiency."

TABLE OF CONTENTS

Preface

Table of Contents

Introduction... 1

Chapter I: La Chaux-de-Fonds, 1900-1907.................. 4

Chapter II: Italy, Vienna and Paris, 1907-1909............ 30

Chapter III: Germany and the Orient, 1910-1911............. 70

Chapter IV: La Chaux-de-Fonds, 1912-1917.................. 105

Chapter V: Paris, 1917-1920............................. 136

Chapter VI: Le Corbusier's Synthesis..................... 169

Notes.. 196

Appendix A: Catalogue of Jeanneret's Library up to 1920.... 232

Appendix B: Chronology of Jeanneret's Reading up to 1920... 239

Appendix C: Jeanneret's Signatures in his Books............ 244

Selected Bibliography...................................... 257

List of Illustrations...................................... 260

Illustrations.. 264

INTRODUCTION

Until now, little has been known about the aesthetic theory
and attitudes to which Le Corbusier was exposed in his early years.
This is particularly unfortunate since theory was fundamental to
Le Corbusier's work, and since his writings and theoretical pronounce-
ments were so influential to the development of modern architecture.
Our lack of knowledge exists largely because Le Corbusier--or Charles-
Édouard Jeanneret[1]-- was not the product of an established school
with known principles and philosophy, but instead made the unusual
choice of educating himself. He acknowledged that Charles L'Eplattenier, his boyhood teacher at the Art School in La Chaux-de-Fonds
(in the French-speaking Jura region of Switzerland), was more of a
"master" to him than any other person; but even the ideas of L'Eplattenier are not very well known except through occasional remarks made
by Le Corbusier later in his career. And the problem is compounded
by Le Corbusier's own tendency to disclaim intellectual influence
and to encourage the view, like so many artists, that his ideas had
sprung full-blown from his creative genius.

One of the principal arguments of this study of Le Corbusier
will be that his attitude toward architecture was fundamentally
intellectual and "idealistic"--that is, that for him architecture
was above all an expression of ideas and transcendent principles,
rather than of those "rationalist" aspects which have been the

ostensible concern of most twentieth-century architects, such as

function, structural and material integrity, or economy.[2] To be

sure, these rationalist concerns were an important component of

Le Corbusier's thought (beginning with his contact with Auguste

Perret in 1908, as we shall see); and in fact a number of critics

have pointed out apparent contradictions in his thinking between

attitudes which could be called rationalist and those which could

be called idealist.[3] But this study will suggest that Le Corbusier

resolved, or synthesized, these two views of architecture in a highly

personal and original way, and that this synthesis can be seen as a

direct product of the different forces in his early training and

education.

In search of clues to the early development of Le Corbusier,

I examined the contents of his personal library, presently at the

Fondation Le Corbusier in Paris.[4] By various means I was able to

determine the approximate acquisition-dates of most of the books,

and thus to arrange them in chronological periods corresponding to

the important phases of his career.[5] This study will examine the

earliest of these periods: his teenage years in La Chaux-de-Fonds,

his years of traveling, his period back in La Chaux-de-Fonds during

the World War, and then his first years in Paris after 1917. These

are the periods which in effect constitute Le Corbusier's "educa-

tion;" for after about 1920 the major outlines of his thinking had

been shaped, and his attention turned primarily to creation and

propaganda.

My examination of Le Corbusier's library has produced a number of "discoveries," but probably the most fundamental of these is the extent to which books and ideas were important to him. This must be emphasized here because of the fact that Le Corbusier himself sometimes pretended that reading had never been very significant to him; for example, he once reportedly boasted that the only books which ever influenced him were the Bible and the works of Cervantes and Rabelais.[6] In reality, as we shall see, his library reveals that books were extraordinarily influential to the development of his thought--especially, as we would expect, during his early years which we shall be examining here. Furthermore, his library shows that throughout his life Le Corbusier read, in a diverse variety of fields, with a deadly serious attitude toward the search for knowledge--often filling his books with extensive annotations revealing the diligence and sincerity with which he pursued this search.

On the one hand, Le Corbusier professed a disdain for academic learning and pictured himself as the Artist who knows by instinct rather than education. Yet on the other hand, the evidence in his library reveals that he possessed an uncommon reverence--even awe-- for books and for the absolute "truth" which he believed they must contain. Perhaps this is typical of the autodidact. In any case, we shall see that it is only one manifestation of Le Corbusier's underlying search for absolutes and universal principles in every aspect of his creative thought.

CHAPTER I

LA CHAUX-DE-FONDS, 1900-1907

Charles-Édouard Jeanneret's early years were spent in the relatively secure, middle-class, and provincial atmosphere of his native
La Chaux-de-Fonds, in the mountainous Swiss Jura close to the French
border.[1] It was there that he received the only formal schooling he
ever was to have--first in the public grade-school, and then in the
civic Art School where in 1900, at the age of thirteen, he was appren-
ticed to learn the traditional local craft of watch-case engraving
which was his father's trade too.[2] Le Corbusier's library reveals that
during his teenage years Jeanneret also began to read seriously, and
that in fact some of this reading was extremely important in laying
the foundations of his later development. This chapter will examine
these early years, up until 1907 when Jeanneret left home to begin his
first series of travels--and will concentrate in particular on a book
which clearly had a great impact on him: Henry Provensal's L'art de
demain, published in 1904.

But before turning to Jeanneret's reading, his early training
in La Chaux-de-Fonds can be outlined briefly here. His drawing-
teacher L'Eplattenier dominates this period, especially after he
became director of the Art School in 1903.[3] As mentioned above,
Jeanneret had been learning the art of watch-case engraving; but

L'Eplattenier believed this was a dying trade, and as part of an attempt to broaden the scope of the Art School, seems to have encouraged the boy to set his sights higher. For a while Jeanneret wanted to be a painter, but then L'Eplattenier turned him toward architecture, as part of the "Cours supérieur" he founded in 1906, as a plan to train a whole community of craftsmen embracing all the arts, apparently on the pattern of Victor Prouvé's school in Nancy.[4]

The formal expression taken by these activities at the Art School was a combination of art nouveau and other contemporary decorative styles, judging from Jeanneret's surviving drawings of that period, and from his skilfully engraved watch case which was exhibited at the Turin decorative arts exposition in 1902.[5] This watch case (Fig. 1) is distinguished by a peculiar juxtaposition of two designs-- one an abstract design of overlapping rectangles, the other a curvilinear design of flowers and a bumble-bee--which reveal two different sources, one French and the other Germanic. The flower-and-bee design must have been inspired by a series of art nouveau watch cases designed by René Lalique (Fig. 2), also with flower and insect motifs, which had been published in 1901 in a periodical to which the Art School subscribed.[6] Le Corbusier later recalled that Lalique, Gallé, and Guimard were among his favorite designers in these early years, and admitted his admiration for the French art nouveau.[7] But the other, abstract part of Jeanneret's watch case reflects a more sober style in Germany and Austria (whose decorative arts were also represented in periodicals in the Art School), in which surfaces were treated as thin overlapping planes (Fig. 3)[8]--and may have been inspired even more directly by Hermann Obrist's strikingly cubic piece of sculpture (Fig. 4) which was illustrated in Die Kunst in 1900.[9]

In retrospect, the rectilinear "Germanic" style seems much more prophetic of Jeanneret's later development. Yet L'Eplattenier was less interested in teaching his students "styles" than an underlying attitude toward nature and art. As Le Corbusier later recalled:

> Mon maître avait dit: 'Seule la nature est inspiratrice, est vraie, et peut être le support de l'oeuvre humaine. Mais ne faites pas la nature à la manière des paysagistes qui n'en montrent que l'aspect. Scrutez-en la cause, la forme, le développement vital et faites-en la synthèse en créant des ornements.' Il avait une conception élevée de l'ornement qu'il voulait comme un microcosme.[10]

On one level, this was a call for understanding the organic structure of natural forms. But we shall see that there was probably a deeper meaning as well: a Platonic conviction that one must penetrate beneath the superficial appearance of nature and discover the ideal, universal reality. Each form thus idealized by the artist would become a "microcosm" of the divine Idea.

A more specific goal of L'Eplattenier's teaching was to lay the groundwork, with his "Cours supérieur," for a regional Jura art style to be inspired partly by local plant forms--related to a notion of his that all great periods of art were based on local forms (such as the lotus in Egypt and the acanthus in Greece.)[11] This attempt at Jura regionalism is reflected in the first house that Jeanneret designed, in about 1906 (Fig. 5)--with its rough stone lower walls, its steep roofs with deep overhanging eaves supported by wooden brackets, and its stucco upper surfaces painted with decorative motifs based on the pine-tree.[12]

But more significant for Jeanneret's development than this regionalist spirit was L'Eplattenier's introduction to him of the world of books and ideas:

> Charles-Édouard Jeanneret entendit pour la première fois parler de l'existence de problèmes d'art. . . Par L'Eplattenier, qui avait installé une bibliothèque dans la salle de dessin, [Jeanneret] eut la révélation des chefs-d'oeuvre du passé et prit le goût de chercher à les comprendre.[13]

Of these books in L'Eplattenier's drawing-class, Le Corbusier later recalled Eugène Grasset's Méthode de composition ornementale, Owen Jones' Grammar of Ornament, and several of John Ruskin's works. In 1925, describing influences on his youth, Le Corbusier remembered Grasset as "le géomètre et l'algébriste des fleurs," adding that because of him it was "de rigueur" to fill all designs with flowers.[14] At the same time, Le Corbusier recalled Jones' Grammar of Ornament as a more significant influence, because of the abstraction and "purity" of its designs:

> L'un après l'autre défilaient les ornements purs que l'homme a créés entièrement dans sa tête. . . Si la nature était omniprésente, l'homme y était tout entier avec ses facultés de cristallisation, avec sa formation géométrique. . . Avec ce livre, nous sentîmes que le problème se posait: L'homme crée une oeuvre qui l'émeut.[15]

Indeed, many of the more abstract plates in the Grammar of Ornament are very similar to designs done by Jeanneret in L'Eplattenier's class (Figs. 6-8). But above all Le Corbusier praised Ruskin. In the 1940s he recalled that he and L'Eplattenier "admiraient passionément Ruskin," and mentioned a passage from the Lectures on Architecture and Painting prompting the citizens of Edinburgh to embellish their city.[16] Le Corbusier's fullest reference to Ruskin, however, is found in L'art décoratif d'aujourd'hui (1925), and reveals that it was Ruskin's anti-materialism that most impressed L'Eplattenier and his students:

> Notre enfance fut exhortée par Ruskin. Apôtre touffu,
> complexe, contradictoire, paradoxal. Les temps étaient
> insupportables. . . c'était d'un bourgeoisisme écrasant,
> bête, noyé dans le matérialisme, enguirlandé dans le décor
> idiot et tout mécanique, décor fabriqué par la machine qui
> [produisait] le carton-pâte et les rinceaux en fonte de fer.
> C'est de spiritualité que parla Ruskin. Dans ses Sept
> Lampes de l'Architecture, brillaient la Lampe de Sacrifice,
> la Lampe de Verité, la Lampe d'Humilité.
>   A cette masse toute bouffie des saturations premières
> d'un machinisme naissante, il leur faisait la démonstration
> de l'honnêteté. . .[17]

The only work of Ruskin's that I found in Le Corbusier's library

was Mornings in Florence (see below). But the library contains other

authors who emphasized the spirituality of art as strongly as Ruskin,

and who can be shown to have influenced the young Jeanneret greatly--

despite the fact that Le Corbusier never mentioned them in his writings.

Jeanneret's Early Reading

There are about a dozen books in Le Corbusier's library

that date from this period in La Chaux-de-Fonds before 1908. Only

three of them are actually inscribed with the year Jeanneret

acquired them: Eugène Müntz, Raphaël, sa vie, son oeuvre et son

temps (Paris, 1900; inscribed 1902); Maxime Collignon, Mythologie

figurée de la Grèce (Paris, n.d., inscribed 1903); and Édouard Schuré,

Les grands initiés (Paris, 1908; inscribed 1907).[18] Four more can

be dated because they contain Jeanneret's signature of this period:

H. Knackfuss, Michelangelo (Leipzig, 1903); Henry Provensal, L'art

de demain (Paris, 1904); John Ruskin, Les matins à Florence (Paris,

1906); and Hippolyte Taine, Voyage en Italie (Paris, 1907).[19] And

several others contain clues of one sort or another linking them to

these early years.[20] Luckily, the books that are of most interest

to this study are among those whose acquisition-dates can be pinpointed most precisely.

The earliest of these datable books contain little or no art
theory per se; but they do suggest that Jeanneret's early training
was by no means divorced from the climate of academic French art
instruction. For example, Eugène Müntz's Raphaël was given to the
boy by his parents in 1902.[21] The author, who was librarian of the
École des Beaux-Arts, expresses the typical academic reverence for
the Italian High Renaissance, for example in stating that Bramante and
Raphael are "the greatest of modern architects and . . . the greatest
of modern painters."[22] And the next year, when Jeanneret was sixteen,
a prize-book was given to him by the Art School--Maxime Collignon's
Mythologie figurée de la Grèce[23]--which was part of a teaching series
published by the École des Beaux-Arts, and like Müntz's book expresses
academic assumptions without ever specifically discussing theory. It
is a kind of text-book of Greek mythology for art students, describing
the standard ways each god was represented in antiquity, and illustrated by line-drawings. Inherent is the concept of classical "norms,"
standard ways of designing which are to be assimilated by the student
and then applied to new problems. Jeanneret seems to have sensed this
message, for he did a sketch (left in the pages of the book), which
transformed a Greek coin illustrated in the work, into a decorative
device picturing a pine-tree (Figs. 9-10), that ubiquitous Jura motif
of these years--thus showing his interest in Classical formats, and a
feeling that the new Jura regionalism could be linked to a larger

tradition. Furthermore, years later Le Corbusier returned to this book, reread part of it, and made some annotations; he apparently was trying to identify the expressive meaning of certain colors, and went back to this childhood text to see how they had been used in antiquity.[24] This is typical. Many of Jeanneret's early books show similar evidence that he later returned to them in search of specific information--a good indication of Le Corbusier's serious attitude toward books and ideas.

L'Art de Demain

The most intriguing book dating from this early period in Le Corbusier's library is Henry Provensal's L'art de demain (Paris, Perrin, 1904.) It contains a La Chaux-de-Fonds bookstore label; Jeanneret's signatures in it are pre-1907; and there are markings by him in the text typical of this early period.[25] Unlike the books mentioned above, this is a theoretical work; indeed it is almost thoroughly devoted to art theory and general philosophical questions. It may well have been the first such book Jeanneret read, and in any case he seems to have been greatly impressed by its ideas, some of which reappear later almost unchanged in the architectural theory of Le Corbusier. Furthermore, as we shall see later, this book may have been suggested to Jeanneret by L'Eplattenier and have reflected some of his own ideas. For all these reasons, and also because the book itself is not well known, its contents will be examined in some detail here.

L'art de demain, which received little notice when it was published and had only one edition, was written by a Paris architect who
had studied under Julien Guadet at the École des Beaux-Arts.[26] It is
an odd book in several ways, and although a few of Guadet's notions
appear in it here and there, most of the ideas seem to have been culled
by Provensal from wide-ranging reading in philosophy, science, and
religion, and then amalgamated by him into a theory of art and life
all his own. In general Provensal's ideas can be characterized as
idealistic, and specifically as being in the nineteenth-century German
philosophical tradition of Schelling and Hegel. Provensal affirms his
belief in spiritual reality, laments the rise of Positivism and Materialism in modern times, and calls on Man to achieve--through art
primarily--an harmonious "uniting" of the spiritual and material
aspects of his nature. The sub-title of the book, Vers l'harmonie
intégrale, refers to this uniting theme, and like many other phrases
in the book seems to foreshadow terminology which was to become standard in Le Corbusier's own writings.

The first part of the book deals with the author's general
philosophy, the second with its implications for the arts (followed
by a rather tedious outline of the history of art as Spirit, which
will be neglected here.) The book opens with an exposition of the
miserable state which the arts have been in for a century--especially
architecture, "l'art primordial," which has been debasing itself by
simply copying the past (p. 1). The true artist's responsibility is
a much nobler one: "Il lui faut accorder la vérité d'hier à celle

de demain et créer de ce fait la chaine invisible qui, unissant à son moi l'infini de l'univers, résout l'équation de l'absolu" (p. 3).

The abstruse language is typical of Provensal. But his point here--that the artist's role is to connect Man with the eternal principles of the "Absolute"--is an essential theme of the book. It is also a theme which was to appear throughout Le Corbusier's writings, sometimes obscurely, sometimes as clearly as when he speaks of art as arousing a "Trace d'absolu indéfinissable préexistant au fond de notre être."[27] Provensal's "absolu" reveals itself in art through divine "laws," which are described as those of unity, number, and harmony ("des lois éternelles d'unité, de nombre et d'harmonie")--all concepts which will play vital roles in the thought of Le Corbusier. All great periods of art obey and express these laws, though never in the same form, for they are subject ultimately to the artist's creative interpretation--"la spontanéité du génie créateur" (p. 6). Provensal stresses that this process is related to both of Man's "deux vies parallèles"--the spiritual and the material. Spirit is the higher of the two; but Man's goal should be to resolve them into an harmonious synthesis:

> Après avoir étudié l'homme dans ses deux principes harmonieusement unis, 'l'esprit et la matière'; après avoir analysé le processus de vie idéale se résolvant au point central de ces deux natures jusqu'ici séparées, l'intérêt de cette étude consistera donc à ramener en un faisceau unique ces forces harmoniques disséminées.[28]

Thanks to Science, Man's comprehension of the material world is greatly increasing; similarly, art must now raise Man "jusqu'à l'idée." The resulting revolutionary step upwards, which Provensal supports with quotations from Spencer, will demand completely new artistic

forms, more "general" and "universal" than those of the present. As

the most abstract of the arts, architecture will thus lead the way:

> . . . la peinture et la sculpture [must be reoriented] vers
> une conception plus abstraite et ce sera vers l'architecture,
> art dominant par excellence, que viendront converger toutes
> les forces intellectuelles des deux arts majeures, afin de
> réaliser, le plus exactement et le plus transcendantalement
> possible, les formes fuyantes de l'absolu (pp. 15-16).

Next, a chapter entitled "L'unité humaine" investigates separ-

ately the two aspects "matière" and "esprit." In the process Provensal

refers to a large number of scientists and philosophers, describing

specific theories of all sorts which he then relates to his theme of

spirit-matter dualism and its ultimate resolution. One of these theo-

ries, large sections of which were bracketed by Jeanneret, relates

creativity to genetics, maintaining that the vast majority of men are

bound to their animal instincts and are thus incapable of original

thinking.[29] Only a very few men even possess the potential for inven-

tion, and they are thus like a race apart, qualitatively superior to

the rest of mankind. These men embody the future, for only through

them is progress possible:

> La majorité signifie le passé, la minorité signifie l'avenir,
> si son originalité fait ses preuves.--La foule est toujours
> conservatrice parce qu'elle agit en vertu d'instincts gén-
> ériques héréditaires, non en vertu de nouveaux procédés de
> pensée individuels . . . (p. 87).

A distinction is made between a "talented" person, who merely

accomplishes traditional activities better than the majority, and a

"genius," who imagines totally new activities or carries out known

activities in a new and original way. A parallel distinction is made

between "emotion," of which all men are capable, and "cogitation,"
which is "le travail d'idéation nette et claire, cette activité du
centre suprême de la conscience, accompli par les individus plus
parfaitement outillés qui possèdent la faculté de former de nouvelles
combinaisons" (p. 88).

The implications of all this are clear. The truly great artist
will reveal himself by, first, his capacity for completely original
invention, and second, his intellectual temperament, which will be
"sharp and clear" rather than emotional. Finally, Provensal closes
this section of the book with advice to the aspiring artist who con-
siders himself one of these gifted few ("l'artiste qui se sent disposé
à créer des activités nouvelles"). First he should seek out an "intellectual minority, a center of action and combat;" then he should
reveal himself to this elite group by the "verbe" which expresses his
own inner self;[30] then he must begin to "formulate in every aspect of
his work, a new personality to replace his former activities." This
naturally reminds us of Jeanneret in Paris after 1917, when he was to
associate himself with other avant-garde figures like Amedée Ozenfant
and Paul Dermée, begin expressing his ideas in L'Esprit Nouveau, and,
as if to consummate his new personality, even change his name.

The role which Provensal envisages for his elite community of
artists is suggested in the last passage of this section which
Jeanneret marked:

> Ce sera donc dans la masse évoluée que l'artiste devra semer
> le bon grain, afin que cette élite intellectuelle, toute
> imprégnée de la haute signification de la vérité, reportant
> cette activité sur la collectivité, la fasse admettre et
> respecter (p. 89).

Jeanneret's interest in these elitist passages is not altogether surprising. Other youthful books of his contain similar references which he also marked--such as Schuré's Grands initiés (see below), and Nietzsche's Zarathustra, which he was to read in Paris in 1909. But L'art de demain seems to be the first; and furthermore, Provensal's elite is to be entrusted with an extraordinarily high purpose; the discovery of spiritual truth, and its revelation to mankind. The magnificence of this vocation could hardly have failed to stir the young artist.

Following this is a chapter in which Provensal presents more theories of a general sort, and further reveals his desire to link art and science, and to bring about a new age in which they will unite to "conquérir une nouvelle harmonie" (p. 99). In the past, the artist's sentiment destroyed reason, just as the scientist's reason destroyed sentiment. Now the two must fuse together into one united activity. There are a number of inconsistencies about this in Provensal's thought (which reveal for example an ambiguity about whether sentiment does actually have a role to play in this new art), but his overall attitude is clear: the artist is an equal of the scientist, and indeed his activity is a fully scientific one, the discovery and application of universal laws: "Et l'artiste, à l'égal du scientiste, résoud une harmonie, chaque fois qu'il crée, car créer n'est-ce pas: DÉGAGER DU MONDE, UNE LOI CO-EXISTANTE ET LUI DONNER L'ESSOR" (p. 104).

Provensal's rather mediaeval concept of "science"--as based on
a priori reasoning rather than empirical method--is evident throughout this book, and is an attitude which also was to be displayed by
Le Corbusier in his own writings, as Reyner Banham has pointed out.[31]
Furthermore, similar non-empirical notions of science appear elsewhere in the early reading of Jeanneret, as will be mentioned later.

According to Provensal, the new utopian age of science-art is
imminent. He predicts a long period of peace, in which the new
leisure time due to prosperity will be devoted to the arts. The
artist will thus become a great directing figure, "le chef éminent,"
who will oversee the elevation of Man's soul "vers la vie toute
harmonieuse" (p. 101). At the same time, Provensal has been describing two ways of thinking: the "analytic," which concerns "the individual and the specific;" and the "synthetic," concerned with "the
collectivity and the general" (p. 91). The great periods of the past
were characterized by "synthetic" thinking--with temples and cathedrals
rising as expressions of the collective spirit. But now individualism
reigns, making great monuments impossible. The imminent new art will
again be a collective expression:

> Les âmes ne s'immolent plus volontiers à un idéal collectif
> et c'est pourtant ce vers quoi nous tendons de tout l'effort
> de notre volonté. L'art de l'avenir sera, comme aux différ-
> entes stages de l'humanité, le résumé splendide de l'idée
> morale collective, la conscience religieuse des peuples
> (p. 109).

These ideas and phrases are to reappear in Le Corbusier's early
writings; but it is interesting to observe how he was to modify them,

to apply to the new Machine Age and to the pride which it was to engender in the masses:

> Cette fierté collective remplace l'antique esprit de l'artisan en l'élevant à des idées plus générales. Cette transformation nous paraît un progrès; elle est l'un des facteurs importants de la vie moderne. L'évolution actuelle du travail conduit par l'utilé à la synthèse et à l'ordre.[32]

It is worth simply mentioning here that in the thinking of both Le Corbusier and Provensal, there is an apparent contradiction between this ideal of collective, impersonal endeavor, expressing a common mass spirit, and the elitist concept of the individual, inspired artist, whose duty, as we saw in the case of Provensal, is to reveal his wisdom to the mass of humanity and "see that it is admitted and respected." These two attitudes are to be found in various forms throughout Le Corbusier's writings, and to remain essentially as unresolved as they are in Provensal.

Next comes a chapter in which Provensal focuses specifically on aesthetic theories, elaborating on many of the ideas discussed earlier, and referring to the aesthetic systems of philosophers from Plato to Kant, Fichte, Schiller, Schelling, and especially Hegel, as we might have guessed. He elaborates on the notion of "beauté idéal," that is, beauty which expresses mind and spirit rather than simply appealing to the physical senses--the same distinction which Jeanneret and Ozenfant were to make in 1918, between Cubism as merely an art of "sensation," and the new Purism as an art of the "intellect."[33] Provensal laments the contemporary lack of understanding of this kind of "ideal beauty," and Jeanneret bracketed a long passage here, of which this is part:

Il serait indispensable de proclamer bien haut cette esthétique [that is, ideal beauty]; car beaucoup d'artistes et
même de maîtres ne savent pas analyser le comment et encore
moins le pourquoi; il leur est donc impossible de synthétiser,
et le plus clair de leurs arguments se trouvent au bout de
leurs crayons ou de leurs pinceaux.
   Un admirable instinct peut aider le génie créateur, mais
de moins en moins cet instinct suffira l'accomplissement des
grandes oeuvres. C'est que la science étend sur tout, sa
grande aile. C'est à son ombre que devra s'amplifier la conscience de l'artiste. La science a commencé par affaiblir le
sentiment, elle finira par le fortifier (pp. 143-144).

Two ideas are of interest here: that mere instinct will no

longer suffice for the artist (an idea to which Provensal will re-

turn); and that not even the "masters" today understand ideal beauty

--a remark which sounds like Le Corbusier's own later attacks on the

Establishment art community, and which indeed may have contributed

to Jeanneret's decision to avoid architectural schools altogether.

Provensal then addresses himself to the definition of beauty, and

naturally his formulations are all idealistic. Beauty reveals the

underlying universal principles in nature. "Ce qui est vraiment

beau . . . est éternal et général." And the artist must seek out

nature's "formes essentielles." Provensal quotes from the major

idealistic philosophers; and the definitions attributed to Plato

and Plotinus, which Jeanneret bracketed, are typical: "Le beau,

c'est la splendeur du vrai, a dit Platon.--C'est la qualité de

l'idée se reproduisant sous une forme symbolique (Plotin.)"[34]

   Finally, Provensal turns to the individual arts, and how they

are to express the new aesthetic. By far the longest section is on

architecture, and as we would expect, Provensal feels architecture must express the "Idea" underlying reality, and that its forms should

be universal and general. Indeed, architecture is the most abstract

of the arts (along with music) and thus is particularly close to the

ideal source:

> Avec la musique, l'architecture partage la haute mission de
> résoudre des abstractions. En tant que manifestation de
> l'idée, besoin moral ou idéal d'un peuple, elle n'est plus
> à l'échelle du corps humain, lieu passager où l'individu
> abrite son existence, mais bien à l'échelle de sa pensée,
> lieu où la collectivité enclôt son âme (p. 159).

This distinction between a mundane "échelle du corps humain" and

an ideal "échelle de sa pensée" reminds us of Le Corbusier's life-long

call for "l'échelle humaine" in architecture. And indeed, Le Cor-

busier's use of this phrase (when applied to some of his gargantuan

urbanistic forms, for example) is more comprehensible when seen, as

in the idealistic context of Provensal, as referring to the scale of

Man's spirit and mind more than to the scale of his body.

But Provensal's primary concern in this chapter is for the actual

form which the new architecture is to take; and surprisingly, the term

he continually uses is "cubic." This is a very early date for the use

of this term, in a theoretical context[35]--but in any case it must have

had special appeal for Jeanneret, whose attraction to cubic decorative

forms has been pointed out already. For Provensal, "cubic" forms are

the most perfect and universal, and thus the most expressive of ideal

reality. The opening sentence of this chapter, underlined for

emphasis, defines architecture as ". . . l'expression cubique harmoni-

euse de la pensée" (p. 158). Despite the fact that architecture is

essentially abstact and does not copy nature, Provensal says that
"nature has given architecture invariable forms, as a point of departure, from which it can draw the first elements of its conceptions."
And as the principal example of these natural sources of inspiration,
he suggests mineral crystals:

> Le règne minéral nous offre dans ses cristallisations, des
> exemples nombreux et invariables de volumes initiaux aux-
> quels l'architecture peut emprunter des renseignements.
> C'est donc dans la combinaison rationnelle de ces volumes,
> que s'effectuera toute l'aspiration de l'art, et c'est bien
> ce que la nature veut nous donner comme point de départ.
> En outre, les formations géologiques peuvent inciter
> l'artiste à des adaptations, à des modèles architectoniques
> capables d'être inscrits au sein de l'espace.[36]

We know that at about this time Jeanneret himself was sketching
rock formations in a very cubistic, crystalline manner (Fig. 11); and
as we saw, his fascination for geometric designs went back at least
to 1902 and his engraved watch case. The effect of Provensal can only
have been to strengthen this existing tendency, by giving it an ideo-
logical foundation, and even more important by suggesting its appli-
cability to architecture. The full implications of this suggestion
may not have been felt by Jeanneret immediately; for the Fallet House
which he designed in 1906, with its spirit of Jura regionalism, shows
no evidence of Provensal's "cubism"--except for one tentative detail,
a small supporting bracket composed of cubic volumes (Fig. 12), which
again harks back to Obrist's piece of sculpture. But Provensal's
impact had been made. Even his specific association of architecture
with mineral crystallizations is an idea which we find Jeanneret
himself expressing only a few years later. For in 1913, in a brief

article by his friend William Ritter on contemporary German architecture, Jeanneret is quoted as saying:

> Rien, depuis des ans que j'étudie ce peuple [that is, the
> Germans] dans ses oeuvres, ne m'a semblé autre que les
> cristaux durs et brutaux des phénomènes géologiques; rien
> n'a pris encore dans l'assemblage et la structure des
> pierres, la forme en racines, tige, feuilles et tête d'un
> épi de blé ou d'une fleur de lin bleue. C'est le triomphe
> de l'organisme obscur avec la cristallisation géométrique
> infrangible. Quelle dureté, quelle brutalité, quelle
> unité, quelle inexorabilité.[37]

Of the many interesting aspects of this hitherto unnoticed quo-
tation--not the least of which is its superabundant imagery--it could
be noted here that Jeanneret's characterization of crystalline architecture as possessing "unité," Provensal's key term, suggests that he
had assimilated not only Provensal's _formal_ suggestions, but also the
thinking that underlay it--the idea that cubic, crystalline forms
achieve that unity of matter and spirit which is the highest aim of
all art. Provensal proceeds to give some more specific idea of how
this new "cubic" architecture is to look. It is to rely on the composition of volumes, with its visual effects produced not by decoration or detail, but simply by the judicious play of volume and void,
light and shadow: "Les oppositions d'ombre et de lumière, de plein
et de vide, les conclusions cubiques de ses trois dimensions, con-
stituent un des plus beaux drames plastiques du monde" (p. 159).

This naturally reminds us of Le Corbusier's later definition of
architecture as "le jeu savant, correct et magnifique des volumes
assemblés sous la lumière,"[38] or as he also phrased it, "des jeux
architecturaux de pleins et de vides."[39] And indeed, the closing

chapter of L'art de demain contains several restatements of this idea
which are surprisingly similar to Le Corbusier's, for example when
Provensal says that "l'édifice résume tout le drame plastique en une
intensité colorée de pleins et de vides, de jeux d'ombres et de
lumières," or that the artist "trouvera les éléments de réalisation
de la matière où le drame plastique se cristallisera sous l'activité
bienfaisante de la lumière. . ."[40]

It is not inconceivable that such phrases, read by the young
Jeanneret in 1905 or 1906, lodged themselves at some level of his
mind and were later extracted and rearranged. But more significant
than the wording is the conviction underlying it--that architecture
is first of all an abstract, sculptural activity, which ought to
employ primary volumes because these are purer and more Ideal. Tony
Garnier's important designs of this period, while superficially re-
sembling Provensal's formal suggestions in some ways, seem to be
unrelated to any such idealistic aesthetic system; but the architecture of Le Corbusier, who turns out to have been immersed in these
philosophical questions, must be understood in relation to them.

Another important aspect in L'art de demain is more of an
attitude than a doctrine. It is the suggestion, throughout the book,
of imminent discovery, progress, and revelation, the idea that whereas
the cultural situation is wretched now, things are about to change, a
new harmony is about to be established, and new artistic giants are
about to reveal themselves and assume their rightful roles. This
Messianic faith could not have failed to arouse the excitement of the

young Jeanneret on the threshold of his studies. Typical of this
attitude is the idea that new architectural "laws," presently still
undiscovered, will soon be revealed. When the formal play of volumes
which constitutes architecture is determined according to "certain
rapports," the spiritual Idea is allowed to manifest itself; but these
"rapports" have not yet been precisely formulated:

> Ces rapports . . . sont impossibles à définir pour l'instant,
> du moins la mathématique n'a pas encore pu nous en tracer la
> loi, mais il est parfaitement possible de supposer que bien-
> tôt des lois harmoniques viendront subjuguer le concept et
> affirmer la résolution de ces rapports (p. 159).

The challenge could not have been more clear: to discover and
define these harmonic "rapports" so that the architect would no longer
need to rely totally on his intuitive sense. This in fact is precisely what Le Corbusier spent a good deal of energy, throughout his
career, attempting to accomplish--first through his "tracés régulateurs," and then in the more complex "Modulor" system. In fact, his
earliest definition of the "tracés régulateurs," in 1921, is amazingly
close to the spirit of Provensal's challenge: "Un tracé régulateur
est une assurance contre l'arbitraire: c'est l'opération de vérifi-
cation . . . Le tracé régulateur est une satisfaction d'ordre spirituel
qui conduit à la recherche de rapports ingénieux et de rapports harmonieux."[41]

Throughout his life, Le Corbusier was to search for universal
formal principles which he felt could bring perfect order into architectural form. His firm belief that these principles are indeed
universal and absolute is revealed for example by the fact that he

went to great trouble, in his later years, really seriously attempting
to prove that certain buildings of the past conformed, in minutest
detail, to the specific dimensions laid down in his "Modulor" system.[42]
The idealistic assumption that there exist perfect formal principles
or Ideas, which can ultimately be discovered and embodied by the artist,
was probably the most fundamental influence of Provensal on Jeanneret.
All of the more specific influences--such as the preference for "cubic"
forms and the definition of architecture as a play of volumes under
light--are corollaries, in Provensal's aesthetic, of this idealistic
assumption.

Les grands initiés

Why did Jeanneret read Provensal's book in the first place? The
possibility that it was suggested to him by L'Eplattenier is plausible
in light of the fact that a similar work in Le Corbusier's library,
Edouard Schuré's Les grands initiés, was actually inscribed to Jeanneret
by L'Eplattenier, apparently given as a kind of farewell gift in 1907
(Fig. 13).[43] Despite the fact that Jeanneret probably did not read this
book until he was settled in Paris the next year, its ideas can be outlined briefly here since they must have reflected, to at least some
degree, the views of L'Eplattenier himself.

Sub-titled Esquisse de l'histoire secrète des religions, this
work appears to derive from German Idealism as much as did L'art de
demain, with which it has much in common.[44] But Schuré's hero, rather
than being the artist, is the mystical prophet, appearing throughout

history in different guises but always bearing the same esoteric

truths. Eight of the greatest of these prophets are examined in turn:

Rama, Krishna, Hermes, Moses, Orpheus, Pythagoras, Plato, and Jesus.

Schuré's main theme, like Provensal's, is the need for the spiritual

revival of modern civilization and the rejection of the prevailing

Materialism, which Schuré blames on the "positivisme" of Auguste

Comte and Herbert Spencer (p. xi). In philosophical terms, Schuré

differs somewhat from Provensal in his attitude toward material

reality; whereas Provensal tended to grant validity to both spirit

and matter and emphasized their ideal unity, Schuré views matter

more strictly Platonically as merely an inferior reflection of

spirit:

> On peut formuler comme il suit les principes essentiels de
> la doctrine ésotérique:--L'esprit est la seule réalité.
> La matière n'est que son expression inférieure, changeante,
> éphémère, son dynamisme dans l'espace et le temps (p. xx).

Jeanneret was not uninterested in these metaphysical issues. In

one of his few annotations in Schuré's book, he associates this spirit-

matter dualism with religious doctrines with which he was already

familiar; next to a passage describing the mystical journey of one's

soul toward goodness or evil, Jeanneret wrote "Évangile: le péché

contre l"Esprit."[45] Not much is known about Jeanneret's early reli-

gious training, except that it was Protestant. But this annotation

is thoroughly consistent with the Calvinist tradition in this part of

Switzerland--with its emphasis on the Gospels ("Évangile") as the

source of religious doctrine; and its opposition of two primal forces,

Man's innate sinfulness on the one hand, and God's grace (granted by the Holy Spirit) on the other. The fact that Jeanneret thought to make this comparison with Schuré's mysticism suggests that his religious training had not been superficial, and that it influenced the way he interpreted new ideas. We know that a devoutly religious maiden aunt lived in the Jeanneret household when Charles-Édouard and his brother were boys;[46] and also that there was a Jeanneret family legend that their ancestors had belonged to the heretical mystical sect in Southern France known as Catharism[47]--a sect which Le Corbusier's library reveals him to have been extremely interested in, especially in his later years.[48] So Jeanneret's "Évangile" annotation undoubtedly represents a familiarity with religious ideas going back to his earliest training at home. The idealism of both Provensal and Schuré would thus have appeared quite normal and proper to him, and we can better understand his attraction to their philosophies.

Several specific aspects of Les grands initiés can be mentioned here. One is Schuré's emphasis on an elite--even stronger than in Provensal's book, since it is naturally basic to the notion of esoteric doctrines and "initiates." Schuré claims that throughout history certain rate men endowed with extraordinary abilities have been able to penetrate the most profound spiritual mysteries, enter the realm of the Initiated, and as a result acquire "une force presque illimitée, une magie rayonnante et créatrice."[49] Of all the great Initiates of the past, according to Schuré, the one most relevant to modern Man was Pythagoras, whose "esprit scientifique" was closest to "l'esprit

moderne" (p. 431). Like Provensal, Schuré means "scientifique" not
to refer to empirical activity, but to quite the opposite: abstract,
a priori thought, and in the specific case of Pythagoras, mystical
numerology. Jeanneret seems to have been particularly interested in
the chapter on Pythagoras, and all of his markings and annotations
are found in it. Schuré's descriptions of Pythagorean numerology
often call to mind Le Corbusier's "Modulor" system, for example when
Schuré describes it as a system unfolding mathematically from simple
divine numbers:

> Pythagore poursuivait beaucoup plus loin l'enseignement des
> nombres. En chacun d'eux il définissait un principe, une
> loi, une force active de l'univers. Mais il disait que les
> principes essentiels sont contenus dans les quatre premiers
> nombres, puisqu'en les additionnant ou en les multipliant
> on trouve tous les autres.[50]

Another interesting aspect is the emphasis Schuré places on the
youthful voyages of Pythagoras, his years spent traveling to all the
ancient centers of learning in search of the knowledge which would
allow him to become one of the Initiated (pp. 326-365). When he was
given this book in 1907, Jeanneret was embarking on his own voyage
of discovery. Was L'Eplattenier perhaps thinking of this parallel
when he gave him the book? In any case, Jeanneret himself thought
of his travels in very much the same spirit as that of Schuré--as
an heroic search for knowledge, and specifically for abstract, universal knowledge. Le Corbusier later recalled this youthful search
for "Truth," as well as the inevitable periods of despair which
accompany such quests:

Recherche de la vérité dans les Bibliothèques. Les livres.
Les livres sont innombrables; où est le commencement? Ces
heures de bibliothèques ou l'on poursuit dans les livres,
la vérité! Et l'on tombe tout à coup dans un trou. Il fait
nuit, on ne comprend plus rien.[51]

This remarkable dedication to the discovery of abstract know-

ledge will be equally apparent in annotations made by Jeanneret in

Paris the next year--such as his inscription in one book that he was

buying it "pour apprendre, car sachant, je pourrai alors créer."[52]

This reveals the extent to which he had absorbed the idealism of Pro-

vensal and Schuré. Architecture for him was not to be the mastery of

technical skills or the solving of specific problems, but simply the

knowledge of "la vérité" which would then allow him to "create."

In Paris, Jeanneret was to meet and work for Auguste Perret, the

most progressive representative at that time of the French tradition

of architectural "rationalism"--the attitude that architecture ought

to be primarily a logical expression of the structural, material, and

social forces which produce it in any given time and locale. Perret

was to influence Jeanneret in a number of ways; but the essential

spirit of his rationalism was to have little effect on Jeanneret's

deeply-rooted idealism, which would shape Le Corbusier's thinking

throughout his career. From his "Dom-Ino" system of 1914, and his

"Purist" forms and utopian urbanism of the 1920's, to his sculptural

architecture and obsession with the "Modulor" in his later years,

Le Corbusier's work was to be characterized most essentially by a

search for generalization, universality, and absolute formal truths

which would put Man in touch with a harmony underlying nature--a divine

"axis," as he called it, which "leads us to assume a unity of direction in the universe, and to admit a single will at its source."[53]

Jeanneret's own library reveals that even in his earliest years
in La Chaux-de-Fonds, his training was pervaded with a spirit of philosophical idealism, and that this had many specific influences on his
thinking. Henry Provensal's vision of a new art uniting matter and
spirit, his deductive notion of "science," his definitions of architecture as a cubic play of volumes, and his challenge to discover
formal "harmonic rapports"; and Edouard Schuré's descriptions of
Pythagorean numerology and of a priestly elite of Initiates charged
with the revelation of truth--these were not isolated ideas but
integral parts of an idealistic world-view, for which the true aim
of art was the expression not of material but of spiritual forces.
Jeanneret himself seems to have associated this idealism with his own
Protestant upbringing; and even his teacher L'Eplattenier encouraged
this thinking, as shown by his gift of Les grands initiés to his
favorite student. In sum, all of the important forces in the education of Jeanneret in this early period conspired to inculcate in him
a very special notion of the nature and role of art.

CHAPTER II

ITALY, VIENNA, AND PARIS, 1907-1909

In June 1907, Jeanneret left La Chaux-de-Fonds, spent several
months traveling in Northern Italy, went on to Vienna where he spent
the winter, and in February 1908 went to Paris for the first time.[1]
Accompanying him on this trip was a fellow-student from L'Eplattenier's
"Cours supérieur," Léon Perrin;[2] but Le Corbusier never mentioned this
in his later recollections of this voyage. Perhaps this suppression of
Perrin was due to a later falling-out of the two of them (a familiar
story with Le Corbusier's associates throughout his life), but more
likely it simply reflects Le Corbusier's desire to view this voyage as
an heroic, individual quest, like that of Pythagoras, rather than just
an educational hiking-trip by two school companions. For when Le Corbusier later recalled this trip (in his own writings and through his
biographer Gauthier), it was always in the most romantic terms:

> La brutalité des grandes villes explorées alors, l'une après
> l'autre, pour apprendre, pour vivre, pour chercher le point
> d'application d'énergies avides de produire.[3]

> Voici donc Édouard Jeanneret, à dix-neuf ans et quelques mois,
> partant pour l'Italie, sans autre pécule que celui qu'il a
> gagné, sans autre soutien qu'en lui-même.[4]

In Italy, Jeanneret and Perrin's itinerary included Florence
(where they apparently were based for a while), Pisa, Siena, Ravenna,
Ferrara, Verona, Padua and Venice.[5] Near Florence, Jeanneret visited

the Monastery of Ema, which he later recalled as having impressed him
greatly[6]--to the extent that later, in 1910 on his return from another
voyage in Greece, he was to visit it again. The possible influences
of this monastery on Le Corbusier's urbanistic concepts have been
examined by Peter Serenyi;[7] but it is difficult to know for certain,
from these influences or even from Le Corbusier's own later remarks,
just what his impressions and attitudes were in 1907. Nevertheless,
we can speculate that the simple, almost cubic forms of the individual
cell-units of the monastery (Fig. 14) would have appealed to him; and
we can also suggest that he was attracted simply to the concept of a
"monastery"--with its implications of sanctity, dedication to the
Absolute, and of course of genuine "initiates." Four years later,
Jeanneret was to spend some time at the monastic complex on Mount Athos
in Greece (see Chapter III), and his accounts at that time will reveal
a strong attraction to the monastic life and discipline in and for
themselves. Furthermore, a book of John Ruskin's which Jeanneret was
reading on this 1907 voyage (see below) contains long passages prais-
ing the beauty and purity of the life of monks and mystics, such as
St. Francis; and this, following on the heels of L'Eplattenier's farewell gift of Les grands initiés, must have made Jeanneret react to a
monastic center such as Ema in much more than simply formal architectural terms.

Nevertheless, in general Jeanneret and Perrin seem to have sought
out the more conventional monuments and tourist attractions, such as
the Siena Baptistery and the Campo Santo in Pisa--many of which

Jeanneret sketched. These drawings were to prove very useful to Jeanneret in the next several years, as we shall see; and something should be said about them here. There are basically two different styles into which they fall; and since Jeanneret was to return to Italy in 1911 and visit many of the same monuments he visited in 1907, the question naturally arises of whether these two styles correspond to the two different visits. One of these styles, represented for example by a drawing of the Siena Baptistery (Fig. 15), is a traditional kind of watercolor style for rendering architecture, and everything suggests that it can be associated with the 1907 trip.[8] It is a style which concentrates primarily on the surface effects of architecture (such as decorative patterns and different types of stone and coloration), and is thus very similar to the drawings which illustrated Ruskin's books (e.g. Fig. 16)--drawings which of course emphasized those architectural aspects which interested Ruskin most. We can imagine that this appreciation of the more decorative or "superficial" aspects of architecture was also shared by L'Eplattenier (we recall for example the pine-tree decorations and other details of the Fallet House, designed under L'Eplattenier's direction), and that Jeanneret learned this style of drawing in L'Eplattenier's classroom, aided no doubt by Ruskin's books which we know L'Eplattenier "admired passionately."[9]

Jeanneret's other style of drawing--represented for example by the well-known pencil sketches of Pisa which Le Corbusier later reproduced in his books (Fig. 17)--is very different, concentrating on the overall architectural form, and hardly at all on surface decoration.

By 1911, this was to be Jeanneret's principal drawing style; but the
question of whether Jeanneret may also have done drawings of this
type in 1907 (perhaps at that time he had one style for watercolor,
and another for small pencil sketches) cannot be resolved here.[10]
What is of more interest here is that this second style clearly corresponds to the architectural theories of Provensal--with his emphasis
on architectural volumes as they are seen in light and shade--just as
the other, decorative style corresponds to the architectural theories
of Ruskin. Probably it would be unwise to infer from these correspond-
ances too much about Jeanneret's attitudes at this time. But it is
interesting that, as mentioned above, Jeanneret seems to have taken
one of Ruskin's books along with him to Italy; and at this point we
can examine its possible influence on him.

Actually, there are two books in Le Corbusier's library which
apparently were used by Jeanneret at this time as guidebooks in Italy:
Ruskin's Matins à Florence (Mornings in Florence) and Hippolyte Taine's
Voyage en Italie.[11] Both of them are inscribed with Jeanneret's early
La Chaux-de-Fonds signature; and both contain itineraries and interests
which seem related to Jeanneret's activities in Italy. Ruskin's book
on Florence, for example, is devoted principally to the Florentine
frescoes of Giotto and his contemporaries; and according to reported
recollections of Léon Perrin, it was precisely the Trecento "Primitives"
which he and Jeanneret sought out above all else in Florence.[12] And
the only architectural sketches by Jeanneret which we know of as dating from this stay in Florence are several pages of drawings of the

interior of Sta. Croce (Fig. 18),[13] which is the only building Ruskin discusses architecturally in this book--although Jeanneret's independence from Ruskin is shown by the fact that Sta. Croce's wood-trussed roof, which Ruskin calls "the ugliest Gothic" he ever saw,[14] was precisely what interested Jeanneret most and what he drew most carefully. It is hard to understand why Jeanneret chose this book as a guide to Florence when its few architectural comments are so notably uninspired, just as it was hard to understand how Ruskin's Edinburgh Lectures (which contain perhaps the most superficial of Ruskin's architectural criticism) were later recalled so fondly by Le Corbusier. This suggests to us the degree to which Ruskin must have been worshiped in L'Eplattenier's classroom (and elsewhere in this period as well), and his legend perpetuated, while his specific ideas about architecture were more or less ignored.

The same could be said for Ruskin's attitudes toward painting. In Matins à Florence he discusses painting in anecdotal, moralizing terms which could hardly have appealed to a student of L'Epplattenier (with his desire that art seek out the underlying forms in nature), or to a reader of Provensal. Like Provensal--and like Le Corbusier himself, in Après le cubisme in 1918--Ruskin condemns painting which is merely sensual, and calls for noble and meaningful painting; yet for him the question is simply one of the choice of subject matter--a "preference of worthy things to unworthy" (p. 52)--rather than of any underlying formal or aesthetic principles.

Nevertheless, a couple of attitudes in this book may have

impressed Jeanneret at this time. One is Ruskin's theory of two
temperaments, one Northern European, the other Southern or Mediterranean; the Northern is active, domestic, practical and level-headed,
the Southern contemplative, monastic, mystical and what Ruskin calls
"insane" (pp. 52-61). Although Ruskin suggests that the greatest art
sometimes succeeds in combining these two temperaments, his own personal preference is clearly for the "mysticism" of the South. Le Corbusier himself was to succumb to a similar attraction to the Mediterranean region and to the aesthetic qualities which he thought it
embodies--an attraction which was to affect in certain ways his thinking and his designing. This turn to the Mediterranean by Le Corbusier
is somewhat odd, considering the Northern-ness of his native region,
his trip to Germany to study the Werkbund in 1910, and particularly
the Germanic philosophy underlying much of his reading. It seems to
be at least partly due to specific books Jeanneret read which presented aesthetic theories of Mediterranean superiority. The most
important of these was to be Alexandre Cingria-Vaneyre's Entretiens
de la Villa du Rouet (see Chapter III); but Ruskin may well have suggested this notion to Jeanneret first.

Related to this is Ruskin's concept of the artist as Mystic, and
specifically the idea that truly heroic and saintly figures are destined to be misunderstood by the common mass of humanity. Inherent
of course is the idea of an Elite, which as we saw was already a common theme in Jeanneret's reading; but in contrast to Provensal's
optimistic view of his Elite, Ruskin's saints are men persecuted and

shunned by the world:

> . . . if you will obey God, there will come a moment when the
> voice of man will be raised, with all its holiest natural
> authority, against you. The friend and the wise adviser--the
> brother and the sister--the father and the master--the entire
> voice of your prudent and keen-sighted acquaintance--the
> entire weight of the scornful stupidity of the vulgar world
> --for one, they will be against you, all at once. You have
> to obey God rather than man. The human race, with all its
> wisdom and love, all its indignation and folly, on one side,
> --God alone on the other. You have to choose. (pp. 81-82)

This sounds very much like the bitterness which was to develop

in Le Corbusier over the years, and which was to become so charac-

teristic of his disappointment over what he considered to be the re-

jection of his ideas by a vulgar world. As early as 1908, he was to

express similar feelings toward his colleagues in La Chaux-de-Fonds

and even toward L'Eplattenier (see below). Jeanneret seems to have

had a temperament which allowed him to become very easily embittered

and disappointed with people in whom he once had great trust--whether

they were teachers, clients, government figures, or simply collabora-

tors and friends. Le Corbusier's bitterness has often been defended

as an understandable reaction to adversity, and usually is traced to

his shabby treatment in the 1927 League of Nations competition;[15] but

in reality it was part of his personality long before that, and seems

to be unrelated to specific incidents in his public career. For this

kind of personality, with a tendency to see himself as being perse-

cuted and rejected, there would be an inevitable attraction to any

theory which represented rejection as indeed the mark of genius or

saintliness. In these early years Jeanneret himself was to write,

in a letter:

. . . je veux me battre avec la vérité elle-même. Elle me
martyrisera peut-être--surement. Ce n'est pas la quiétude,
qu'aujourd'hui j'envisage et me prépare pour l'avenir. Et
peut-être moins encore le triomphe de la foule. Mais moi,
je vivrai--sincère--et de l'invective je serais heureux.[16]

Other aspects of this element of Jeanneret's temperament will be

discussed below, for example in connection with his reading of Nie-

tzsche. It should be suggested here that this is not simply a psycho-

logical question having no bearing on Le Corbusier's architectural

thought. For, just as Provensal's claim that the great artist creates

radically original forms would naturally have encouraged Jeanneret to

search for such forms, so the claim that the great prophet is he whose

ideas are rejected by the world could naturally have encouraged him

(perhaps not consciously) to seek out forms that were likely to be

rejected. Often, we can actually see this happening in specific ways,

for example when we examine those cases in Le Corbusier's career in

which he submits a proposal (as in a competition), sees it rejected,

and then reacts with anger and bitterness; sometimes it is almost as

if the proposal or design had been made in such a way as to invite

rejection.[17] Whether we wish to label this as simply an "épater le

bourgeois" phenomenon, or to consider the explanation advanced here,

it suggests an intimate and complex relationship between psychic

aspects of the artist's personality and the forms which he presents

to the world.

Taine's Voyage en Italie

The second book which Jeanneret took to Italy was Hippolyte

Taine's Voyage en Italie--which he must have bought right before

leaving La Chaux-de-Fonds, since his edition of it was published in
1907.[18] Furthermore, he apparently prepared for his trip by reading
parts of this book before leaving home. For in Gauthier's description
of Jeanneret's first impressions of Italy in 1907, and how they dif-
fered from his pre-conceived notions from books and photographs,
Le Corbusier recalls that:

> A Pise, par exemple. où, sur la foi de Taine, il s'attendait
> à un éblouissement de blancheurs, de "marbres immaculés," il
> découvre, au contraire, tout un caressant mirage de bruns
> dorés, de roses, de bleus en sourdine, et c'est ainsi qu'il
> apprend à se méfier, en même temps, des textes littéraires,
> apropos d'art, et des images sans indication d'échelle, de
> dimensions, dont on les accompagne. Vacciné pour la vie
> contre les opinions toutes faites, cet intellectual de la
> bonne espèce s'efforcera désormais de fonder ses raisonne-
> ments et ses raisons sur des sensations personnelles. (p. 22)

In Jeanneret's copy of Taine, the chapter on Pisa contains no
marks or annotations by him; but the passage referred to above is
obviously the following: "Tout est marbre et marbre blanc, dont la
blancheur immaculée luit dans l'azur. Partout de grandes formes
solides, la coupole, le mur plein, les étages équilibres, la ferme
assiette du massif rond ou carrée. . ."[19] Ironically, the conclusion
which Jeanneret drew from his disappointment in Taine's description
of Pisa--namely that in matters of art one should distrust books and
"opinions toutes faites," and instead base one's judgments on "sensations personelles"--is in fact an idea of Taine's himself, related to
his aesthetic theory based on individual "sensations" rather than
a priori values. And most ironic of all, one of the two passages which
Jeanneret bracketed in his copy of Taine is actually an expression of
this very notion:

> Le ciel nous préserve des législateurs en matière de beauté,
> de plaisir et d'émotion! Ce que chacun sent lui est propre
> et particulier comme sa nature; ce que j'éprouverai dependra
> de ce que je suis.[20]

It is easy to understand why Jeanneret would have found this
passage appealing, with his distrust of authority and especially of
academic authority. But beyond that, we can question whether Jeanneret was even aware of the full implications of this passage, since
it refers to an aesthetic doctrine which Taine exposed in other works
but which is not explicitly to be found in the Voyage en Italie[21] --
a doctrine representing to a large extent the "Positivist" side of
nineteenth-century thought, which this thesis suggests had little
fundamental influence on Jeanneret. The principal tenets of Taine's
aesthetic--that there are no absolute standards of beauty and that
artistic form at any given time and place is simply the determined
result of the influences of "race," "milieu," "moment," and all the
other specific forces which these subsume--preclude the kind of search
for universal formal principles which we shall see characterizes Le
Corbusier's early career.

Yet certain peripheral aspects of Taine's thought which are
found in the Voyage en Italie could be seen as possibly influencing
Jeanneret's early thinking. Oddly enough, some of these aspects seem
almost contrary to the positivist nature of Taine's formal theory (a
fact which incidentally reflects a contradiction in Taine's thought
itself, between his formal doctrine and his more conventional preju-
dices and taste.[22]) Thus, the aspects which seem to have interested
Jeanneret in 1907 are for the most part unrelated to the specific

doctrines for which Taine is normally remembered.

One of these aspects is an attitude toward "sublimity" in nature and art. Aside from Taine's remark on aesthetic authority discussed above, the only passage which Jeanneret marked in this book is one in which Taine describes the Bay of Naples and Mount Vesuvius:

> Impossible de rendre ce spectacle. Lord Byron a bien raison:
> on ne peut pas mettre de niveau les beautés des arts et celles
> de la nature. Un tableau reste toujours au-dessous et un pay-
> sage toujours au-dessus de l'idée qu'on s'en peut faire. Cela
> [i.e. the Neapolitan landscape] est beau, je ne sais pas dire
> autre chose, cela est grand et cela est doux; cela fait plaisir
> à tout l'homme, coeur et sens; il n'y a rien de plus voluptueux
> et il n'y a rien de plus noble.[23]

The distinction between art-objects, whose beauty can be conceptu-alized and understood, and nature, whose beauty is so grand and noble that it is beyond analysis, is an attitude revealed by Taine throughout this book by the difference between the way he describes nature, often in awe-inspired and reverent tones, and his description of art which are generally rather coldly analytical (consistent with a theory that art is simply the result of specific "forces.") The notion behind this distinction seems to be that there are two types of beauty: one simply the result of all the environmental forces at play; and another, which transcends this, and could be called "sublime." Normally, Taine finds this "sublime" beauty only in nature; but occasionally he also sees in in works of Man--and it is these exceptional works of art which natu-rally impress him most. There are certain specific qualities which seem to arouse this reaction in Taine; and furthermore, it is archi-tecture which is most likely to have this sublime effect on him. Spe-cifically, Taine describes the Colisseum in Rome as having this effect, and even compares it with natural landscape forms:

> Au milieu de cet étonnant silence, on dirait qu'il existe seul,
> que les hommes, les plantes, toute vie passagère n'est qu'une
> apparence; j'ai éprouvé autrefois cette sensation dans les
> montagnes; elles aussi semblent les vrais habitants de la
> terre. . .[24]

Taine's romantic reaction seems to be inspired particularly by

grand scale and extremely simple architectural forms. Elsewhere, he

says of the Colisseum that

> La beauté de l'édifice consiste dans sa simplicité. Les voûtes
> sont le cintre le plus naturel et plus solide, avec un bordure
> unie. L'édifice s'appui sur lui-même, inébranlable, combien
> supérieur aux cathédrales gothiques avec leurs contreforts qui
> semblent les pattes d'un crabe![25]

Taine's innate preference for Classical forms over Gothic forms

(and especially over Baroque forms) is evident throughout this book--

as it was to be in Le Corbusier's writings as well.[26] For Taine,

Classical forms are those which are the simplest, the least decor-

ated, the "purest."[27] The Renaissance in Florence returned to "les

formes sveltes et simples de l'antiquité paienne;" and its artists

strove to attain "la perfection classique."[28] In his chapter on Roman

villas and palaces, he finds the Palazzo Farnese the simplest and most

noble--and in Jeanneret's copy of the book this page is marked by a

slip of paper.[29] To Taine, the beauty of the Palazzo Farnese resides

in its "vigueur virile. . . . ce qu'on aime, c'est la beauté male et

sérieuse."[30] It is the absence of this simplicity and sincerity in

Baroque architecture which makes that period defective for Taine. In

St. Peter's "on a compliqué les formes, multiplié les colonnes, pro-

digué les statues, entassé les pierres, en sorte que la beauté a dis-

paru sous l'encombrement;" and Taine adds that

A mon gré, toute oeuvre architecturale ou autre doit être
comme un cri, comme une parole sincère, l'extrémité et le
complément d'une sensation, rien d'autre.[31]

This idea that architecture ought to be an expressive art,
revealing the artist's emotions and sincerity and arousing these in
the viewer, is a notion which was to underlie much of Le Corbusier's
thinking (though in a completely different theoretical framework from
that of Taine), as revealed for example in his many descriptions of
architectural beauty as being a matter of "emotion."[32] Despite the
fact that it is an attitude clearly inconsistent with Taine's formal
doctrines, its expression in this book of his may well have helped
shaped Jeanneret's conception of architecture.

One other aspect of the Voyage en Italie should be mentioned
briefly here: the great interest which Taine has in describing
country-side, village life, local customs, and especially the life
of cities, with all of their individual sights, sounds, smells and
impressions. Unlike the aspects discussed above, this is closer to
being an expression of Taine's formal theories; for the environment
in which art develops is obviously of major importance in a theory
which sees art as the product of specific forces. Long passages in
the Voyage en Italie are devoted to descriptions of the cities Taine
visited, to local cultural characteristics, and to what we would call
vernacular or anonymous architecture. This approach must have
impressed the young Jeanneret, for when he traveled through Eastern
Europe four years later, the articles he wrote about this journey--
which he later published as the book Voyage d'Orient--consist principally of descriptions of towns, cities and vernacular architecture

in a style very similar to that of Taine. The <u>Voyage d'Orient</u> will
be examined later in this study.

Thus Taine's book appears to have impressed Jeanneret in several ways--reinforcing his admiration for simple geometric architectural forms, presenting architecture as a fundamentally expressive
art which arouses emotions, and emphasizing the importance of environmental and urbanistic observation--but that these aspects are hardly
characteristic of the "positivist" aesthetic doctrines for which Taine
is generally known.

Jeanneret in Vienna

In late summer or fall, 1907, Jeanneret and Perrin took the
train to Vienna, where they were to stay through the winter.[33] It is
not totally clear just what Jeanneret did during those months in
Vienna. It has been claimed that he worked in Josef Hoffmann's office
there;[34] but the account in Gauthier's biography maintains only that
right before leaving Vienna he went to see Hoffmann, was offered a
job (on the strength of his Italian drawings), but rejected it in
favor of going on to Paris (pp. 23-24). This account (which, like
all other accounts coming from Le Corbusier himself, again suppresses
Perrin and gives the impression that Jeanneret was heroically alone)
says that Jeanneret had gone to Vienna because of the "intense artistic
life" which he had read existed there, but that he found the new Viennese architecture disappointing, and was still captivated by the
"masterpieces of the Quatrocento" (p. 23). He spent six cold winter
months in "the solitude of a comfortless room, drawing up projects

for his native country undoubtedly more ambitious than original;"
and his "only precious memories of these six months" were his regu-
lar visits to the Opera and Philharmonic Concerts (p. 23). It has
also been claimed that Jeanneret became familiar with the ideas of
Adolf Loos here in Vienna;[35] but if they really had made a strong
impression on him, he probably would have mentioned this to Gauthier
as one of the redeeming aspects of this bleak period--just as he mentioned his offer from Hoffmann, and also an introduction to several
Viennese artists such as Koloman Moser and Klimt. Furthermore, there
are no books in Le Corbusier's library which give any evidence of
having been either purchased or read by Jeanneret during this period.

On the other hand, there are two private houses in La Chaux-de-
Fonds which are said to have been designed by Jeanneret and constructed during the time he was in Vienna (Figs. 19-20).[36] Their style is
so close to Jeanneret's 1906 Fallet House--in their combination of
stone and stucco surfaces, their overhanging eaves supported by big
wooden brackets, and their picturesque massing and details--that they
surely do date from about this time, or perhaps were even designed
by Jeanneret before he left home. Their "execution" is said to have
been carried out by René Chapallaz, the same architect who was associated with the Fallet House.[37]

But whatever may be the precise date of these houses, they would
not appear to be the "over-ambitious" projects which Le Corbusier later
recalled as having worked on in Vienna. The only clue we seem to have
to the nature of these projects is a remark which Jeanneret made, in

a letter written from Paris the next year, which disparages his stay

in Vienna as the last gasp of "ma conception purement plastique

(faite de la recherche seule des formes) de l'architecture."[38]   The

full significance of this remark must be understood in relation to

Jeanneret's new attitudes toward architecture in Paris (which will

be discussed below); but in brief, the suggestion is that in Vienna

he had been composing purely abstract, formalistic designs--perhaps

influenced by the cubic arrangements advocated by Provensal, and

perhaps also evoking the Italian Renaissance whose spell he says he

was still under.

Throughout Le Corbusier's life there were to be periods when

he withdrew into himself, to absorb the ideas and stimuli to which

he had just been exposed, and to come to some conclusion about them.

The winter in Vienna seems to have been the first of these periods.

Paris and Jeanneret's first contact with rationalism

In February 1908, Jeanneret left Vienna for Paris--inspired,

he later said, by a performance of La Bohème at the Vienna Opera.[39]

Again he was accompanied by Léon Perrin, who proceeded to find a job

in Paris with Hector Guimard.[40]   Jeanneret went to Franz Jourdain

(architect of the Samaritaine department store), who did not have a

place for him but was as impressed as Hoffmann had been with his

Italian drawings--which, if we are to believe Le Corbusier, acted

unfailingly as a kind of open-sesame in these early years.   Jourdain

sent him to Charles Plumet, who had no room in his office but referred

him to Henri Sauvage (later architect of the stepped-back apartment buildings in the rue Vavin and the rue des Amiraux), who offered him

work drawing architectural decoration; but Jeanneret apparently con-

sidered this beneath his dignity and refused the job.[41] Then he found

the address of Eugène Grasset, the furniture and decorative designer

whose book had been used in the Art School in La Chaux-de-Fonds; he

went to see him, was at first rudely treated, but then impressed him

with his portfolio and was well received. Grasset spoke to him about

the "complete decadence" of contemporary architecture--except for one

small ray of hope: a new construction method called "béton armé,"

which yielded "des formes pures"[42]--and he referred Janneret to the

foremost practitioners of this new technique, the Perret brothers.[43]

When Auguste Perret met Jeanneret and saw his drawings, he

apparently was very impressed;[44] and he offered him a job in his

office--which was located on the ground floor of his first important

reinforced-concrete building, the apartment house on Rue Franklin

(Fig. 21). At this point, a new realm of experience opened up for

Jeanneret, consisting of ideas, techniques, and attitudes of which

he had never even known the existence before. They were to influence

him and change his thinking in many ways, affecting the whole future

development of Le Corbusier--although this thesis will contend that

they were to remain fundamentally superficial changes, grafted onto

more basic thought-patterns already too deeply ingrained to be altered.

Much happened to Jeanneret in this crucial period, and the details and

chronology are not always easy to reconstruct. But some important

facts are clear: new concepts were introduced to Jeanneret primarily

by Auguste Perret; these represented an approach toward architecture
which can be characterized as positivist or rationalist;[45] and judging
from Jeanneret's unusual response to these new concepts, he seems
never to have been exposed to them before. This last point is odd
since these concepts were nothing new in France, and indeed in many
ways were part of the architectural "establishment," through the writings of Viollet-le-duc, Hippolyte Taine, the courses taught by Anatole
de Baudot, and those taught at the École des Beaux-Arts by Julien
Guadet--Perret's teacher.

Briefly stated, the central notion of this architectural "rationalism" was that above all else architectural forms are shaped by the
specific functional and programmatic requirements, available materials,
and structural technology of any particular age and locale. Guadet,
in his Éléments et théorie de l'architecture (a compilation of his
lectures) stresses constantly that architecture is first of all "construction;" and when he defines beauty as "la splendeur du vrai" (that
phrase which Provensal interpreted so idealistically), he carefully
makes clear that for him "le vrai" principally means the rational
expression of programme and construction.[46] Despite his personal
prejudice for Classical forms (which however he always attempts to
justify as the most rational), Guadet has an unshakable faith that
good architecture will emerge directly from the proper handling of
functional and programmatic requirements ("composition") and good
construction. Auguste Perret shared these attitudes of his teacher,
prided himself on being a "constructeur" rather than an architect,

and as we shall see, impressed on his young employee Jeanneret the
idea that architecture is principally the solving of practical problems with available technology.

These rationalist notions seem so commonplace to us now, that
we almost find it hard to believe Jeanneret's first reactions of
shock, astonishment, and excitement over the contemplation of them.
In a long, revealing letter to L'Eplattenier from Paris, Jeanneret
berates his former master for teaching his students false doctrines,
says that he suddenly realizes he knew nothing at all, and that only
now has he suspected "that architecture is not a matter of the
'eurythmie' of forms but... something else...what?" Then he describes the new doctrine which Perret has revealed to him, and lectures on it to L'Eplattenier:

> Je le sais--et personne de vous ne me l'a dit: . . .
>   L'architecture égyptienne a été telle, parce que la reli-
> gion était telle et que les matériaux étaient tels. Religion
> de mystère, appareil en plates-bandes--temple égyptien.
>   L'architecture gothique a été telle, parce que la religion
> était telle, et que les matériaux étaient tels. Religion
> d'expansion, et matériaux petits--la cathédrale.
>   Comme conclusion aux lignes précédentes. Si on emploie la
> platebande, on fera le temple égyptien, ou grec ou mexicain.
> Si le petit matériau s'impose, la cathédrale s'impose . . .

It is truly astounding that a young man who had felt that his
formal education was over, who had designed and built several houses
and considered himself a trained architect ready to take up a respon-
sible job in a Paris office, could suddenly be so devastated by this
proposition. It reveals, I believe, not so much the provincial quality of his education back at La Chaux-de-Fonds (although that may be
part of it), but especially the nature of that education--so formal

and non-"architectural" (L'Eplattenier himself had no architectural
background) and so steeped in the aesthetic idealism represented by
Provensal and apparently shared by L'Eplattenier.

That this reaction in Paris was, indeed, devastating for Jeanneret is revealed throughout his long letter to L'Eplattenier, in
which he laments over and over again his realization of knowing
nothing, his bitterness against L'Eplattenier's formalistic teaching,
and his resolve to start anew and to study for years if necessary in
order really to understand architecture. Besides turning to the
study of historical architectural periods (he was following history
courses at the École des Beaux-Arts and reading in the libraries), he
says that he was studying statics, mathematics, and the strength of materials. As strange as it sounds, his descriptions of these technical
studies suggests that they were all totally new to him and that he had
never before even suspected their importance:

> Et j'étudiai la mécanique, puis la statique; oh ce que j'ai
> transpiré la-dessus pendant tout l'été. Combien de fois me
> suis-je trompé, et aujourd'hui, avec colère, je constate les
> creux dont est formée ma science d'architecture moderne.
> Avec rage et joie, parce que je sais enfin, que là est le
> bon, j'étudie les forces de la matière. C'est ardu, mais
> c'est beau, ces mathématiques, si logiques, si parfaites![48]

Later, Le Corbusier recalled that it was Auguste Perret who had
told him to study mathematics, saying that it "forms the mind;"[49] and
it is clear that in many ways Perret was like a teacher to Jeanneret
at this time. Instead of simply hiring Jeanneret, he took a special
interest in him, and did all he could to promote and direct his studies.
The fact that Le Corbusier later turned against Perret probably ex-
plains why Le Corbusier's own accounts of this early relationship

are sketchy at best; but the outlines can be made out. Perret let Jeanneret work part-time in his office (five hours each day, at any time of the day or evening he wished), leaving the rest of the time for him to attend courses, read in the libraries (especially the Bibliothèque Ste. Geneviève and the Conservatoire des Arts et Métiers), visit museums, and study examples of new architecture in Paris.[50] Furthermore, Jeanneret may have gone to Lyon, soon after arriving in Paris, to see Tony Garnier;[51] and if this is true, it was surely at the instigation of Perret, who would have been one of the few men in Paris at that time interested in, or even aware of, Garnier's revolutionary "Cité Industrielle" project, which had been exhibited in 1904 among other Prix-de-Rome projects at the École des Beaux-Arts but had attracted little notice then and was not to be published until 1917. Jeanneret later acquired this 1917 publication of the project and reproduced parts of it in his Esprit Nouveau articles;[52] and there can be little doubt that Garnier's forms (if not his principles) influenced Le Corbusier. But Perret must have been the primary transmitter of Garnier to Jeanneret.

Perret also seems to have directed Jeanneret's reading at this time. In his letter to L'Eplattenier, Jeanneret says that he spent three months in the library, at night, studying Romanesque architecture; and a notebook, found in the Fondation Le Corbusier, containing extensive notes which Jeanneret took at that time, shows that he was studying Édouard Corroyer's L'architecture romane (Paris, 1888.) This book, which presents Romanesque architecture as an evolution of

simple structural elements (walls, columns, arches, and domes) which
were then modified and combined in various ways with corresponding
formal results, could well have been suggested by Perret in order to
introduce Jeanneret to the fundamental notion that architectural forms
express structural principles. Corroyer's illustrations, many of
which Jeanneret copied out faithfully (Fig. 22), are primarily plans
and sections; and again Perret probably wanted to emphasize the relationship between structure and form--as well as simply familiarizing
Jeanneret with the most basic graphic tools of the architect.

Perret also seems to have told Jeanneret to read Viollet-le-duc
(whose works, to be sure, had been in the Art School library in La
Chaux-de-Fonds, but which we have no evidence of Jeanneret having
read there.) We do not know whether he read the Entretiens; but he
actually bought the Dictionnaire raisonné de l'architecture française
--all ten volumes of it--and inscribed in it that he had purchased it
with his first pay-check from "Mr. Perret" on 1 August 1908.[53] In
fact, it is thoroughly reasonable that Perret should have urged
Jeanneret to buy this work, for it had provided his own introduction
to architecture in his youth, and had shaped to a large extent his
own attitudes.[54] Perret must have pointed out specific passages for
Jeanneret to read, passages which most clearly expressed the relationships between structure and form; and at one of these passages,
in which Viollet describes the functioning of the flying buttress,
Jeanneret inserted an annotation (Fig. 23), in typically Perret
language:

> Ces quelques lignes font voir que tout cet <u>art vit par sa
> carcasse</u>.
>   C'est un monolithe aussi, une cage de fil de fer,--où
> les pressions verticales et les poussées obliques tiennent
> lieu du ciment des blocages romains, et des ronds d'acier
> du béton.
>   <u>Or</u>, me disait Aug Perret, <u>tenez la carcasse</u>, et vous
> tenez l'Art (ce qui n'est peut-être pas faux du tout, étant
> bien compris.)[55]

This "carcass," for Perret, is the essential underlying structural shape of any building; and by "holding to the carcass," you
automatically are in conformity with "art."[56] Pure Perret--and pure
architectural rationalism. Besides having Jeanneret take courses in
statics and mathematics, and introducing him to fundamental architectural notions he had missed in La Chaux-de-Fonds, Perret was trying
to inculcate in his young employee-student his own architectural
philosophy.

But it did not quite take. Or at least not the way Perret
meant it. Jeanneret did indeed adopt certain specific principles
of Perret's rationalism, such as an emphasis on structural systems,
and a fascination for new materials and their potentials; and these
were of course to shape his thinking from then on. Yet these new
principles seem to have been grafted onto, or laid over, Jeanneret's
existing idealism, rather than replacing or modifying it. The proof
of this is in all of Le Corbusier's later thought and work; but even
in the meagre evidence which we have from this early period in Paris
in 1908, we can see how Jeanneret's innate idealism integrates with
the new ideas and distorts them.

In his letter to L'Eplattenier, for example, right next to his paraphrases from Perret, his attacks on L'Eplattenier's teachings, and his resolutions to learn and study, he proclaims that he is now searching out "la vérité elle-même"--a concept which he means in the absolutist sense of Provensal or Schuré. For Jeanneret also proclaims here, several times, that "L'art de demain sera un art de pensée"--an art which will be formulated not by going into the world and studying specific problems, as Perret would do, but rather by retreating into thought, in a profound attempt to discover universal principles. This retreat into one's inner self ("le moi"), which was so important to Provensal's aesthetic--but which is obviously irrelevant to Perret's-- is in fact stated by Jeanneret (in his letter to L'Eplattenier) to be the very essence of the New Art he is formulating:

> Ils [others] ne savent pas ce que c'est que l'Art: amour intense de son moi; on va le chercher dans la retraite et la solitude, ce "moi" divin qui peut être un moi terrestre quand on le force--par la lutte--à le devenir. Ce moi parle alors, il parle des choses profonde de l'Etre: l'art naît et, fugace--il jaillit.
> C'est dans la solitude que l'on se bat avec son moi, que l'on se châtie et qu'on se fouette.

Quite aside from the weird, almost mystical emphasis here on the self-punishment which the Artist must undergo (an emphasis which occurs throughout this letter), it is perfectly plain that Jeanneret is in a totally different world from that of Perret, even though he seems sincerely to think he is expounding Perret's notions. The same thing can be seen, though not in as extreme a form, in Jeanneret's inscription in Viollet's Dictionnaire (Fig. 24):

> J'ai acheté cet ouvrage le 1 août 1908 avec l'argent de ma première paye de Mr. Perret. Je l'ai acheté pour apprendre, car sachant je pourrai alors créer.

Jeanneret will not be able to create until he <u>knows</u>--a theme which also runs through his letter to L'Eplattenier and is associated with the "vérité" he is seeking. To Viollet-le-duc or Perret, architecture would be basically the patient empirical solution of problems by a rational and economic application of the materials and techniques at hand; but to Jeanneret it is a solitary search for Truth (like Schuré's "initiates"), which when found then allows one to "create" and thus be an Artist. It is of course ironic that Jeanneret should have written such an inscription in his copy of Viollet, since their two attitudes toward architecture are so essentially opposite. As we would expect, Viollet's works appear to have had no particular influence on Jeanneret's development.

It should be pointed out here that this overlapping of two aesthetic systems by Jeanneret--with certain rationalist ideas from Perret laid over an idealistic foundation--was not simply a transitional phase after which Jeanneret was to slough off his idealism and bring his thinking into consistent order. Rather, this odd fusion was to persist, and indeed I believe, become one of the characteristic qualities of Le Corbusier's work throughout his career. This will be elaborated later; but it is worth mentioning here that I believe that part of the very <u>power</u>, and attraction, of Le Corbusier's work and thought resides precisely in the specific way he fuses these two things --for example in the way he takes the superficial <u>objects</u> of the rationalist doctrine (a structural system, or a mundane functional requirement), but then <u>treats</u> them idealistically, with awe and art and as if they were absolute principles like the "Idea" of Provensal.

Jeanneret's reading in Paris, 1908-1909

In his letter to L'Eplattenier, Jeanneret emphasizes that his stay in Paris is to be a period of study and reflection. This is borne out by the fact that Le Corbusier's library contains at least a dozen books which, like Viollet's Dictionnaire, are inscribed by Jeanneret as having been acquired during this period. And these do not represent the sum of his reading, since we know he was working in the Paris libraries--although unfortunately, except for Corroyer's book on Romanesque architecture, we do not know exactly what he was reading there. The books which survive in Le Corbusier's library, however, provide interesting clues to Jeanneret's concerns during these two years. Contrary to what we might expect, there are no books on construction or other technical matters, and in fact none which are specifically about architecture, except for the Viollet. For the most part, the books are literary "classics" from various periods--as if Jeanneret was trying consciously to fill out gaps in his general education. He read Homer (both the Iliad and the Odyssey),[57] Rousseau's Confessions,[58] Baudelaire's Fleurs du mal,[59] Flaubert's Salammbô,[60] Claudel's Connaissance de l'Est,[61] a collection of literary essays by Jules Laforgue, Moralités légendaires,[62] Nietzsche's Thus Spake Zarathustra,[63] Huysman's La cathédrale,[64] as well as a few others which may or may not have been acquired at this time.[65] The rest of the books could be characterized loosely as

"historical:" Renan's <u>Vie de Jésus</u>,[66] Ménard's <u>Histoire des anciens</u>
<u>peuples de l'Orient</u>,[67] and LeBon's <u>Civilizations de l'Inde</u>.[68] Two
of these books are of particular interest and will be examined here.

Nietzsche's Zarathustra

Jeanneret put no date in his copy of <u>Zarathustra</u>,[63] but signed
it and inscribed his address in Paris (3, quai St. Michel), thus showing that he acquired it in either 1908 or 1909. The earlier of these
two years seems more likely, however, judging from the apparent influence of some of Nietzsche's ideas on Jeannert's thinking as seen in
his letter to L'Eplattenier discussed above, written in November 1908.
I see no evidence that Jeanneret was influenced by the overall nature
of Nietzsche's philosophy (which in any case is not very clearly exposed
in <u>Zarathustra</u>), but he does seem to have been struck by some of Nietzsche's notions and images, which seem to have responded to Jeanneret's
own thinking at this time. That Jeanneret read Nietzsche in a very
personal, subjective way is further suggested by the fact that years
later, at the end of Le Corbusier's career, when he seems to have been
thinking a lot about his youth and early development, he took this book
to Southern France one summer, reread parts of it, and wrote a second
inscription in it:

Cap Martin, 1 août 1961.
je n'ai pas lu ce livre depuis 1908 (Quai St Michel Paris)
= 51 ans = ma vie d'homme. Aujourd'hui ayant butiné ces pages
je devine des situations, des faits, des décisions, des destin-
ations qui sont des faits d'homme. Je décide d'en noter les
pages.[69]

Le Corbusier noted some page-references here; and in the text, on these and other pages, passages are marked and underlined in pencil and occasional annotations are made. These markings all date from 1961 (being in Le Corbusier's later hand), but for the most part they are next to the passages which most likely impressed Jeanneret in 1908, so we sense that Le Corbusier reread this book in 1961 much as he had read it fifty-three years earlier.

As we might expect, Jeanneret was struck most by Nietzsche's conception of the "Superman" (translated "le Surhumain" in this edition, rather than the "Surhomme" of most French editions)--a new type of man, noble and totally in control of himself, who embodies the Future, and who makes present-day Man seem bestial in comparison with his own spiritual qualities. In these terms, Nietzsche's hero is hardly much different from Provensal's artist of the future. What seems especially to have appealed to Jeanneret was Nietzsche's fiery and poetic enthusiasm for this Hero of the Future, his passionate hatred of the old form of Man, and his resulting attitudes toward past and future. Le Corbusier later marked several passages in which Nietzsche speaks of the need to prepare the way for the future by destroying the past, and of the resulting link between destruction and creation. For example:

> Voyez les bons et les justes! Qui haïssent-ils le plus?
> Celui qui brise leurs tables des valeurs, le destructeur,
> le criminel:--mais c'est celui-là le créateur.[70]

This must have been fresh in Jeanneret's mind when he wrote to L'Eplattenier in November 1908, for in much the same spirit as that of Nietzsche he identifies his former teacher and colleagues as men

of the past, whom he will soon have to renounce, finding new values

by turning all the old ones upside-down:

> La réalité sera un jour (sous peu, peut-être) cruelle: car
> la lutte contre ceux que j'aime s'approche. . .
>
> Ces 8 mois de Paris me crient: Logique, vérité, honneteté,
> arrière le rêve vers les arts passés. Les yeux hauts, en
> avant! . . . Paris me dit "Brûle ce que tu as aimé, et
> adore ce que tu brulais.

Nietzsche also emphasizes the great work and sacrifice which one

must undergo (awarded only by the vilification of other men) in order

to prepare the way for the Superman; and the same theme of work, pain,

and the inevitability of vilification are found in Jeanneret's letter

to L'Eplattenier:

> La vie de Paris est solitaire pour moi. Et depuis 8 mois je vis
> seul--seul à seul avec cet esprit fort qui est en chaque homme,
> et avec qui je veux chaque jour causer. Et aujourd'hui je puis
> parler avec mon esprit--heures fécondes de solitude, heures où
> l'on sape et où le fouet cingle. Oh que n'ai-je un peu plus de
> temps pour penser et apprendre! La vie réelle, mesquine, est
> dévoureuse des heures.
>
> Ce n'est pas la quiétude, qu'aujourd'hui j'envisage et me pré-
> pare pour l'avenir. Et peut-être moins encore le triomphe de
> la foule. Mais moi, je vivrai--sincère--et de l'invective je
> serai heureux.

The state of mind which Jeanneret reveals in this letter, with

its peculiar combination of withdrawal from the world, self-punishment,

Utopianism, and hatred of the past, is in all ways typical of what

Erik Erikson has characterized as a type of young man (often destined

for creative greatness), in his late adolescence, in a period which

Erikson calls a "moratorium," when he purposely withdraws into contem-

plation and refuses to commit himself to specific action.[71] This kind

of "moratorium" is in fact clearly revealed by Jeanneret in his
letter; for he criticizes L'Eplattenier several times for wanting
him to create too soon, and proclaims that he still needs a long
period of thought and study before he will be ready to act.[72]

Jeanneret was apparently also struck by passages in which
Nietzsche speaks of Zarathustra as a Christ-like figure, descend-
ing to the level of humanity and voluntarily choosing to sacrifice
himself in order to bring men the Truth. Le Corbusier marked many
of these passages in 1961, and next to a couple of them wrote "la
main ouverte"--that phrase which recurs so often in his later writings (and which, as a visual image, is a recurring theme in his
paintings and sculptural works [e.g. Fig. 25])--and which here is
indicative of Le Corbusier's identification with Zarathustra's
magnanimous sacrifice to Mankind. There is no reason to suppose
that this identification was not also present in Jeanneret's mind
when he originally read Nietzsche as well--especially since we shall
see an even clearer identification with a Savior-figure in another
book Jeannert read at this time (see below.)

Underlying all of these specific aspects which appealed to
Jeanneret in Zarathustra, and tying them together, is the notion of
two kinds of Man: the "beast" of Man's past, and the Superman of
his future--aspects which can be seen not only in terms of past and
future, but also as two coexisting parts of Man's nature (an interpretation which Nietzsche too shared, in his concepts of Dionysian and
Apollonian temperaments.) Present-day Man is in a transition stage

between the two: he is "une corde tendue entre la bête et le sur-

humain;" and the choice he must make is whether to "retourner à la

bête [or] surmonter l'homme."[73] We find a very similar concept

throughout Le Corbusier's writings, in which he reveals that he con-

siders Man to be composed of two natures, which he sometimes calls

"la bête" and "la tête." At times Le Corbusier suggests that the

"mind" should overcome the "beast," like Nietzsche, whereas at other

times he suggests that the two can be reconciled; but the Nietzschean

imagery always seems detectable:

> L'homme s'arrète devant la machine, la bête et le divin s'y
> rassasient.[74]

> . . . la maison est notre gîte; elle est un objet qui inter-
> esse en nous la bête et la tête, parce qu'étant dedans, nous
> subissons sa contrainte.[75]

> L'homme régit son sentiment par la raison; il réfrène ses
> sentiments et ses instincts en faveur du but qu'il a. Il
> commande à sa bête par son intelligence.[76]

This last view, of a noble Man ruling his own brute nature by

sublimating it into intelligent purpose is especially Nietzschean,

and underlies much of Le Corbusier's thought. It is easy to under-

stand why this concept would have appealed to Jeanneret in Paris in

1908, since he was filled with intense but undirected desires for

sacrifice and the realization of some noble purpose. But it is also

evident that this aspect is not actually very far removed from the

elitist notions which Jeanneret was already familiar with from Pro-

vensal and Schuré. The fact that Nietzsche's philosophy, in reality,

was opposed to the idealism represented by these men, is more or less

irrelevant to us, since Jeanneret seems to have picked out from
Nietzsche only what interested him and was appropriate to his needs.
If anything, Nietzsche reinforced Jeanneret's view of himself as
destined to belong to an artistic elite seeking out ideal principles
and absolute truth--itself a most un-Nietzschean notion. What
Jeanneret did get from Nietzsche which had not been in his reading
before, was an attitude of disdain toward the past, of wild hope for
the future, and a fascination with destruction as necessary to creation. Furthermore, he seems to have been influenced by Nietzsche's
style of writing--characterized by passionate language, striking
aphorisms, violent challenges and attacks against opposing ideas,
and the fervent advocacy of oneself. Le Corbusier's writing-style
(which was so important to the popular appeal and dissemination of
his ideas) was also to be influenced by Futurism and perhaps Guillaume
Apollinaire as well; but of these influences, Nietzsche's is probably
the strongest, and suggests the great impact Zarathustra had on
Jeanneret in 1908.

Ernest Renan's Vie de Jésus

Like Zarathustra, this book is inscribed only with Jeanneret's
signature and his Quai St. Michel address--and thus must date from
1908-1909.[77] Throughout the text, passages are bracketed in pencil,
in the margins, but there are virtually no annotations (a pattern
typical of Jeanneret's markings in his early books); and this fact,
together with the substance of the marked passages, indicate that

these markings date from 1908-1909--unlike Le Corbusier's later markings in _Zarathustra_. Taken all together, these marked passages in Renan's book reveal the rather startling fact that Jeanneret actually identified himself with the figure of Jesus, and was seeking parallels between Jesus's career and that which he himself was embarking upon.

It should be emphasized here that Jeanneret's interest in this book was obviously very different from the interest which the general public had in it, and by which it is remembered as an important milestone in nineteenth-century scholarship. Renan's courageous examination of Jesus as an historical personality subject to objective study --which so scandalized the Church, delighted unbelievers and positivists, and strengthened the position of Taine and his followers-- was not the aspect of this work which attracted Jeanneret (if, indeed, he was even _aware_ of its significance in the world of scholarship). Throughout his life, Le Corbusier read books very selectively and tended to find in them only what reflected his own concerns. In this case, Jeanneret's markings reveal that he was reading Renan's book simply because it contained a great many details about Jesus's career (especially his early career), his ideas and personality, and his struggles to promulgate his beliefs and gain adherents to them.

Jeanneret marked or bracketed about thirty passages in the _Vie de Jésus_, scattered throughout the text; and these passages fall into several definite categories. One of these categories concerns Jesus's youthful years, when he withdrew into solitude and meditation

(". . . de méditer sur les montagnes et dans les lieux solitaires,"
p. 91), trying to discover what pattern his life was to take--just
as Jeanneret describes doing at that very time in his letter to
L'Eplattenier. Similar passages marked by Jeanneret describe the
young Jesus's search for "perfection" in everything (p. 86), just
as Jeanneret seems obsessively to have been trying to learn everything; and claim that Jesus's lowly origin was no hindrance to his
high destiny (p. 75), a point which could have impressed Jeanneret,
himself understandably anxious in 1908 about his lack of a proper
French education.

Another category--comprising the largest number of the passages
which Jeanneret bracketed (about ten of them)--characterizes the ideas
of Jesus as being "revolutionary." Renan felt that Jesus was revolutionary in two different senses of the word: first, that he wanted
men to renounce earthly concerns and devote themselves to the Spirit;
but at the same time, that he was a Utopian social reformer who wanted
to create an actual earthly "Kingdom of God" in which the social
classes would be turned on end, the rich disinherited, and men live
in communal brotherhood.[78] Renan admits that these two revolutions--
the spiritual one and the earthly communist one--are ostensibly incompatible; but he claims that Jesus's originality, and the power of his
thought, lay precisely in his espousal of both of them at the same
time (p. 131). Jeanneret was interested in Renan's descriptions of
both of these revolutions; and it is worth noting that Le Corbusier's
later thought is itself characterized by an ostensible contradiction

between an architectural revolution based on the "earthly" concerns
of function, efficiency, urban planning, etc., and another revolution
in which architecture was to be raised above mere function and become
"pure création de l'esprit."

Whether or not Jeanneret in 1908 was cognizant of this two-fold
implication in Renan's analysis, it is clear that he considered Jesus
the Revolutionary to have personal significance for himself and his
own career; and a number of the passages he marked in Renan are similar to his own description of the revolutionary role he saw for himself. For example, Renan's statement, bracketed by Jeanneret, that

> . . . cette Jérusalem nouvelle qui descend du ciel, ce cri:
> "Voila que je refais tout à neuf!" sont les traits communs
> des réformateurs (p. 130)

reminds us of Jeanneret's remark to L'Eplattenier that "Ces 8 mois de
Paris me crient: 'Brûle ce que tu as aimé, et adore ce que tu brû-
lais'"--which also of course was related to Nietzsche's _Zarathustra_.
Indeed, Jeanneret seems to have read Nietzsche and Renan together,
seeking out in both books the traits of the archetypal revolutionary
prophet and reformer--and then relating these traits to his image of
his own similar destiny.

Jeanneret's letter to L'Eplattenier reveals considerable anxiety
over the problem of _how_ he ultimately would put his ideas into effect,
how he would gain recognition and adherents, and whether on the other
hand he was doomed to be rejected and misunderstood (even claiming
defensively, as we saw, that "de l'invective je serai heureux.") The
second-largest category of passages which he marked in the _Vie de Jesus_

concerns precisely this problem in Jesus's own career; for example:

A qui s'adresser, de qui réclamer l'aide pour fonder le règne
de Dieu? (p. 132)

En somme, l'influence de Jean sur Jésus avait été plus facheuse
qu'utile à ce dernier. . . Peut-être, si le baptiste, . . fut
resté libre, n'eut-il pas su rejeter le joug des rites et des
pratiques matérielles et alors sans doute il serait demeuré un
sectaire juif inconnu. . .(p. 119)

Le royaume de Dieu se réalisera-t-il par la force ou par la
douceur, par la révolte ou par la patience? (p. 124)

Other passages of this sort bracketed by Jeanneret include a

description of Jesus's early failure to win followers in his own

native Gallilee (p. 138; Jeanneret's letter reveals how sensitive

he was to the gulf which he saw between his ideas and those of L'Eplat-

tenier and his former colleagues in La Chaux-de-Fonds), and also

Renan's observation that it is not enough for a prophet simply to have

great ideas, but he must also suffer if necessary to put them into

effect:

La palme est à celui qui a été puissant en paroles et en oeuvres,
qui a senti le bien et, au prix de son sang, l'a fait triompher.
(p. 97)

This is amazingly close to the spirit of Jeanneret's letter to

L'Eplattenier, in which he continually refers to the pain and suffer-

ing which he will have to undergo, and as we saw, even suggests that

his struggle may lead to martyrdom (". . . je veux me battre avec la

vérité elle-même. Elle me martyrisera peut-être--surement").

Finally, it is worth mentioning two other categories of passages

which Jeanneret marked. The first concerns architecture directly.

Renan believes that Jesus considered architectural decoration (as well

as all lavish forms of art) to be sinful vanities, incompatible with
"son spiritualisme absolu" (p. 219)--an attitude which reminds us of
Le Corbusier's own moralistic objections to decoration in his writings of the 1920's (as well as of Adolf Loos's "Ornament und Verbrechen" of course.) And in another passage Renan combines this idea
with a familiar climatic theory of art, saying that warm climates like
that of Galilee produce a temperament less materialistic and more
"idéaliste," which thus eschews material decoration and prefers the
most simple houses. (p. 175) That Jeanneret marked these passages
would not be particularly significant, except for the fact that he
himself was later to become interested in the simple house-types of
the Near-East and the Mediterranean region--which he was to study
only three years later on his "voyage d'Orient."[79]

The remainder of the passages marked by Jeanneret are less specific in their substance; but they all emphasize the spiritual "perfection" of Jesus, his total "idealism," and especially his "purity:"

Une idée absolument neuve, l'idée d'un culte fondé sur la
pureté du coeur. . . (p. 94)

Ce qui distingue . . . Jésus . . . c'est son parfait idéalisme. (p. 131)

Jésus est l'homme qui a cru le plus énergiquement à la réalité de l'idéal . . . C'était la religion pure. . . (p. 296)

It would undoubtedly be wrong to suggest a causal relationship
between these characterizations of Jesus's teachings as "pure," and
Jeanneret's first formulation of his aesthetic theory in 1918 as
"Purism"--especially since this name seems to have been chosen as

much by Ozenfant as by Jeanneret (see Chapter V.) Yet it is amazing
how often the term "pure" occurs in Jeanneret's early reading in reference to philosophical or religious idealism--as in Provensal,
Schuré, and here in Renan. Furthermore, the mediaeval Catharists
(Jeanneret's youthful interest in whom has been mentioned already)
were actually known as "les Purs" and the concept of "purity" was
central to their doctrines.[80] What we can suggest is that when Jeanneret began to employ the terms "Purism" and "l'art pur" to describe
his new aesthetic, they likely had connotations to him beyond their
merely formal meaning, and implied all the religious and philosophical
associations with which they had been invested in his early reading.

Jeanneret's reading of the Vie de Jésus has been examined in
detail here because it suggests so clearly his state of mind at this
crucial period in Paris: his intensity, his spiritual preoccupation,
and above all his conviction that he was destined to play a revolutionary role and to be the prophet of a new order.

Summary

What, exactly, was the significance of these two years in Paris
to Jeanneret's education and development? He himself, at the time,
saw this as a period of great crisis, in which all of the teachings
of his former Master were shown to be false, making it necessary to
formulate the "art of tomorrow" all by himself, starting only with the
bold new principles which Auguste Perret had announced to him. Yet as
we saw, these new principles--that architecture is the expression of

the structural "carcass" of a building, of the materials one uses, and
of the laws of statics and mechanics--were assimilated by Jeannert
only superficially, to say the least. His letter to L'Eplattenier reveals that essentially he still thought of architecture, like Provensal,
as a manifestation of absolute "truth" and formal principles which were
to be discovered by solitary meditation and communion with "le moi,"
and whose ultimate purpose was the salvation of Man. And the books he
read at this time which seem to have impressed him most, rather than
tempering these ideas, actually intensified them--Zarathustra by con-
tributing the passionate image of an imminent higher form of Man, and
the Vie de Jésus by linking earthly and divine "revolution" and suggesting an identification with the Christ himself.

Jeanneret's letter to L'Eplattenier reveals that he was in a
state of considerable mental and emotional turmoil at this time--
precisely the sort of crisis which Erikson describes as typical of
the "moratorium" period. But it would be wrong to conclude from this
that nothing definite was gained from this period, or that Jeanneret's
sense of working toward an aesthetic formulation was self-delusion.
For the fact is that he did adopt aspects of Perret's thinking--not-
ably a fascination with reinforced concrete as the material of the
future, a concern for structural systems, and an interest in city-
planning--although he altered and reshaped these to fit his own needs
and preferences. These transformations by Jeanneret will be examined
later in this study. But the point to be made here is that Jeanneret's
emotional state during this period in Paris, and his reactions to

books like _Zarathustra_ and the _Vie de Jésus_ are by no means irrele-

vant to his later career as Le Corbusier, because they clearly influ-

enced his perception of Perret's ideas, and determined to a large

extent what he _did_ to these ideas in the following years. Indeed,

one could suggest that the essential quality of Le Corbusier's archi-

tectural thought was to be the result of the distortion of Perret's

rationalist notions of architecture by their absorption into Jeanneret's

idealistic view of himself and the world.

CHAPTER III

GERMANY AND THE ORIENT, 1910-1911

Sometime toward the end of 1909 Jeanneret returned to La Chaux-de-Fonds, where he was to stay until the next April.[1] His reasons for leaving Paris (where he had told L'Eplattenier he could devote himself so effectively to learning), and returning home (where he felt the views of his former teacher and colleagues were so mistaken) are hard to imagine, especially since Jeanneret then joined these colleagues in an undertaking, called the "Ateliers d'art," in which they all were to design and execute projects in the decorative arts and architecture -- precisely the sort of thing Jeanneret had attacked so vehemently in his letter to L'Eplattenier as premature creativity which an artist in his twenties should avoid at all costs. Perhaps Jeanneret had a sudden reaction against Perret's ideas, or simply a change of heart about L'Eplattenier and his friends back home. But whatever his motives, the activities which were envisioned for these Ateliers d'art ("sculpture sur pierre, sculpture sur bois, mosaïque, vitrail bronze, métal repoussé, peinture murale, lustrerie, etc.") do not suggest the industry-oriented program of the Bauhaus, as Le Corbusier later claimed,[2] but rather L'Eplattenier's decorative interests or the English Arts-and-Crafts movement. So in joining this enterprise, Jeanneret was in a sense renouncing Perret's dedication to advanced new materials and techniques.

Even the well-known design which Jeanneret drew up at this time, for a building to house these "Ateliers d'art,"[3] which at first glance seems to be in the spirit of Perret because it seems designed to be constructed of concrete, actually has little to do with Perret when we examine it more closely (Fig. 26). For one thing, the drawings reveal that in reality no thought had been given to how the building would be constructed: the walls of the second-level studios, for example, are all above voids and could hardly have been built regardless of the material used. And even formally, the design harks back to Jeanneret's pre-Paris days. The separate studios (as Peter Serenyi has pointed out) are like the cells of the monastery at Ema which Jeanneret visited in 1907. But even more than this, the overall composition of volumes looks exactly like a blown-up version of the bracket-detail on Jeanneret's Fallet House of 1906 (Fig. 27), which as we saw seems to have been related to Provensal's call for a new "cubic" architecture. Even the proportions of the blocks comprising these two compositions are amazingly similar--the vertical faces seeming to be based roughly on golden rectangles. Thus, in effect, this "Ateliers d'art" design is as formalistic and abstract as Jeanneret's Vienna-period projects must have been, which in Paris he had deemed worthless because of their "conception purement plastique."

This contradiction is puzzling. Perhaps the most we can suggest about it is that Jeanneret at this time was unsuccessfully trying to reconcile the theoretical positions he had adopted in Paris, with his inherently formalistic attitudes toward design. It must have been an extremely frustrating experience--and perhaps this frustration was one of the reasons Jeanneret suddenly left La Chaux-de-Fonds again, after only a few months there, and headed off on another voyage, this time to Germany.

Jeanneret in Germany

It is sometimes assumed that Jeanneret was sent to Germany, by the Art School in La Chaux-de-Fonds, with the mission of studying the decorative arts there--his report on which was to be published by the Art School in 1912.[4] But he went to Germany in April 1910, and only two months later received the commission to undertake this study.[5] In Munich, he had already become friendly with the architect Theodor Fischer, through whose auspices he was to meet the leading figures in the Werkbund and other artistic movements in Germany at that time.[6] So it seems likely that Jeanneret himself may have proposed this study, while already in Munich and realizing that his new contacts could lead to a travel-study project paid for by the Art School--which L'Eplattenier then may have proceeded to secure for him (just as he probably had secured Jeanneret's early architectural commissions.) However it was accomplished, we have here the first example of what was to become Le Corbusier's life-long genius for selling his architectural observations and theories, or publishing his own unexecuted design projects, or simply financing a journey by writing about what he had learned from it.

Jeanneret spent the next year in Germany: first in Munich,
where besides Theodor Fischer he met Baron Gunther von Pechmann
(director of the Vermittelungsstelle dur angewandte Kunst); then
Berlin where he met Hermann Muthesius and Peter Behrens (in whose
office he was to work at the end of 1910 and the beginning of 1911);
Dresden, where he met Wolf Dohrn (then director of the Werkbund) and
Heinrich Tessenow (architect of the garden-city and art-colony Hellerau, where Jeanneret's brother Albert happened to be studying at
that time[7]); and Hagen, where he met Karl Ernst Osthaus, director of
the Folkwang Museum.[8]   And he saw many exhibitions--the most important of which was probably the Allgemeine   Städtebau-Ausstellung
in Berlin in 1910.[9]

The report which Jeanneret made of these studies, and which
was then published in 1912, consists primarily of factual information
about the applied arts in Germany, the organizations he investigated,
the exhibitions he saw, and especially the art schools he visited.
This rather unexpected interest in education suggests that Jeanneret
perhaps had already been approached by L'Eplattenier about teaching
in his projected "Nouvelle Section" of the Art School (see Chapter IV),
and that Jeanneret was already thinking of himself as a teacher. As
for Jeanneret's own opinions of what he saw in Germany, few are expressed directly in this report. Of those which are, the most per-
sistent is an admiration for the technical skill and organizational
ability which the Germans were able to bring to bear on the arts, but

at the same time a conviction that in the final analysis, French
artistic taste remained superior: "Si Paris est le foyer de l'Art,
l'Allemagne demeure le grand chantier de production" (p. 74). Related to this attitude is Jeanneret's belief that the "esprit bourgeois" is stronger in German art than in French (pp. 9-11), a notion
which appears in Jeanneret's somewhat confused introduction to the
report, in which he also speaks of the French Revolution as having
destroyed aristocratic refinement and as having been "désastreuse
pour l'Art" (p. 9)--a judgment which probably could have been shared
by the more reactionary students at the École des Beaux-Arts.

Jeanneret's commission was specifically to investigate the
"applied" arts; so it is hardly surprising that a large part of his
report describes exhibits of jewelry, decorative ceramics, printed
wrapping papers, candy boxes, and other ornamental objects. Yet
when we remember that in the early twenties Le Corbusier was to
detest the very notion of "decorated" arts,[10] it is useful to point
out that in 1910 he found nothing to criticize in these things--and
even spoke admiringly of "une merveilleuse collection" of ladies'
toilet objects and jewelry (p. 28) and of boxes covered with "papiers
ornementés gaiement, encadrant une vue typique d'un grand nombre de
villes d'art célèbres. . ." (p. 27.)

But we naturally are more interested in Jeanneret's reactions
to the new architecture (especially Behrens' work) and city-planning
in Germany. As for Behrens, Jeanneret writes that he first visited
his A.E.G. factory buildings (e.g. Fig. 28) in June 1910, and then

became more familiar with them while working in Behrens' office.[11]
He was impressed with the fact that Behrens was asked to supervise
the design of all the company's products and buildings; but his reaction to the designs themselves is strangely neutral--remarking on
their sobriety and cleanness, but speaking almost as if they had
little to do with architecture. Behrens' overall work for the A.E.G.
is

> . . . une création architecturale intégrale de notre époque,
> --locaux d'une sobriété et d'une propreté admirables, au
> milieu desquels de superbes machines apportent une note
> grave et impressionante. [And it all has] un aspect modeste,
> sobre, presque impersonnel.[12]

We sense here an attitude of surprise, and of uncertainty about
just how he should react to Behrens' forms--very similar, in fact, to
those attitudes which we observed (see Chapter I, p. 21) in Jeanneret's
1913 quote in which he was to speak of German architecture as ". . . les
cristaux durs et brutaux." In fact, we shall discover, when we examine
Jeanneret's annotations in a book which he read while working for
Behrens (Cingria's Entretiens, see below) that rather than being favorably impressed with the new German architecture, he actually was re-
acting against it rather strongly.

In his report, Jeanneret's remarks about German town-planning
are similar to those about Behrens' architecture. He speaks of the
intense activity and spirit of "reform" in German town-planning--which
he contrasts with the continuation, in France, of "une tradition jugée
parfaitement adequate et bonne à perpétuer" (p. 35)--but it is primarily the neatness, convenience, and again "sobriety" of these new

towns which impresses him.[13] He is impressed with the concept of

"garden cities" (which he was to study carefully in the next few

years (see below) but then was partly to react against) and speaks

with praise of plans he saw at the Berlin "Städtebau-Ausstellung"

for new towns with curving roads, single-family houses, and large

green spaces. (p. 48) He says that the most impressive of the

constructed new towns in Germany is Hellerau, near Dresden (Fig. 29)

--which, as mentioned above, was designed by Heinrich Tessenow and

others, and included a school where Jeanneret's brother was study-

ing--and which Jeanneret visited at Christmastime 1910. His remarks

about Hellerau are particularly interesting because they are the

first evidence we have of any interest on his part in the social and

economic aspects of low-cost housing, and especially in the notion

of "collectivist" communities. He describes how the construction

of the town was financed, how the workers who live there all own

their houses simply by paying their rent, and how civic decisions

are voted on by the whole community:

> Les ouvriers sont maîtres de la société, puisque pour être
> locataire il faut faire partie de la société. . . S'ils
> veulent hausser ou baisser le prix de leur loyer, ou créer
> quelque modification, ils le décident eux-mêmes en assem-
> blée générale.--Hellerau est proprement une manifestation
> collectiviste. C'est le détournement du capital jusqu'ici
> canalisé vers un but égoiste,retournant à ceux qui le pro-
> duisent. (p. 50)

The term "collectivist" was to recur later in Le Corbusier's

writings, beginning in 1918;[14] and especially in the late 1920's and

1930's he was to become intensely concerned with social and political issues. This aspect of Le Corbusier's career will not be examined in this study, but it is important to note that Jeanneret had begun to be aware of these questions at least as early as 1910 in Germany.

Jeanneret and Muthesius

Reyner Banham has pointed out some important similarities between the aesthetic theory of Hermann Muthesius--as seen in his influential speech to the Werkbund Congress in 1911--and Le Corbusier's thinking in the 1920's. He points especially to Muthesius' assertions that architectural beauty is ultimately a spiritual quality, transcending material or functional considerations--for example when he says that:

> Far higher than the material is the spiritual; far higher than function, material and technique, stands Form. These three material aspects might be impeccably handled but--if Form were not--we would still be living in a merely brutish world.[15]

Muthesius is, indeed, very close to Le Corbusier here--not only in his characterization of architecture as a supra-material activity, as Banham points out, but also in his contrast of brute nature and spiritual Man, like Le Corbusier's "la bête" versus "la tête." And there are other aspects of this speech which sound like Le Corbusier, such as its attack on Impressionism for concerning itself with the "individual" rather than the "typical" or universal.[16] It is not however clear, as Banham assumes, that Jeanneret would have attended this 1911 Werkbund Congress and heard Muthesius's speech--especially since Jeanneret left Germany in May 1911.[17] But in any case, Muthesius is not really crucial to Jeanneret's development, since as we now know,

all of these attitudes which could be called idealistic or formalistic were thoroughly familiar to Jeanneret from his reading long
before he went to Germany. It is true that Germany, around the turn
of the century, was the acknowledged center of philosophical idealism in all of its manifestations, and so Jeanneret's contacts with
figures like Muthesius may well have strengthened or modified his
idealism--but did not create it.

In fact, Jeanneret does seem to have been interested in the
thinking of the Werkbund leaders--for he apparently arranged to have
Werkbund publications sent to him in La Chaux-de-Fonds, after his
departure from Germany. The 1913 Werkbund Jahrbuch was one of these;[18]
and it contains another speech by Muthesius which even more specifically than his 1911 speech expresses ideas which can be found in Le
Corbusier's later writings. Despite the fact that Jeanneret did not
read this until a couple of years later, it is worth discussing here
because some of its ideas may well have been expressed by Muthesius to
Jeanneret in Germany.

This 1913 Werkbund Jahrbuch, devoted to the subject "Kunst in
Industrie und Handel," also contains articles by Walter Gropius,[19]
Peter Bruckmann, and others, on rather specific aspects of industrial
architecture; but Muthesius's article stands out as being more general
and theoretical. Entitled "Das Formproblem in Ingenieurbau," it first
traces the nineteenth-century development of these "engineering structures"--bridges, warehouses, factories, etc. Muthesius of course
damns the early period when eclectic decorative forms were applied

to these constructions; but he also criticizes a newer attitude (he

obviously is referring to architectural "rationalism") that merely

by expressing the function one inevitably produces acceptable form:

> Vielleicht ahnte man damals noch nicht, dass die Erfüllung
> des reinen Zweckes an und für sich noch keine das Auge be-
> friedigende Form schafft, vielmehr hierzu noch andere Kräfte,
> sei es auch unbewusst, mitwirken müssen. (p. 25)

The suggestion here that this necessary, non-functional, aesthe-

tic element may be used by the artist even unconsciously, is taken up

later. But first Muthesius elaborates on his distinction between

Function and Form--indeed, taking us to an amazingly extreme position,

where the two are considered to be totally unrelated, although both

are necessary:

> Die Vorstellung, es genüge für den Ingenieur völlig, dass ein
> Bauwerk, ein Gerät, eine Maschine, die er schafft, einen Zweck
> erfülle, ist irrig, noch irriger ist der neuerdings oft gehörte
> Satz, dass, wenn sie einen Zweck erfülle, sie zugleich auch
> schön sei. Nützlichkeit hat an und für sich nichts mit Schön-
> heit zu tun. Bei der Schönheit handelt es sich um ein Problem
> der Form und um nichts anderes, bei der Nützlichkeit un die
> nackte Erfüllung irgend eines Diestes. (pp. 27-28)

Muthesius goes on to say that both of these aspects must be sat-

isfied and combined in good design; but what is surprising is the

categorical distinction he makes between them: "Beauty is concerned

with the problem of form and with nothing else." Our examination of

Jeanneret's background suggests that this attitude must have appeared

perfectly normal and proper to him (despite his exposure to Perret);

and in Le Corbusier's writings we find very similar expressions of

the sharp separation between formal questions and functional questions:

Nettement formuler, animer d'une unité l'oeuvre, lui donner
une attitude fondamentale, un caractère: pure création de
l'esprit. On l'admet pour la peinture et la musique; mais
on rabaisse l'architecture à ses causes utilitaires: bou-
doirs, w.-c., radiateurs, ciment armé, ou voûtes en berceaux
ou arcs ogifs, etc. Ceci est de construction, ceci n'est
pas d'architecture. L'architecture, c'est quand il y a
émotion poétique. L'architecture est chose de plastique.[20]

Muthesius' article goes on to describe the aesthetic sides of

this duality in somewhat more specific terms than he had in his 1911

speech:

Unser Auge ist der ständige Kontrolleur dessen, was wir
sichtbar tun, wobei wir die Form nach einem unserm Gehirne
eingepflanzten Gesetze bilden, beurteilen und handhaben.
Dieses Gesetz wirkt selbsttätig, wir können uns ihm nicht
entziehen, selbst wenn wir es wollten. (p. 28)

The description of this form-controlling element as a "law"

implanted in our mind, suggests further links with Le Corbusier's

thinking--as well as with Provensal, for whom aesthetic "laws" were

also an important notion. Yet for Muthesius, this concept remains

rather vague. Only once in this article does he start to describe

the nature of this form-sense in Man, and then only very cursorily:

. . . gute Proportionierung, Abstimmung der Farben, wirkungs-
vollen Aufbau, Rhythmus, ausdrucksvolle Form. Die Tendenzen,
die bei allen diesen Gestaltern wirken, sind allgemeiner,
sozusagen kosmischer Art, sie sind unserer Gehirntätigheit
immanent. (p. 30)

But if these principles have hitherto been "immanent," "selbst-

tätig," and "unbewusst," Muthesius claims that now this will no longer

suffice--precisely the same point which Provensal had made about his

"rapports harmoniques" which artists hitherto had followed instinctively

but which now had to be formulated scientifically. For Muthesius, the

great problems now facing designers also require that "[Der Schaf-
fender] unbedingt diese Gesetze nich nur unbewusst wirken lassen,
sondern sie bewusst befolgen muss." (p. 30) As in Provensal's book,
the challenge here for Jeanneret clearly would have been to search
out the precise shape and workings of these formal laws.

There are a number of other ideas in Muthesius' article which
seem related to Le Corbusier's later thinking, for example the notion
that certain engineering-buildings can have high aesthetic value--if
they express the universal form-principles. Muthesius lists "bridges,
railroad stations, lighthouses, and grain-elevators" as particularly
likely to do this (p. 30); and in particular his mention of grain-
elevators suggests that like Le Corbusier he considered strong simple
geometric forms to be most satisfactory aesthetically. In fact, the
illustrations accompanying Muthesius' article included several pictures of American grain-elevators; and in the first issue of L'Esprit
Nouveau in 1920, Le Corbusier was to reproduce several of these illus-
trations--retouching them, however, to make them look even starker and
more cubic (e.g. Figs. 30-31).[21]

Thus Muthesius' influence on Jeanneret seems to have consisted
mainly of reinforcing his belief that architectural form must be a
creation of Man's spirit and mind, following innate plastic laws.
Inherent in this idealistic view of form is the suggestion that this
spirituality of plastic problems raises them to the highest level of
human achievement. As Muthesius said:

[Our aesthetic sense] strebt, das Unharmonische harmonisch zu machen, das Störende zu beseitigen, das Fehlende zu ergänzen und das so einen höheren Ordnungssinn darstellt, der unsere Leistungen erst zur menschlichen Arbeit im höheren Sinne erhebt. (p. 31)

Like Provensal and Schuré before him, Muthesius seems to have contributed to Jeanneret's conviction that his work as an architect was to concern Man's spirit much more essentially than Man's body.

Jeanneret's reading in Germany

Le Corbusier's library contains four books which are clearly inscribed as dating from this 1910-1911 period in Germany. Several other books, with no inscriptions, may well have been acquired by Jeanneret at this time too;[22] but they are less certain. All four of the dated books are in French; and one of them was in fact ordered by Jeanneret from Geneva, thus showing that Jeanneret continued serious reading even during his travels in Germany. Two of these books are typical of the kind of general cultural works Jeanneret had read in Paris: Victor Cousin's Du vrai, du beau, du bien (see below), and Dante's Divine Comédie.[23] Another is a lengthy essay on the future of the arts in French-speaking Switzerland, Alexandre Cingria-Vaneyre's Entretiens de la Villa du Rouet (see below). And the fourth is a novel, L'entêtement slovaque (see below), by William Ritter, an art-critic and dilettante whom Jeanneret seems to have met in Germany at this time, and who in the next several years was to become his closest friend and intellectual confidant.[24]

Victor Cousin's Du vrai, du beau, et du bien,[25] would be of interest to us--with its strong case against empiricism and its

idealistic aesthetic doctrine derived from Hegel--if we had some idea
of what Jeanneret's attitude toward it was. He inscribed it "Munich,
mai 1910" (thus only a month after he had arrived in Germany), but
made no annotations, and furthermore read only part of it (the pages
of the last chapters were left uncut.) The chapters which he did read
are primarily philosophical, concerned largely with defending the
absolute existence of Plato's "Ideas" (against Kant's "scepticism");
and it is all so similar to what Provensal talked about (who must have
been influenced by Cousin), that Jeanneret may simple have stopped
reading it out of disinterest. Nevertheless, there are some aspects
in the chapters he read which could have impressed him--such as
Cousin's fascination with the perfection of mathematics and geometry
(p. 94); his statement that a truly beautiful form has a simple, clear
shape which is easy to perceive at a glance (p. 133); or his idea that
beauty is based on a subtle opposition of elements of "variety" versus
elements of "unity" (pp. 155-58), an idea which Le Corbusier was later
to stress in his own writings.[26] Yet, we must confess that we simply
do not know what Jeanneret's reactions were toward this work.

Cingria-Vaneyre's Entretiens de la Villa du Rouet[27]

The case with this book is totally different from that of
Cousin's. For one thing, this is the book which Jeanneret ordered
from Geneva, thus suggesting some special interest in it.[28] But more
important, he marked passages in it and made annotations--in fact the
most extensive and significant annotations which we find in any

of his books up to this time. These annotations reveal that Jeanneret
reacted very favorably to the argument of the book, and that it actually convinced him to modify his plans for his career--deciding to make
of himself a Swiss regionalist architect. This is such an unexpected
and unknown aspect of Jeanneret's development that it is worth examining the book in some detail here--especially since it throws a good
deal of light on Jeanneret's activities in the next several years.

The _Entretiens_ is written as a series of "dialogues" between
several upper-class French-Swiss art-lovers, set in a Florentine villa.
Its sole theme is the need for creating a local artistic identity for
the "Suisse-romande"--that is, the French-speaking part of Switzerland,
around Geneva and Neuchâtel (and of course including La Chaux-de-Fonds.)
To Cingria-Vaneyre, this was a problem of crucial importance; and he
seems to have convinced Jeanneret of this. Large parts of the book
are devoted to singing the praises of the Suisse-romande region, and
claiming for it an illustrious artistic tradition and great potential
genius. But the single most important idea, which is reiterated
throughout the book, is that the true spirit of this region is Mediterranean, not northern, and that its art must be reoriented away
from Germany, and toward the Classicism of the greco-latin civilizations:

> Notre âme classique, en effet, ne peut qu'évoluer dans une
> formule gréco-latine. (p. 9)

> La vocation de rendre ma patrie à ses vraies harmonies
> m'avait alors investi. J'avais réfréné tout ce qui pou-
> vait me porter loin du Sud, de Rome et de la Méditer-
> ranée; c'était le salut par la culture classique.
> (p. vii)

Geneve doit être greco-latine. (p. 23)

Linked with this is an attack on "Romanticism," which has per-
verted the true Classical spirit of the region, and on Germany, which
is the source of this perverting influence and has had a cultural
"domination" over the region.[29] These charges are repeated many times,
and while it is often difficult to pinpoint very precisely just what
Germanic influences Cingria is referring to, Jeanneret clearly
responded to the challenge. For at the end of the book he carefully
wrote out a kind of profession of faith (Fig. 32)--even dating it
("23 nov 1910")--stating that this book had unlocked the German "vise-
grip" from him and reoriented him toward a "Jura discipline:"

> . . . Pour moi, ce livre vient favorablement aider à mon
> orientation. Il provoque un examen, les déductions normales,
> claires, lumineuses; il desserre pour moi l'étau germanique.
> Dans une année, à Rome, je le relirai, et, par des esquisses,
> je fonderai ma discipline jurassique, neuchâteloise.[30]

Aside from the regionalist aspect, this is fascinating because
it reveals that already in November 1910, while he was working in
Peter Behrens' office, Jeanneret had strong doubts about Germany and
was planning some kind of trip to the South (where he was to go in
May 1911.) And in fact, there are some striking parallels between
specific remarks in this book and the actual itinerary which Jeanneret's "voyage d'Orient" followed in 1911--suggesting that Jeanneret's voyage may actually have been inspired by this book. For
example, Cingria spends a good part of the book describing the physical nature of the Jura region, with its mountains and valleys, and
maintains that it is a "classical" topography which requires and

inspires a very specific kind of architecture; in search of geo-
graphical parallels to the Suisse-romande landscape, he suggests only
two--on the one hand, Greece,[31] and more surprisingly, the area around
Constantinople.[32] Greece and Constantinople, in fact, were to be the
two highlights of Jeanneret's voyage the next year, the two places
where he was to spend the most time and experience the most significant architectural insights--as we shall later see.

As for the specific sort of architecture which is appropriate
to this kind of mountainous landscape, Cingria calls for a calm,
simplified Classicism, which while composed of some traditional elements like columns and friezes, will be stamped with a new "geometric" character:

> . . . la montagne appelle à ses flancs des architectures regu-
> lières et calmes qui la reposent du désordre inférieur de ses
> bases. Et c'est pourquoi les vallées alpestres devraient
> être décorées de longues colonnades, d'hypogées tranquilles
> et puissants, de bas-reliefs taillés dans le roc, avec une
> facture géométrique et grandiose. (p. 262)

Next to this passage Jeanneret wrote: "Des idées analogues au
Zugspitz [sic], puis ensuite absolument positives au Haut Jura"--a
somewhat enigmatic annotation, but which seems to refer to similar
ideas which Jeanneret himself had recently had.[33] In any case, it
shows that he was receptive to the kind of Classical mountain-archi-
tecture which Cingria is advocating. And indeed, the two houses which
Jeanneret was to design next, in La Chaux-de-Fonds in 1912 (see ahead,
Figs. 35-36), were to follow very closely the prescription which
Cingria proposes--with their large, calm forms (so different from

the picturesque details of his three earlier houses), and simplified classical elements such as the pedimented porch of the Favre-Jacot House.[34]

Cingria goes on to make more specific suggestions for the new Suisse-romande architecture he envisages. Colors, when used, should be earthy colors, such as ivory, olive green, and ochres.[35] But preferable are white walls--which can be either marble, or rubble or brick covered with "crepi à la chaux" and painted white. (p. 290) Other materials, like wood, are discouraged (p. 292)--probably for tending toward picturesqueness. Wall-surfaces should be large and unbroken; and the main lines of a building should be horizontal (pp. 308-09.) But the most important ideal is of a simplicity based on the right angle:

> . . . la simplicité rectiligne caracterise le classicisme
> dans ce qu'il a de plus pur. (p. 306)

On the other hand, Cingria does not want the new architecture to be composed solely of "des masses cubiques avec des sculptures carrées, comme les architectes berlinois" (p. 307). This reference is probably to the nineteenth-century work of Schinkel and his followers; but in a sense it could also include Behrens, for whom Jeanneret was of course just then working. It underlines our problem of knowing exactly what Jeanneret meant when he wrote that this book had unlocked the "German vise" from him--for this could refer either to German picturesque Romanticism (which Cingria attacks) or to the overly stark tradition of Berlin classicism (which he also attacks.) Actually,

however, these two are apparently linked in Cingria's view. His
criticism of the "Berlin architects" seems to be that their buildings are too harsh and brutal; and he says for example that some
curved forms should be employed in architecture, though sparingly
(p. 307)--and in this sense, all German architecture for him shares
a lack of gracefulness and calm order. Jeanneret may well have
agreed with this view. This would explain not only the "German
vise," but also his remarks in the Werkbund report that Germany
had fine organization but little sense of "art"--and furthermore
would help explain the character of his next houses, with their
judicious use of simple curved forms which distinguishes them from
the work of Behrens and Tessenow. (Indeed, even in the 1920's,
Le Corbusier's designing was to be characterized by a careful use
of curved forms which would distinguish his work from that of the
Bauhaus and "Germanic" work in general.)

Cingria also seems to object to what he sees as a bleak industrialism in German architecture; for later in the book, there are
tirades against utilitarianism (p. 338), and against machines and
"the ideal of uniformity" which is attacked as "l'américanisme
naissant" and "cette dégénérescence du goût" (p. 360). Cingria's
point of view, in fact, is aristocratic: for him "l'américanisme"
is a euphemism for class-leveling, and the French Revolution with
its "idées égalitaires" destroyed all artistic refinement (p. 360)
--the same idea which Jeanneret was to express in the introduction
to his Werkbund report. Cingria is a reactionary in many other

ways as well--dreaming of escaping from the vulgarity of modern industrial life by recreating the calm beauty and elegance which he
finds in the Classical art of the South.

Jeanneret shared a good deal of this sentiment. This is revealed in a long and emotional annotation which he wrote in a section
of the book which, in ironic fashion, is ostensibly defending "le
modernisme" against romantic reactionaries. Cingria's characters are
speaking of the powerful beauty of watching, from an isolated "poste
de vigie," a railroad train at night as it crosses deep valleys on
iron viaducts, and tunnels through snow-capped mountains; and this
leads to an attack on those Romantics who love Roman engineering-
works but hate their modern equivalents. Cingria does not seem to
sense the irony of his own Romantic view of this nocturnal mountain-
train "modernism;" but nevertheless, this passage struck a responsive
chord in Jeanneret, and he wrote around the margins:

> Vive le modernisme. C'est beau, c'est juste, c'est vivant!
> Cependant si le poste de vigie est belle évocation, mon
> esprit, mes besoins, "monacals" me font redouter la cime
> envahie. Si je pouvais y monter seul ou avec quelques uns
> de mon acabit, par un soir, en I classe, oui, ce serait
> splendide, très beau, grand. Mais diable, je fus, voici
> trois mois, au Zugspitz. [sic] La désillusion fut
> cruelle, motivée. Ce ne fut pas un banal sentimentalisme.
> Et quand je lis ces lignes, j'ai deux pianos qui sonnent
> là, tout près. Ceci me rend fou-furieux, et je jure, et
> l'Art s'en va: le sentiment est refoulé.--Cependant, une
> nuit même de pluie au sommet de la Jungfrau, je me la
> paierai et sacrificerai alors à notre brave siècle.
> (soir 2/11/10.)[36]

This is a most candid revelation by Jeanneret of his attitudes.
First is his desire to be isolated and alone on this metaphoric

"look-out post," or at most accompanied only by several others of
his "quality" ("de mon acabit")--a remarkable expression of the elitist notion of artistic genius which we have seen throughout Jeanneret's
reading. It is impossible for us to know just what the "disillusionment" was, at the Zugspitze three months earlier, but we can guess that
it was some kind of vulgar intrusion on Jeanneret's artistic sensibil-
ity--like the discordant pianos which just then were driving away his
sense of "Art." The second remarkable attitude is Jeanneret's assumption that this isolated, trance-like sensitivity to Art is what "le
modernisme" is all about. In this regard, it is totally appropriate
that his resolution to "sacrifice" to "our gallant century" does not
envisage this being done in a factory or on a building-site, but on
the summit of another snow-capped mountain.

These attitudes, in reality, are hardly any different from those
we examined in Jeanneret's letter to L'Eplattenier written in 1908
from Paris: the same vague Romantic conception of the "art of tomorrow,"
the same conviction that it will be created by isolating oneself in
ecstatic meditation, and the same fascination with pain and "sacrifice."
Just as we found it peculiar that Jeanneret would have preserved these
attitudes after having been exposed to Perret's ideas in Paris, it is
even stranger than he should be preserving them in Germany, after studying the Werkbund movement and while working in Behrens' office. Whatever their limitations or biases, the Werkbund leaders recognized that
the great problem facing architecture was its role in the industrial
and urban society of the twentieth century. Despite this, Cingria's

Romantic call for an elegant Classicism set in an unspoiled mountain
landscape was apparently accepted wholeheartedly by Jeanneret--even
to the extent that he rededicated himself to a "discipline jurassique
neuchâteloise" and to a future in the mountains of his homeland rather
than in Paris or Berlin. Only this can explain why Jeanneret was to
return to La Chaux-de-Fonds after his southern voyage the next year,
and stay there for six full years--a retreat which up until now has
been inexplicable (the World War is sometimes given as a reason; but
Jeanneret had been home for three years before it began.) That this
return to La Chaux-de-Fonds was the result of free choice (and not,
for example, financial problems) is proven by the fact that in late
1911, when Jeanneret was in Constantinople, he was to meet Auguste
Perret (there to supervise the construction of the French Embassy),
who urged him to return to Paris to work with him, but that Jeanneret
declined the offer.[37] This refusal by Jeanneret to pursue his career
in a progressive environment, with Perret in Paris, and his choice
instead to return to the mountains and a "discipline jurassique,"
can make sense only in light of Cingria's Romantic vision of a new
Suisse-romande Classicism.

The Voyage d'Orient

In May 1911, Jeanneret left Berlin and started on a trip with
a friend, August Klipstein, which was to last until the end of the
year, and lead them to Bohemia, Serbia, Rumania, Bulgaria, Constantinople, Mount Athos, Athens, and then through Italy back to Switzerland.[38] Later accounts of this trip have suggested that Jeanneret

had been growing tired of Berlin and Germany and that a letter from
Klipstein (who was writing a thesis on El Greco and wanted to go to
Budapest and Bucharest to look at paintings) caught his fancy and
made him decide, on the spur of the moment, to go along.[39] But we
have seen that already, six months before, his reading of Cingria
had convinced him that the South was the place to be rather than
Germany; and that he even had foretold (in his annotation dated
23 Nov 1910) that in "one year" he would be in Rome--a prediction
which oddly enough he seems to have fulfilled precisely. It apparently was Jeanneret who suggested to Klipstein that they enlarge the
trip to include specifically Constantinople and Greece;[40] and as we
saw, these two places were of special importance in Cingria's argument. And there may have been another influence on their itinerary
as well: William Ritter, Jeanneret's friend mentioned above, who
was a connoisseur of the folk-art and culture of Eastern Europe and
wrote articles on this region for French and German art magazines.
In fact, in July 1910, Ritter had presented Jeanneret with a copy of
a newly-published book of his--L'entêtement slovaque[41]--which is a
Romantic novel of peasant-life in Slovakia. It contains long descriptions of peasant art and of the white-washed houses of peasant villages (which are like "un premier avant-goût de l'Orient," p. 8),
often in language similar to that with which Jeanneret was to describe
such villages in the letters which he wrote during his trip. Later,
Jeanneret put these letters together and published them as Le voyage
d'Orient--which in effect is the first book written by him which

expresses his own attitudes (the Werkbund report having consisted
mainly of factual information), and as such it is of considerable
interest to us.[42]

One of the most striking things about Jeanneret's account of
his voyage, in fact, is its reverent attitude toward peasant art
and culture. With the exception of the Parthenon and the mosques
in Constantinople, everything he admires is anonymous folk-art or
"architecture without architects" (and even the Parthenon and mosques
are considered by him in some ways as anonymous, universal forms, as
we shall see.) A large part of his account is devoted to descriptions of peasant villages (both in Eastern Europe and Turkey), their
houses, their artifacts (pottery, silver-work, costumes, etc.), their
rituals and celebrations, and their life in general. In many passages, Jeanneret expresses the feeling that this peasant-culture is
somehow superior to "civilized" culture, because it is universal and
fundamental and, we sense, in touch with deep spiritual forces:

> . . . cet art populaire comme une immuable caresse chaude,
> enveloppe la terre entière. . . Les formes sont expansives
> et gonflées de sève; la ligne toujours synthétise les
> spectacles naturels ou offre, tout à côté et sur le même
> objet, les féeries de la géométrie: étonnante conjonction
> des instincts rudimentaires et de ceux susceptibles des
> plus abstraites spéculations.--La couleur, elle aussi,
> n'est pas de description mais d'évocation; symbolique
> toujours. Elle est but et non moyen. . . . elle bouscule
> les grands géants empêtrés, les Giotto même, les Greco
> même, les Cézanne et les Van Gogh! --Considéré d'un
> certain point de vue, l'art populaire surnage les civilisa-
> tions les plus hautes. Il demeure une norme, sorte de
> mesure dont l'étalon est l'homme de race,--le sauvage, si
> tu peux. (p. 15)

This "savage" is a kind of universal Man, stripped of all irre-
levance; and at the end of this letter, Jeanneret says "Je te dis
Perrin [to whom this was written] que nous sommes, nous autres civil-
isés du centre, des sauvages et je te serre les mains" (p. 22). To
Jeanneret, in fact, this universal peasant-art is such a perfect
expression of the forces of nature and of Spirit, that he despairs
of ever being able to reach such a level himself:

> A gérer ces simples et éternelles forces, n'y a-t-il pas pour
> moi le travail d'une vie et la certitude même de n'arriver
> jamais à une proportion, à une unité, à une clarté dignes
> même d'une toute petite masure de province batie selon les
> lois inestimable d'une seculaire tradition? (p. 127)

In some ways, of course, this sounds like Adolf Loos--for whom
peasant architecture and art also attained a perfection seldom if
ever found in the "civilized" world.[43] But for Loos, peasant forms
were superior simply because they satisfy so precisely all of their
functional and material requirements with the maximum of economy--
basically the same notion which Christopher Alexander has recented
elaborated in more scientific terms.[44] This thoroughly materialistic notion is totally different from Jeanneret's attitude, which
sees in peasant forms not only economy and efficiency but, much
more important, spiritual and formal verities. We find this throughout the Voyage d'Orient, for example in Jeanneret's characterizations
of forms or colors as "symbolic," but even more specifically in his
obsession with geometry. Needless to say, the most efficient, functional, or economic objects will not necessarily be those which are
most geometric; yet everywhere Jeanneret looks, the forms which

interest him most are those ruled by the purest geometry (e.g.

Fig. 33), and in particular those based on circles and squares:

> Le sanctuaire blanc pousse ses domes sur ses grands cubes
> de maconnerie, en sa cité de pierre.
> Une géométrie élémentaire discipline les masses: le carré,
> le cube, la sphère. (p. 78)

The fact that Jeanneret is also most attracted to buildings

which are pure white (a preference expressed in literally dozens

of passages) is a corollary of this, since geometric forms proclaim

themselves most clearly under light when they are white. Like Henry

Provensal (who is surely the source of much of this), Jeanneret

feels that geometric volumes--as defined by the horizon and illu-

minated by the sun--express the eternal Ideal, or "absolute:"

> Je crois que l'horizontalité du toujours même horizon et
> surtout, en plein midi, l'uniformité imposante des maté-
> riaux perçus, installent en chacun la mesure la plus
> humainement perceptible de l'absolu. Dans l'irradiation
> de l'après-midi, voici qu'apparut la pyramide d'Athos!
> (p. 125)

Jeanneret in fact is so obsessed with the symbolic implications

of geometry, that he uses it metaphorically to describe even non-visual

phenomena--if he finds them spiritually moving--such as the singing of

a group of peasants in Serbia:

> Tout d'un coup, le bloc s'ébranle, et un cube de musique en
> sort; toutes les voix partent à l'unisson et les instruments
> ornementent le fond. . . la nuit tombe toute bleue; l'hor-
> izontale infrangible, sépare en les unissant, bien loin, la
> terre bourdonnante et le ciel illuminé d'étoiles. Le barde,
> seul est debout. Tout s'est fini sur une géométrie grandiose.
> . . . Les hymnes ont été comme de grands carrés posés ainsi
> que des tours. (p. 43)

Jeanneret's style of writing in these letters--poetic, Romantic,

often over-blown--is interesting because it is a style that crops up

now and then in Le Corbusier's later writings as well, and also
because it reveals such an emotional, expressive, and intense personality. Despite his frequent disclaimers of not knowing how to
write (pp. 7, 32, 37), Jeanneret clearly feels a great desire to
express his feelings verbally (just as he would throughout his life)
--and we actually feel ourselves more in the presence of a born poet
or essayist, than of a born architect. Indeed, it is amazing how
much of what attracted Jeanneret on this voyage, including the architecture, attracted him in thoroughly non-architectural ways. Typical
of this is Mount Athos--which, along with the Acropolis, impressed
Jeanneret more deeply than any other stage of his voyage. He and
Klipstein stayed there eighteen days; and although Jeanneret was
greatly impressed with the Byzantine murals there, and also with the
beauty of the landscape, it was really the monastic life and discipline itself which fascinated him most. His most impassioned language is reserved for descriptions of the solitude, silence, and inner
struggle which one submits to on Mount Athos:

> O cet Athos trop voué à la mort. . . Oui, y aller, la force
> dans les poings et non pour somnoler dans la lente narcose
> de la soi-disante prière, mais commencer l'immense vocation
> du trappiste--le silence, le combat tout en soi, surhumain
> presque, pour arriver à tirer sur soi, avec un sourrire
> antique, la dalle de la tombe! (p. 124)

> Car cette terre. . . n'est vouée qu'à des sombres ou pauvres,
> . . qu'à des rêveurs, des extatiques, des solitaires! (p. 130)

This attraction to solitude and to "combat tout en soi" sounds
precisely like Jeanneret's letter to L'Eplattenier from Paris--and
of course also recalls Jeanneret's early reading, and especially

Schuré's concept of mystical "initiates." The community at Mount
Athos actually lived this unworldly spirituality and anti-materialism, and this was what attracted Jeanneret so strongly, rather than
anything specific about its architecture. In fact, we sense that
the kind of architecture which most appealed to Jeanneret on this
trip was indeed that which was most unworldly, most unsubstantial,
most spiritual. The precise construction and structure of buildings are almost never discussed in the Voyage d'Orient; buildings
instead are "squares," "cubes," "spheres," or "cylinders"--volumes
whose very abstraction and perfection remove them from the realm
of substantiality. That Jeanneret should also have heard music in
terms of geometry is simply another aspect of this. As Provensal
had said, music and architecture are the most abstract of all the
arts, and the most easily expressive of the divine "Idea." Jeanneret's own mother was a musician, and he often made references to
this fact, and clearly felt that music and architecture were very
similar disciplines: both "pure création de l'esprit."

The Parthenon

With this de-materialized conception of architecture, it is
obvious how Jeanneret would perceive the Parthenon: as refined
Spirit, rather than refined structure or construction as did the
rationalists.[45] Jeanneret and Klipstein stayed in Athens several
weeks;[46] and Jeanneret seems to have spent virtually all of this
time on the Acropolis, studying its architecture, and especially
submitting to the power of the Parthenon. His immediate impressions

of it are contained in the Voyage d'Orient; but its impact stayed
with him, and even grew stronger with time, for these first impressions were eventually transformed into one of the most idealistic
professions he ever made: the article "Architecture: pure création
de l'esprit," published in L'Esprit Nouveau in 1921 and then reprinted in Vers une architecture. Furthermore, Jeanneret in Athens
seems to have purchased a short essay on the Parthenon, Ernest Renan's
Prière sur l'Acropole,[47] --which, while sharing Jeanneret's basic
idealism, presents it even more extremely than Jeanneret had before,
and seems to have influenced his specific attitudes toward the
Parthenon, as we shall see.

In the Voyage d'Orient account, many of Jeanneret's remarks
about the Parthenon are similar to those about other buildings
earlier on his trip. Its form is described as pure geometry (most
often as a "cube"), and there is an emphasis on the psychological
feelings of solitude, isolation, and removal from the world which
one experience in its presence[48]--a reaction also revealed by
Jeanneret's sketches of the Acropolis done at the time (Fig. 34).
But beyond this, the Parthenon begins to have a new and special
significance for Jeanneret. His descriptions become less vague,
and for the first time he talks about a building expressing "law"
and eternal principles of form related to mathematics; and he sees
the Parthenon as the most perfect expression of these eternal
principles:

Les huit colonnes obéissent à une loi unanime. . . (p. 162)

. . . la suprême mathématique du temple. (p. 166)

Je sais mesurer la perfection de ses temples et reconnaître
qu'ils ne sont nulle part ailleurs si extraordinaires; et
j'ai de longtemps accepté que ce soit ici comme le dépot
de l'étalon sacré, base de toute mensuration d'art. (p. 158)

These ideas are presented rather tentatively; but it is essen-

tially the same idealism which Le Corbusier was to state more clearly

in 1921--the notion that the Parthenon moves us because its form is

perfectly attuned to a universal harmony and thus "sounds an internal

chord" in us, and touches what Le Corbusier will call the "axis,"

the divine universal principle. Everything which stikes this chord

or axis provokes

au fond de nous, par delà nos sens, une résonance, sorte de
table d'harmonie qui se met à vibrer. Trace d'absolu indéfinissable préexistant qu fond de notre être.
Cette table d'harmonie qui vibre en nous est notre critérium
de l'harmonie. Ce doit être cet axe sur lequel l'homme est
organisé, en accord avec la nature et, probablement, l'univers, cet axe d'organisation qui doit être le même que celui
sur lequel s'alignent tous les phénomènes ou tous les objets
de la nature; cet axe nous conduit à supposer une unité de
gestion dans l'univers, à admettre une volonté unique à
l'origine. Les lois de la physique seraient consecutives
à cet axe. . .[49]

This is similar to the idealism which Jeanneret had read in

Provensal; but in some ways it is even more explicit. For one thing,

Provensal had not described any specific building as most perfectly

embodying the "absolute"--as Jeanneret describes the Parthenon here.

For this reason, it is significant that the Parthenon is, indeed,

described this way in Ernest Renan's essay--Prière sur l'Acropole[50]--

which, as mentioned above, Jeanneret seems to have read in Athens.

Renan, in fact, represents the Parthenon as the one perfect manifes-

tation on earth (aside from the advent of Christ) of the universal

"Ideal:"

>Il y a un lieu où la perfection existe. . . C'était l'idéal
>cristallisé en marbre pentélique qui se montrait à moi.
>Jusque-là, j'avais cru que la perfection n'est pas de ce
>monde; une seule révélation me paraissait se rapprocher de
>l'absolu [i.e., Christ]. . . Or voici qu'à cote du miracle
>juif venait se placer pour moi le miracle grec, une chose
>qui n'a existé qu'une fois. . . mais dont l'effet durera
>éternellement, je veux dire un type de beauté éternelle,
>sans nulle tache locale ou nationale. . . Quand je vis
>l'Acropole, j'eus la révélation du divin. (pp. 1-2)

>Cette révélation de la grandeur vraie et simple m'atteignit
>jusqu'au fond de l'être. (p. 3)

What Renan describes as "révélation" is virtually the same
experience which Le Corbusier later describes as the sounding of a
"corde interne" and the touching of the "axis." Both strike one
"jusqu'au fond de l'être," and both put one in touch with the "absolute." Renan's statement that the Parthenon is an eternal form free
of all "local or national" aspects, is also like Jeanneret's conviction that it is the "étalon sacré" of all art--as well as his
later rejection of the rationalists' idea that the Greek temple can
be traced back to local natural forms such as trees.[51] And other
parallels between Renan's essay and Jeanneret's attitudes could be
pointed out (such as Renan's frequent references to the Parthenon
as "art pur" and as embodying universal "règles"); but the one
fundamental factor is their common belief in the Parthenon's perfect
expression of the Absolute.

It is significant that Jeanneret should speak of the Parthenon's
perfection so consistently in terms of "mathematics" (see quotes above),
for this emphasis was also a new departure for him. Geometric forms

are themselves related to mathematics of course, but pure mathematics is totally abstract--and in Jeanneret's view this makes it more
spiritual and more "austere," a term which will recur throughout
his later writings. "Austerity," in fact, is a quality which Le
Corbusier associates specifically with the Parthenon;[52] and we sense
here a link with the puritan fascination for self-denial which was
so evident in Jeanneret's letter to L'Eplattenier from Paris and in
his account of Mount Athos. Indeed, when Jeanneret in the Voyage
d'Orient speaks of "la rectitude des temples," and "la rectitude
d'une mathématique évidente" (pp. 154 and 162), we sense that the
moral meaning of the word "rectitude" is intended as fully as the
geometric meaning--and perhaps even that the two are bound up inextricably for Jeanneret. And just as Puritan "rectitude" is enforced
by a kind of terror of punishment, and of predestination (in Calvinism), Jeanneret's fascination with the superhuman purity of the
Parthenon contains similar elements:

> Voici que se confirma la rectitude des temples. . . L'entable-
> ment d'une cruelle rigidité écrase et terrorise. Le sentiment
> d'une fatalité extra-humaine vous saisit. Le Parthénon, ter-
> rible machine, broie et domine. . .[53]

This, by the way, seems to be the first time that Jeanneret
refers to a building as a "machine," or even as possessing machine-
like qualities. The metaphor is echoed later in the same chapter,
when the Parthenon is described as having "la rectitude d'une mathématique évidente et la netteté qu'apporte à son labeur, le mécani-
cien" (p. 162; my underline.) The "machine," in this context, is
not only a symbol of precision, mathematics, and geometric rectitude,

but also of the super-human presence, austerity, and _moral_ rectitude which we have seen are associated with them. Le Corbusier's later attraction to machines, as we shall see, is motivated by very similar associations--and can only be understood in relation to his under- lying search for formal equivalents of the Absolute.

The Parthenon represents a milestone in Jeanneret's youth because, for the first time, he seems to have experienced first- hand the conviction that an architectural form can perfectly embody the divine Ideal, or "absolute." Ernest Renan's essay undoubtedly aided him in perceiving the Parthenon this way; but in fact his whole education, as we have seen, had been preparing him for years for this experience.

Summary

As Jeanneret headed back to Switzerland by way of Italy in late 1911 (on the way visiting Pompeii, Rome, and the Monastery of Ema again),[54] was he really any closer to formulating his architectural thought--despite his experience of the Parthenon--than he had been for example in Paris? His travels and work in Germany had exposed him to some new currents of thought and to Behrens' industrial architecture; but then he had made the strange decision to reject the progressive big-city concerns epitomized by Behrens and Perret, and to return to La Chaux-de-Fonds and devote himself to a "discipline jurassique." His long voyage through the peasant country of Eastern Europe and Turkey was a natural adjunct to this return to L'Eplattenier's Jura regionalism--just as his strong affirmation of idealism on the

Acropolis was in a sense a return to Provensal and his childhood

training. Was it all as reactionary as it looks? We can perhaps

never know exactly what was going on in Jeanneret's mind. But it

should be emphasized that Jeanneret had by no means abandoned his

ideal of "modernism"--as Romantic or vague as this ideal may have

remained with him. It is amazing how seldom, in the whole Voyage

d'Orient, he alludes in any way to contemporary architectural issues

(only three times), or even alludes to himself as an architect (only

twice);[55] yet these allusions do show that he still considered him-

self devoted to a new architecture. At one point he and Klipstein

engaged an architectural student in argument, defending the hardy

beauty of several "ponts de fer" on the Danube; and Jeanneret went

on to defend "la belle technique moderne" and to describe

> tout ce que lui doivent les arts, d'expressions plastiques
> nouvelles et de réalisations hardies et le champ splendide
> qu'elle offre au bâtisseur dès lors affranchi des servi-
> tudes classiques. La Halle aux Machines de Paris, la gare
> du Nord comme celle de Hambourg, les autos, les aéroplanes,
> les paquebots et les locomotives nous paraissent des argu-
> ments décisifs.[56]

And in another passage, he refers to himself as "poussé vers

l'action par la voie impérative du constructeur qui rêve d'amalgamer

en fortes cadences le fer et le béton" (p. 138). This seems to be

the one specific thing which Jeanneret had retained faithfully from

his contact with Perret in Paris: a devotion to the idea that re-

inforced concrete was the material of the future. But how was he

going to advance its cause in La Chaux-de-Fonds? What relevance

could reinforced concrete have for a "discipline jurassique," totally removed from the centers of industry and population? And

even if Jeanneret were to abandon his regionalist resolution (as

he eventually was to do, of course), how would he resolve his dream

of a concrete architecture of the future with his idealism of pure

forms whose principal purpose is the expression of the Absolute?

None of these questions could really have been resolved in Jeanneret's

mind at this time. And just as he had spent a winter in Vienna try-

ing to synthesize his first impressions from Italy, he now was to·

spend several years in La Chaux-de-Fonds trying to synthesize all the

parts of his education into a new architecture.

CHAPTER IV

LA CHAUX-DE-FONDS, 1912-1917

These five-and-a-half years spent in La Chaux-de-Fonds are in
many ways the most mysterious years of Jeanneret's life. There are
few sources of information on this period, and Le Corbusier seldom
specifically referred to it later, as he did with his early years
under L'Eplattenier or his "Voyage d'Orient."[1] It was a period when
Jeanneret must have been crystallizing much of the thought which he
began publicizing soon afterwards, in Paris, where he was to estab-
lish himself permanently in 1917; and yet his activities, his state-
ments, and even his notebooks from this period (which I examined at
the Fondation Le Corbusier, and which constitute the main source of
information for this period) seem to a large extent more consistent
with Jeanneret the Jura regionalist, than with Jeanneret of the
1920's.

Some of Jeanneret's preoccupations at this time, however--such
as his "Dom-Ino" system, developed from about 1914 on--reveal many
characteristics of his later thinking, and are of great significance
as the beginning steps of important parts of his work. Thus this is
a complex period, with seemingly contradictory aspects; and this complexity is compounded by the great variety of activities in which
Jeanneret was involved at this time: teaching, designing, organizing

business ventures, writing, etc. To try to clarify our examination of this period, these various activities will be discussed under separate headings.

Design and execution of houses

Designing must have been one of the first activities which Jeanneret took up after returning from Italy at the end of 1911. For in 1912, two houses were constructed by him: a house for his parents (Fig. 35); and the "Favre-Jacot" House (Fig. 36) in Le Locle, near La Chaux-de-Fonds.[2] He did not construct another house until 1916, when he built the Schwob House (Fig. 37)--the only product of this early period which Le Corbusier later deemed worthy of inclusion in his oeuvre.[3] But Von Moos (p. 48) speaks of other projects for local buildings which Jeanneret designed at this time, including an unbuilt project for a museum of 1913, and also a movie-house which was indeed built in 1916 (Fig. 38)--although reportedly, when first constructed, its roof collapsed and had to be rebuilt.[4] In most respects, the two houses of 1912--and indeed, to a large extent the 1916 Schwob House as well--are what we would have expected from Jeanneret's contacts in Germany, combined with his enthusiasm for Cingria's book with its specifications for a new Jura architecture. As Von Moos points out (pp. 37, 47), the 1912 houses have much in common with the more classical houses of Behrens (such as his 1911 Schröder House   ) and of Tessenow--as well as with the houses of local architects such as René Chapallaz and others.[5] Yet, as mentioned above (in Chapter III), these houses in many ways even more

closely reflect the ideas in Cingria's book--for example in their
simple massing, large areas of white stucco walls, their conscious
Classicism (seen most literally in the pedimented portico of the
Favre-Jacot House), and especially the use of simple cylindrical
volumes (in the Jeanneret and Schwob Houses) which distinguishes
them sharply from the work of Behrens and Tessenow.

Thus, these houses can be considered "regionalist"--even though
their regionalism is not the picturesque-chalet regionalism of Jeanneret's first houses, but rather the Classical Suisse-romande regionalism proposed by Cingria. To be sure, the 1916 Schwob House does
contain some new formal elements--such as its flat roof; and more
fundamentally, its plan (Fig. 39) reveals the influence of Frank
Lloyd Wright's centrifugally-composed house-plans, which Jeanneret
had recently seen published.[6] Yet the house as a whole, with its
rigidly composed geometric masses, thorough symmetry, and Classical
spirit, expresses none of the Wrightianism suggested by the plan;
and in reality it is quite similar to the 1912 houses.

Even many of the house-types which Jeanneret designed around
1915 for his "Dom-Ino" system (which will be discussed separately
below) are very similar to these La Chaux-de-Fonds houses--for
example in their banked windows, their symmetry, and their heavy
projecting cornices (e.g. Fig. 40).[7] The fact that by this time
Jeanneret was probably no longer thinking of himself as a Jura
regionalist, and that these house-types were not intended specifically for the Suisse-romande, does not alter the fact that most of

their formal characteristics were first conceived by Jeanneret under the inspiration of Cingria's book.

Contact with Suisse-Romande artistic circles

This is an aspect of Jeanneret's activities at this time which is relatively unknown, and which for the most part is revealed only in references in the "Sketchbooks" which Jeanneret kept during these years.[8] In a sense it is a minor aspect; but it does shed light on Jeanneret's image of his career at this time. It seems that his friend William Ritter may have been his main link to the intellectual and artistic circles with which Jeanneret was apparently trying to associate. As we saw, he had known Ritter already in Germany, but their friendship became closer during these years in La Chaux-de-Fonds; and judging from a later tribute written by Le Corbusier, Ritter's role seems primarily to have been that of encouraging the young artist in a period when he was beset by self-doubts and frustrations:

> Dans la période trouble où l'on apprend à connaître les hommes, où l'on quitte les années d'études pour se lancer avec confiance dans le grand jeu de la vie que l'on croit ouverte aux hommes de bonne volonté, où toutes les forces . . . sont offerts sans restriction avec la naïve pré- tention de secouer la muraille de l'indifférence quo- tidienne--à ce moment j'ai trouvé un vieil ami pour acueillir mes incertitudes. . .[9]

Ritter's encouragement took somewhat more concrete forms as well--for example his reference, in one of his articles in 1913, to "the Swiss architect Charles-Édouard Jeanneret"[10]--undoubtedly an attempt to bolster his young friend's reputation and boost his ego. For similar motives Ritter may also have introduced Jeanneret to a

group of noted Suisse-romande figures which Jeanneret mentions in
his "Sketchbooks" in 1916--a group which included the orchestra-
director Ernest Ansermet, the actor Jacques Copeau, the regional-
novelist Ferdinand Ramuz, and Alexandre Cingria himself.[11] Jeanneret met with these figures at intellectual suppers ("agape," as
they called them in allusion to the Ancients), held in old country-
houses in the mountains; and Jeanneret's diary descriptions of these
gatherings, their charm, and the gossip overheard there, suggest
that even as late as 1916, one side of his temperament still rather
liked the prospect of settling into a role as a respected member of
the regional artistic elite. As a matter of fact, throughout Le
Corbusier's life there was to be a peculiar contradiction between
his disdain for the Establishment, on the one hand, and on the other
a real desire to be a respected member of this Establishment--revealed
by many remarks and incidents, such as the great importance which he
sincerely attached to his honorary degree from Cambridge University
in 1959.[12] But in these early years in La Chaux-de-Fonds, Jeanneret's
association with the regional artistic Establishment seems also related to his planned future as a Jura regionalist.

The Nouvelle Section

In 1911, L'Eplattenier established a "Nouvelle Section" of the
Art School, as an expansion of his "Cours supérieur," and a continuation of his efforts to orient the Art School away from watch-making
and toward a more general program of fine and applied arts. He chose
three of his former students to teach with him in this "Nouvelle

Section:" the sculptor Léon Perrin (Jeanneret's former traveling

companion), the interior-decorator Georges Aubert, and Jeanneret

himself. This teaching-position, even though only part-time, must

have been one of the inducements to Jeanneret to return to La Chaux-

de-Fonds rather than going to Paris at that time.[13]

But the program met resistance from the beginning--and actually

collapsed in 1914--mainly from opposition by the Socialist-Democratic

political leaders in the city, who complained that it would merely

produce artists unable to earn an honest living, and also that the

three younger instructors were unqualified. And other objections

apparently came from older teachers at the Art School, who simply

resented the young usurpers.[14] The arguments, charges, and counter-

charges which ensued are not worth going into; but it is interesting

that we find here the first example of a phenomenon which was to

recur throughout Le Corbusier's career--his reaction to a real or

imagined injustice to himself by creating a gigantic cause-célèbre

out of it, and by waging a campaign of polemics and bitterness against

his enemies which in the total amount of energy expended often over-

shadowed the original offense. In this case, the "Nouvelle Section"

climaxed its defense with a lengthy publication--entitled Un movement

d'art à La Chaux-de-Fonds[15]--refuting the charges leveled against it,

accusing its opposition of stupidity and dishonesty, and reproducing

solicited letters of support from noted European artists. The hand

of Jeanneret is clear behind all this. For one thing, the solicited

testimonials all came from men Jeanneret had known (Eugène Grasset,

Rupert Carabin, Karl Osthaus, Theodor Fischer, and Peter Behrens)[16]
--except for a letter from Hector Guimard (added at the last minute)
which no doubt was solicited by Perrin. Furthermore, the language
of this publication, and its lengthy recital of charges and counter-
charges, is thoroughly reminiscent of Le Corbusier's later similar
publications, such as the brochure he was to write after the League
of Nations fiasco in 1927.[17] We sense in this language a great bitterness brought on by a sheer inability to comprehend how the Artist's
activities could be criticized or questioned--surely at least in part
a result of Jeanneret's early training which viewed the artist as an
inspired prophet and as belonging to a privileged elite.

Aside from this combattive aspect, however, the most interesting
thing about the "Nouvelle Section" was the nature of Jeanneret's own
course. It was meant to train architects, decorators, and designers
in general; and its catalogue description reveals the extent to which
Jeanneret believed that geometry was the basic key to all of these
disciplines:

Éléments géométriques, leurs caractères, leurs valeurs rela-
tives, décoratives et monumentales.
Applications diverses à l'architecture, au mobilier, à divers
objets (dessins d'exécution, plans, coupes, perspectives,
etc.)
Exécution pratique d'oeuvres d'architecture, de décoration
d'intérieur et d'objets divers.[18]

The way in which Jeanneret actually taught this course is suggested by some photographs (discovered at the Fondation Le Corbusier)
of the projects executed by students in the "Nouvelle Section."[19]
Unlike the more realistic and curvilinear designs executed in the

classes of L'Eplattenier, Perrin, and Aubert, those in Jeanneret's class are all geometric, whether they are architecture, garden-designs, or simply abstract decoration. In fact many of them are odd architectural elements with no apparent function--things which look like isolated columns or pedestals or fountains--with a different design produced by each student, but all more or less based on the same geometric forms. Clearly, Jeanneret's assignments were something like: "Design a pedestal (or fountain, or whatever), based on a cube and a cylinder." Even the designs for houses look essentially the same, and show no evidence of having plans or a structure.

The abstractness of this approach is remarkable, and reveals a belief that design (even of architecture) is essentially the formalistic arrangement of geometric elements--an attitude which of course we saw originate in Provensal, but which Jeanneret had said he was renouncing in his 1908 letter to L'Eplattenier. In Jeanneret's notebooks of this period 1912-1917, he was to write "La plus haute architecture est cubique" (see below); and many of his sketches in these notebooks are of abstract geometric decoration which is amazingly similar to his students' projects. The reason this is emphasized here is that it contrasts dramatically with the ostensibly pragmatic and down-to-earth nature of the Dom-Ino system which Jeanneret was working on at about the same time (although, as we shall see, even this Dom-Ino system is a good deal more formalistic than it first appears.) The whole question of whether architecture is primarily structure (Perret), or pure form (Provensal) underlies this period, and Jeanneret still had not really found a way to resolve it.

The Ateliers d'Art

When the "Nouvelle Section" finally closed in 1914, much of
the energy devoted to it shifted to the "Ateliers d'Art Réunis"--
that organization for which Jeanneret had designed a fanciful building in 1910 (see above, pp. 71-72), and with which he had continued
to be associated since his return to La Chaux-de-Fonds.[20] In the
meantime, it seems to have become less educationally-oriented, and
more simply a profit-making association of young artisans who primarily executed interior decoration for well-to-do citizens and public
buildings in the locality.[21]

Jeanneret's notebooks--from about 1914 to 1916[22]--show that he
devoted much of his attention to this enterprise (doubtless primarily
to make up for the loss of his teaching income.) And whereas the
work that was done was very traditional in nature, this fact in itself is interesting since this represents a large part of Jeanneret's
activity in this period. One thing Jeanneret did was to buy antique
furniture for clients; for his notebooks are filled with drawings
of chairs and other objects, with notations of their styles ("Louis
XIII," "Directoire," etc.), their condition ("bonne paille," etc.),
their prices, and the names of prospective buyers and sellers. We
can imagine that Jeanneret might have found this business degrading
(after all, this kind of furniture is precisely what Le Corbusier was
to attack so vehemently after 1920); but he seems not to have felt
that way, and even picked out especially fine pieces for himself and
his family (for example: a "Louis XV" organ--"pour notre salon.")

Another large group of sketches in these notebooks are of lamps, of various types and styles--but some of these seem to be designed by Jeanneret himself, and were probably related to another business enterprise he began at this time: a "Société pour la Fabrication de Lustrerie d'Art."[23] The notebooks also contain sketches for a kind of exhibition pavilion--which Jeanneret seems to have planned as part of the promotion of this "art-lamp" business.

All of this activity suggests that Jeanneret intended to stay in La Chaux-de-Fonds for some time, and that he was setting up businesses which could support him until his reputation as an architect was established.

Trips to Paris

Throughout these years in La Chaux-de-Fonds, Jeanneret seems to have made relatively frequent visits to Paris. In 1912 he is said to have exhibited a group of his travel-drawings at the Salon d'Automne there.[24] An inscription in a book shows that he was also there at Christmas-time in 1913.[25] And he continued visiting there after the War had begun, judging from his notebook remarks about buildings he saw in Paris, and also about engravings--which he is said to have studied at the Bibliothèque Nationale in the summer of 1915.[26] He also seems to have kept in touch with Auguste Perret--since in one of his notebooks, next to his early sketches for the Dom-Ino system, he wrote: "demander Aug Perret."

Jeanneret also seems to have visited Germany at least once in this period (Dresden, in June 1913, to see an exhibition.)[27] But it was primarily through trips to Paris that he kept in touch with the outside world. Furthermore, his notebooks reveal that toward the end of his stay in La Chaux-de-Fonds, the attraction of Paris became stronger and stronger, and he started to make plans to move there. All in all, this period was not as isolated for Jeanneret as we might imagine--although it seems to have been as late as 1915 or 1916 that he seriously questioned his Jura-regionalist plans and began to think of moving to Paris permanently.

Reading

In a sense, Jeanneret's reading becomes less significant during this period in La Chaux-de-Fonds. He still reads a great deal (as he was to do throughout his life), but we do not sense as we did earlier that his reading directly shapes his thinking. In general, his basic attitudes seem to be more or less formed by now--even if not yet resolved--and his interest in books begins to be transformed into a search for specific information, to be used in the process of synthesis in which he was engaged. Still, we can identify some of his reading in this period as providing him with important ideas, and (in the case of town-planning) as turning his interests in new directions.

There are eighteen books in Le Corbusier's library which are inscribed as dating from this period--and nearly as many more which are uninscribed but may date from then as well.[28] A large number of these are not of great interest (and in fact several of them are nineteenth century books which were apparently given to Jeanneret by a relative in 1916, and which he probably never even read.)[29] But aside from Le Corbusier's own library, there are other works which we know Jeanneret read at this time--mainly through references to them in his notebooks.[30] Of all of these books, only a few seem really to have interested Jeanneret much. These include: Georges Benoît-Lévy's books on garden-cities (which will be discussed in a separate section below); Maurice Denis's Théories, 1890-1910; Auguste Choisy's Histoire de l'architecture; Marcel Dieulafoy's L'art antique de la Perse;[31] and possibly Julius Meier-Graefe's Cézanne.[32] Furthermore, it is possible that Jeanneret may have come in contact with Futurist writings in Paris at this time; but this possibility, and Jeanneret's relationship to Futurism in general, will be examined below in Chapter V.

Maurice Denis's Théories, 1890-1910--which Jeanneret acquired in 1912[33]--seems not to have had a profound effect on his thinking, for the simple reason that Denis's basic philosophy of art was not very different from Jeanneret's. Nevertheless, a number of Denis's specific ideas were to reappear in 1918 in Après le cubisme (which will be analyzed in Chapter V); and in general, Denis seems to have got Jeanneret more interested in painting--for which he had shown surprisingly little interest (for a future painter) in his early years.[34] Denis's attitude toward art, like Jeanneret's, was essentially classicist and idealist. "Symbolism," as he conceived of it and propounded it, was a reaction against the materialistic nature of Impressionism which had concerned itself simply with superficial

"sensations," and was an attempt to find symbolic visual embodiments
("équivalents") of spiritual and emotional realities underlying the
visible world. In Après le cubisme, Jeanneret and Amedée Ozenfant
will say exactly the same thing, except that it is Cubism which they
will accuse of being superficially materialistic, and Purism which
they will offer as the art of emotions and ideas. Indeed, the
formula Symbolism : Impressionism = Purism : Cubism holds true for
a surprising number of the arguments presented in Théories and Après
le cubisme. For Denis, art must renounce the Romanticism and excessive individualism characterized by Impressionism, and must instead
be "idéaliste," searching out "les règles de la vie," "réalities
solides," "idéals collectifs," and "un ordre nouveau."[35] "Order" is
one of Denis's major concepts. Art is to express "l'ordre de l'univers" (p. 277), and is to do this by discovering "rapports numériques"
and geometric proportions (p. 276)--just as in Provensal--all of which
will arouse in the viewer "un plaisir esthétique pur" (p. 163.) One
of Denis's key concepts is "synthesis" (just as it was to be in
Après le cubisme), which for him is a process of generalization and
simplification, in order to arrive at universal truths--or, as he
quotes Sérusier: "La synthèse consiste à faire rentrer toutes les
formes dans le petit nombre de formes que nous sommes capables de
penser: lignes droites, quelques angles, arcs de cercle et d'ellipse;
sortis de là, nous nous perdons dans l'océan des variétés" (p. 260).

Purism, as we shall see, also was to place great emphasis on
replacing chaotic and uncontrolled variety with generalized, "universal" forms and systems of proportioning. The examples could be

multiplied and elaborated, and would simply confirm our impression that Jeanneret was attracted to Denis's specific concepts and terminology because they shared the same idealistic attitude toward art. Nevertheless, one of Denis's points may have struck Jeanneret in a special way. In his attacks on Romanticism, and its excessive emphasis on individuality, Denis ridicules "le culte du moi" (p. 118 et al.)--that ego-worship which Romantic artists cultivate, but which Denis recognized as inconsistent with a search for universal principles. We have seen how the young Jeanneret enthusiastically accepted the idea that the artist's "moi" was his greatest concern and source of inspiration (for example in his 1908 letter to L'Eplattenier.) After he read Denis, he was never to write about his "moi" in this way; and in Après le cubisme, he was to attack Romantic individualism as strongly as Denis did. This is not to say that Jeanneret's attitudes toward himself and his genius were replaced by a new spirit of humility; but he did become careful, in his theory at least, to suppress his "moi" in public--and Denis may well have been the catalyst of this change.

Auguste Choisy's Histoire de l'architecture--Jeanneret's copy of which is inscribed as having been bought in Paris at Christmas, 1913[36]--is of interest to us for a very different reason; for unlike Denis, Choisy represents attitudes which were not particularly shared by Jeanneret. As Reyner Banham has shown, the notion which underlies Choisy's Histoire is that architectural form is above all else the logical consequence of construction and technique[37]--a clear-cut expression of the same "rationalism" which we have associated with Viollet-le-duc and Auguste Perret. In fact, we sense that Choisy's Histoire was precisely the sort of book Perret would have suggested that Jeanneret read in 1908; and perhaps he did. But whether or not Jeanneret had ever read it before, his reactions to it are suggested by a couple of brief annotations he wrote in this copy he bought in 1913--as well as by Le Corbusier's later reproduction of many of Choisy's illustrations in his Esprit Nouveau articles.[38]

First of all, not all the pages of Jeanneret's copy of Choisy are cut--indicating that he read only the parts which interested him. And apparently what interested him most was a section on the formal "laws" of architecture which in many ways is atypical of Choisy's thinking. Jeanneret wrote the word "LOIS" next to one part of this section in which Choisy--describing the Egyptians' method of proportioning based on "tracés" derived from triangles (exactly as Le Corbusier was to do in the 1920's)--says:

Plus grande encore est l'importance de la méthode au point de vue de l'harmonie des formes. L'idée d'unité dans une oeuvre d'art est celle d'une loi qui domine tout l'ensemble: nous sentons l'existence de cette loi alors même que nous en ignorons la formule . . . Que cette loi, en architecture, soit géométrique ou numérique, peu importe: avant tout il faut une loi.[39]

And in the next paragraph, in which Choisy suggests that the use of "combinaisons modulaires" can "éveillent en nous l'idée d'ordre, qui n'est pas loin de l'idée du beau," (p. 57), Jeanneret brackets this and writes "l'idée d'ordre" next to it. It is hard to know whether it was actually these passages which first started Jeanneret

thinking about "tracés régulateurs," for he was reading other books
at this time which also described geometric systems of proportioning (see Chapter VI).[40] But this is clearly what interested him most
in Choisy's book. It is truly amazing how selectively Jeanneret read.
Out of Choisy's whole Histoire, the parts which impressed him most
were these paragraphs which are **not** typical of Choisy's attitudes
toward architecture--and which in fact sound precisely like passages
from Provensal's L'art de demain. Jeanneret the idealist was continually in search of absolute principles, and only that which helped
him in this search was of interest to him.

Writing

When we actually list the writing projects which Jeanneret
undertook in La Chaux-de-Fonds (and include outlines for unexecuted
projects which we find in his notebooks), we realize that writing
was a much more important aspect of his activities in this period
than has been recognized. This writing-activity will be reviewed
briefly here.

First, his Étude sur le mouvement d'art décoratif en Allemagne
was published in 1912; and although Jeanneret had probably written
parts of it in Germany, he undoubtedly revised and completed it right
after returning to La Chaux-de-Fonds. Next he put together his notes
and newspaper articles describing his trip through Eastern Europe, as
Le voyage d'Orient, which according to his later recollections was
going to be published in 1914--although the beginning of the War prevented that.[41] Then, in 1914, came the pamphlet Un movement d'art

à La Chaux-de-Fonds which, as we have seen, appears to have been primarily the work of Jeanneret. Despite its local and topical nature, much of its polemical language, as pointed out above, fore-shadows Le Corbusier's later writings; and indeed, some of its pass-ages read like a general attack on bourgeois attitudes toward art. We sense that Jeanneret's urge to write manifestoes found expression even in this local issue.

After this, Jeanneret did not publish anything during this period in La Chaux-de-Fonds; but several outlines which are found in the notebooks he kept around 1915 and 1916 reveal that he was planning to write at least one book on architecture.[42] Some of these "outlines" are so sketchy that it is hard to know if indeed they really were writing-projects, or simply were jotted-down ideas. And a couple of them seem to be outlines of brochures meant to be pub-lished as advertisement for the Dom-Ino system which Jeanneret was trying to patent at this time. But one is clearly an outline for a real book. It consists of twenty-three pages in one of Jeanneret's notebooks, some of these pages having simply a heading at the top (possibly meant as chapter-titles or section-headings), others filled in with Jeanneret's notes on one side of the page, and lists of in-tended illustrations on the other--an interesting outline method, since it suggests that importance of the visual image which charac-terizes Le Corbusier's later books. In general, this outline is so skeletal that it is impossible to tell just what attitudes Jeanneret was intending to express; but in several places he wrote out complete sentences which are worth noting. One of these is: "l'Acropole qui est une oeuvre d'adaptation, d'appropriation, est-elle construite sur une idée génératrice?"--a question which despite its vagueness reveals Jeanneret's desire to discover "generating" formal principles, just as we saw in his copy of Choisy. In another section of the outline, following some rather mystical notes on "L'asie toujours religieuse," Jeanneret wrote:

L'unité d'idéal
Islam -- Le nomade de race
Stamboul
Unité de concept; éléments cubiques.

La plus haute architecture est cubique: l'intérieur des cathédrales. L'extérieur du temple grec. Le complexe de la mosquée. Les intérieurs du temple égyptien.

As interesting as these notes may be--for their explicit preference for cubic forms, their association of these forms with religious ideals, etc.--probably most significant is simply the fact that Jeanneret at this time was seriously outlining books in which he intended to express his general ideas and theories about architecture-- just as he was to do in the 'twenties. Thus, in this period before he had even built anything of note, Jeanneret was thinking of his role as more than simply that of an architect, but also as that of a propagandizer of the new architecture.

The Dom-Ino System

The design which Jeanneret christened the "Dom-Ino System" was the most important product of his thinking in La Chaux-de-Fonds, and indeed laid the groundwork for many of Le Corbusier's later architectural ideas. He never explained why he chose the term "Dom-Ino;"

but it probably combined the word "domus" with the notion of inde-
finite linkage of similar parts as in the game of dominoes.[43] Le
Corbusier later said that he began developing this system in late
1914 (thus soon after the collapse of the "Nouvelle Section"),
in response to the widespread destruction in Flanders resulting
from the first stage of the War--which everyone thought would soon
be over, and which then would require large-scale rebuilding programs. This dating seems plausible; for in the sketchbook which
Jeanneret kept around 1915 (which I examined at the Fondation Le
Corbusier), there are several pages of drawings related to the
Dom-Ino system--although not including any of the more precise
drawings which Le Corbusier later published in his books.[44]

This "system" (Figs. 41 & 42) is essentially just a structural unit
consisting of three horizontal slabs, each of the upper two supported
by six reinforced-concrete columns, and with concrete stairs connect-
ing the levels.[45] This was to provide two-storey housing units, which
could be linked or expanded in various ways, as Jeanneret suggested
in other drawings and also in a patent which he wrote up in his notebook, which described this design as a "système des constructions
juxtaposables selon d'infinis combinaisons de plans. . ."[46]

One of the interesting aspects of this design is the setting-
back of its columns, away from the edge of the slab--thus suggesting
a separation of the wall from the structure, which was to be one of
Le Corbusier's important later doctrines. Von Moos (p. 49) claims
that this set-back idea was original to Jeanneret; but this is

untrue. It had been used before, for example in Perret's 1905 Garage Ponthieu in Paris (Fig. 43)[47]--and in fact from a structural point of view, it is simply the most economical design for poured concrete structures since the cantilever of the slab produces a better moment-curve than if the slab ended right at the column. Perret, like any structural engineer even in those early days of concrete technology, would have been fully aware of this structural phenomenon, and surely had explained it to his protegé Jeanneret. So in the Dom-Ino system, this set-back may be due simply to Jeanneret's desire for maximum structural efficiency--although, unfortunately, he seems to have mis-understood the principle, since the Dom-Ino slab is not a real mono-lithic slab (see below) and could not actually have supported a canti-lever efficiently.

Despite this technical problem, Jeanneret was later to realize the aesthetic potential of the separation of wall and support which this set-back allows; and in fact it is tempting to assume that he suspected this potential right from the beginning--especially since his patent description of the system includes the phrase "séparation des pouvoirs" and mentions as one of the system's features that "les poteaux à l'intérieur n'apparaissent pas en façade." But despite this, the facades which Jeanneret actually designed for this system (e.g. Figs. 40 and 44), with their conventionally-placed window openings and wall surfaces, reveal no formal recognition of this set-back structure; and we are forced to conclude that the aesthetic implications must have followed, later, from the structural fait-accompli.

In my opinion, the really significant thing about the Dom-Ino
design is the fact that its columns and slabs are completely smooth
--that is, that its columns have none of the splay or brackets, and
its slabs none of the exposed ribs, which virtually all concrete construction had at that time (e.g. Fig. 45). Even in Maillart's revolutionary Zurich warehouse of 1910 (Fig. 46), in which the rib beams
were eliminated (for the first time, apparently) and the flat slab
thus achieved, the columns were given a broadly extended splay to
support this slab. The way the Dom-Ino system is designed, however
--with neither rib-beams nor column-splay--would have been exceedingly
difficult to construct at this time; and Jeanneret himself seems to
have recognized this (or perhaps Perret told him), for instead of
using a poured reinforced-concrete slab, he devised a highly complex,
and dubious, scheme for pouring concrete over hollow blocks which
were to be held in place with a special kind of scaffolding.[48] Furthermore, as mentioned above, this technique eliminates the structural
advantage of the cantilever--and in fact makes the cantilever the
source of numerous construction difficulties.

Because of all these difficulties, it is apparent that the
smooth, simple forms of the slab and the column in Jeanneret's design
were the result of a purely aesthetic choice. Jeanneret's own
descriptions of the system verify this--by their emphasis on the
importance of the "smoothness," per se, of the structural elements:

> . . . il s'agit d'un matériel de chantier special qui permet
> de couler les planchers définitivement lisses dessus et
> dessous. [my underline][49]

And the patent which Jeanneret originally drew up in his notebook stresses three points: the combinability of the units; the
structural "separation of powers;" and the "smooth" ("lisse") and
"monolithic" nature of the slabs and columns:

> Système des constructions juxtaposables selon d'infinis com-
> binaisons de plans grace à un [?] module sous-multiple [?],
> par ossatures monolythes de béton armé à plancher lisse.50

Indeed, this formal simplicity and "smoothness" of the structural elements is the one really distinguishing feature of the Dom-
Ino system. Other reinforced-concrete structural "systems" had long
been in use, such as those of Hennebique and others; other "pre-
fabricated" concrete systems had been designed and manufactured,
although it is not clear to what extent the Dom-Ino
system was meant to be pre-fabricated;[51] and as pointed out above,
the column set-back was not new. What is truly Jeanneret's is the
uncompromising formal decision to strip the structural elements
down to their barest, most generalized, most "ideal" forms: a pure
slab and a pure column. And Jeanneret's desire for "separation of
powers" is simply part of this effort to isolate and idealize each
element. The fact that this simplification could be accomplished
only by an excessively complex (indeed almost perverse) construction
method, was not of great concern to Jeanneret. The important thing
was that the ultimate form should be the simplest, most pure expression of the concepts "slab" and "column"--in other words the Ideal
Slab and the Ideal Column--divested of all particularity. The Dom-
Ino system, in effect, is philosophical idealism applied to architectural structure.

Jeanneret had long conceived of _form_ idealistically--in the geometric terms first suggested to him by Provensal. But this additional concept of idealistic _structure_ was a step of great significance for Jeanneret, and one which was to lead to many of his later doctrines--such as those of "pilotis," the "free façade" and "free plan," and the ramp--all concepts which stress the isolation and idealization of some architectural element. We shall examine this more closely in Chapter VI.

At last Jeanneret had found a key to the synthesis which had hitherto eluded him. The conflict between Perret's rationalism and Jeanneret's idealism--that is between architecture as the expression of structure, and architecture as pure form expressing transcendent ideals--could perhaps be resolved if the structural elements themselves were idealized, purified, and made to transcend their materiality to become Ideas in their own right.

City-Planning

Jeanneret's sketchbooks of this period--and in particular the one which he kept around 1915 and 1916[52]--contain many notes and drawings revealing a strong interest in housing and city-planning issues, which until now had apparently not been one of his major concerns (despite his comments on German city-planning in the Werkbund report.)[53] Perhaps to a large extent this new interest in planning was related to the Dom-Ino system and to Jeanneret's optimistic plans to manufacture Dom-Ino components which would be used to rebuild whole communities devastated by the War. But through this business-interest, he seems to have become concerned with city-planning in its own right.

Jeanneret's notes reveal that he was reading books on housing and planning at this time--mostly in libraries, it seems[54]--and that he was exposed principally to the "garden-city" concepts of planning, just as he had been in Germany. In fact, some quotations in his notebook turn out to have been copied by him directly from the third volume of La cité-jardin of Georges Benoît-Lévy, the leader of the Association of French Garden-Cities.[55] And the fact that Jeanneret's first serious contact with city-planning was by way of the garden-city movement seems to have had a number of important effects on his urbanistic attitudes from then on. For example, the garden-city assumption that housing ought to be set in the midst of large park-like grounds was to be accepted by Le Corbusier as axiomatic throughout his career--from his 1922 Ville Contemporaine to his Unités d'Habitation of the 1950's--and had much to do with his lack of sympathy for the conventional European city of streets and street-façades.

First, some comments can be made about Jeanneret's site-plans which show how he intended the Dom-Ino houses to be arranged and combined into communities. Two different planning-concepts can be seen underlying them: one, a curvilinear, "English-garden" lay-out of the houses and roads (e.g. Fig. 47); and the other a more formal, geometric planning around rectangular courtyards and on axes (Figs. 44 and 48). Both of these concepts can be found in the garden-city plans of that time--for example in English plans by Raymond Unwin and others which were illustrated in the book by Benoît-Lévy which

Jeanneret read (Figs. 49-50). One feature common to both of Jean-

neret's plan-types, however, is the joining-together of standard

house-units at right-angles--a natural result of the Dom-Ino system

based on one standard construction module. It is interesting that

the schematic drawings of Unwin's plans illustrated by Benoît-Lévy

have the same spirit of linking up modular units, and indeed even

look like lined-up dominoes; but it would be impossible to know

whether these plans may have suggested the notion of modular link-

age to Jeanneret.

More significant are the passages in Benoît-Lévy's book which

Jeanneret copied out into his notebook. The longer of these is a

quotation attributed by Benoît-Lévy to the English planner S. D.

Adshead--which recalls Henry Provensal in its demand for totally

new forms:

> La question qui se pose aujourd'hui est d'exprimer en notre
> architecture civique ce qu'il y a d'énergie, d'intensité,
> de raffinement, de beauté, dans la vie urbaine. Nous n'avons
> pas besoin seulement de bâtiments d'un type supérieur, mais
> de type entièrement différent. Nous avons maintenant des
> machines extraordinaires pour la rapidité et le fini de la
> construction. Nous avons des ouvriers d'élite se servant
> d'outils perfectionnés. . . . La cité doit exprimer tout
> cela. Réléguons aux jours du bon vieux temps la ville avec
> ses toits à pente, avec ses fenêtres à vitres lilliputiennes.
> Des telles villes étaient pleines de charme, mais elles ont
> fait leur temps; leurs jours sont passés pour ne jamais
> revenir.[56]

Several things are interesting here: the admiration for the

machine, speed, energy, and modern society (a kind of prefiguration

of Futurism); and more specifically, the attack on pitched roofs and small-paned windows. Jeanneret himself, at this time, had not yet rejected these elements as totally as he later would; the Dom-Ino houses are all flat-roofed, but his notebooks of the period (and even later) contain drawings of pitched-roofed houses; and even his Dom-Ino houses have windows with small panes. But more basic than all this, in Adshead's quote, is the idea that city-planning should "express" something--that is, that it is an art, and like any other art should communicate feelings and ideas, in this case the spirit of modern industrialism. Le Corbusier himself was to have a very similar "expressive" conception of city-planning; and thus it is significant that Benoît-Lévy's book is permeated with this attitude that the city-planner is primarily an artist rather than a planner. In fact, he quotes Adshead again as saying that a city ought to be "la plus grande et la plus noble de toutes les oeuvres d'art" (p. 18)--thus implying that the city-planner is correspondingly the greatest and most noble artist. A quotation from Parker and Unwin's L'art de construire un home, which was the other passage which Jeanneret copied out of this book, expresses a similar idea: that a house, "en tant qu'habitation, appartient au client et doit le satisfaire," but "en tant qu'oeuvre d'art, appartient et doit satisfaire celui qui la dessine."[57] And Benoît-Lévy's opening passage in the book, in fact, is a particularly extreme expression of this idea that the garden-city architect is no mere organizer or engineer, but an artist expressing himself:

[Garden-cities] doivent le meilleur d'elles-mêmes à la per-
sonnalité de leur architectes. Ceux-ci n'ont rien de commun
avec les gens de bureau et les scribes dont le goût a été
formé par l'enseignement artificiel des écoles et des ateliers;
ce sont des artistes qui "expriment leur esprit et leur âme
dans le travail de leurs mains." (p. 16)

Here, Benoît-Lévy goes much further than his more pragmatic

English colleagues could ever have gone. For him, great city-plan-

ners do not express anything even as objective as the spirit of

industrialism; they express their own "esprit et leur âme." It

could be Provensal or Schuré speaking, or Jeanneret's 1908 letter

to L'Eplattenier with its definitions of architecture as the ex-

pression of one's "moi." It is easy to see what attracted Jeanneret

to this book, and what got him interested in city-planning as a

proper concern of the artist. Several pages after his opening

remarks quoted above, Benoît-Lévy describes the architect as "un

artiste d'élite" who shapes the city of the future in "sa main

puissante;" and then he reveals the full extent of his idealism

in an extensive quote from Henri Bergson:

Quel est l'objet de l'art? Si la réalité venait frapper
directement nos sens et notre conscience, si nous pou-
vions entrer en communication immédiate avec les choses
et avec nous-mêmes, je crois bien que l'art serait in-
utile, ou plutôt que nous serions tous artistes, car
notre âme vibrerait alors continuellement à l'unisson
de la nature. . . . Nous entendrions chanter au fond de
nos âmes, . . . la mélodie ininterrompue de notre vie
intérieure. Tout cela est autour de nous, tout cela est
en nous, et pourtant rien de tout cela n'est perçu par
nous directement. Entre la nature et nous...que dis-je?
entre nous et notre propre conscience, un voile s'inter-
pose, voile épais pour le commun des hommes, voile léger, .
presque transparent, pour l'artiste et le poète.[58]

Bergson's metaphor of the artistic soul "vibrating" in unison with the divine principles of nature was of course to be used in the same way by Le Corbusier in his article "Architecture: pure création de l'esprit" (see above, p. 99). Whether or not this quote is actually its source, Jeanneret must have been impressed with the strong idealism of this book, and with the notion that city-planning too could be a vehicle for exposing the underlying, ideal "reality" of nature.

One disappointing feature of Benoît-Lévy's work, however, must be pointed out: the specific garden-cities, housing schemes, and cottage designs which he describes and illustrates (mainly from English examples) are not nearly as revolutionary as his theory would suggest they ought to be. For the most part, they are in the picturesque country-cottage style typical of garden-cities at that time, and quite the opposite of the new industrially-expressive forms called for in Adshead's quote. Like Provensal and so many other men at the turn of the century, Benoît-Lévy had a vague vision of a new architectural style, and even an outline of its doctrines, but no specific forms worthy of this vision. There is a pathetic gap between the romantic Victorian cottages illustrated by Benoît-Lévy, and the visionary ideals suggested in his quotes from Adshead and in his own calls for a grandiose reinforced-concrete city of the future:

> Les architectes des Cités-Jardins sont-ils encore les pala-
> dins des siècles morts, ou ont-ils été assez habiles, en
> sondant l'avenir, pour découvrir un style nouveau; ne re-
> noncent-ils aux cités du vieux monde, ou ont-ils pu engen-
> drer en leur pensée des villes inspirées uniquement, dans

leur armure de fer et de ciment, dans leur structure gigantesque, de formules nouvelles?[59]

This must have had the same effect on Jeanneret as Provensal's
predictions that new architectural laws were about to be discovered.
Benoît-Lévy imagines a new kind of city, of gigantic structure, and
inspired solely by "new formulas"--and the challenge clearly was to
go ahead and formulate these. The fact that Benoît-Lévy specifies
reinforced concrete could only have intensified Jeanneret's interest
in pursuing this vision and discovering these new formulas himself.

Jeanneret's Dom-Ino houses, however, do not fully satisfy these
requirements of Benoît-Lévy's vision. They are made of reinforced
concrete, but they do not have a "structure gigantesque." Thus it
is significant that we find in Jeanneret's 1915 notebook that he goes
back to an idea first suggested by Auguste Perret, of a city of great
towers, and makes the first rough sketches of what was to become his
"Ville contemporaine" project seven years later.[60] There are only
two small pages of these sketches; but most of the essential characteristics of the later "Ville contemporaine" are suggested
here: tall housing towers, spaced out regularly in a park full of
trees, with lower buildings such as schools at their base.[61] Unlike
Le Corbusier's cross-shaped plan for the towers in 1922, these
sketches show some of the towers with square plans and others with
hexagonal plans--just as Perret was reported to have envisaged vari-
ous-shaped plans for his towers.[62] And in the 1922 "Ville contemporaine," the center-city with these towers was to be surrounded by
lower-density apartment buildings forming three-sided rectangular

courtyards--as in his Dom-Ino site-plans--and that then surrounded by a great ring of parkland, with "garden-cities" beyond that.

Thus, nearly all the elements of Le Corbusier's 1922 project can be found in Jeanneret's sketchbooks around 1915; and furthermore, each part of the "Ville contemporaine" is in the spirit of the brand of garden-city thinking which Jeanneret was studying at this time. Even the towers in the center of the city are a kind of realization of Benoît-Lévy's vision of "gigantic" structures of reinforced concrete; and of course their placement in a vast park is just as Benoît-Lévy would have wished.

In these concepts Jeanneret found another key to the synthesis he had been searching for: a kind of resolution of Perret's vision of a new reinforced-concrete architecture on the one hand, and on the other his own anti-urban, regionalist preferences. When he had returned to La Chaux-de-Fonds and dedicated himself to a "discipline jurassique," he had been surrendering to the second of these impulses; but disillusionment must have followed the "Nouvelle Section" fiasco--as well as a realization that his dream of creating a new architecture was not going to be achieved in the conservative atmosphere of his native region, no matter how much he loved its landscape and mountains. His incipient "Ville contemporaine" ideas of 1915 are in a sense a resolution of all this. The concept is revolutionary and daring, thus satisfying his self-image as prophet of a new architecture; and it is to be made of reinforced-concrete, thus satisfying his one real article of faithfulness to Perret;

yet it is essentially a garden-city, one vast park-land full of trees--a rejection of the traditional city and a regionalist's yearning to return to the innocent beauty of nature.

But these concepts represented a kind of synthesis for Jeanneret on a more fundamental level as well. For, as pointed out above, Benoît-Lévy's view of city-planning as a full-fledged "art" --which expresses its creator's personality, his soul, and even the Bergsonian-Reality underlying nature--was precisely what was needed to interest Jeanneret seriously in urbanism. When Perret had conceived his "tower-cities," it was surely with the sole aim of solving specific urban problems and of exploring the potential of reinforced-concrete construction; and he no doubt would have been bewildered by the suggestion that a principal goal of city-planning was to make "our soul vibrate in unison with nature." Just as with the Dom-Ino system, Jeanneret found here another way in which he could place Perret's rationalistic concerns within his own idealistic framework. For just as the Dom-Ino system represents his discovery that architectural _structure_ could be achieved idealistically, so he discovered at the same time that the creation of whole _cities_ could be conceived in the same way.

CHAPTER V

PARIS, 1917-1920

Sometime in 1917, Jeanneret moved definitively to Paris.[1] The
move itself is significant, as a final rejection of the regionalist
career and "discipline jurassique" which had been Jeanneret's main
reason for returning to Switzerland in 1911. There were probably
many reasons for this change of heart--such as Jeanneret's disillusionment over the "Nouvelle Section" fiasco in 1914; his reactions
to the World War; the formulation of his architectural ideas, which
stressed general, universal solutions rather than specificity or
locality; and also a falling-out with L'Eplattenier, which Le Corbusier later described and attributed to L'Eplattenier's desire to make
a "décorateur" out of him.[2] Le Corbusier later said that in 1917 he
was offered a job in Frankfort, and had decided to go there, when,
at the last minute he changed his mind, on sheer whim, and went to
Paris instead.[3] This would be an interesting story, insofar as it
suggests that in the midst of the War Jeanneret had so little fran-
cophilic sentiment that it did not matter to him whether he moved to
France or Germany; but it is contradicted by Jeanneret's own notebooks of 1915 and 1916, which contain many references to his being
able to move to Paris as soon as the Dom-Ino system was properly
patented and the business set up and prospering.[4] These references

clearly reveal that Jeanneret had been wanting to move to Paris for some time, and that finally he just did it, even though the Dom-Ino business had not materialized as planned.

Ozenfant and Purism

Once in Paris, Jeanneret's activities are virtually unknown until he met Amedée Ozenfant--which according to Ozenfant occurred in May 1917, but which according to Le Corbusier was in 1918. Early 1918 is perhaps the most probable; but the evidence is highly inconclusive.[5] Nevertheless, all accounts agree that they were introduced by Auguste Perret--who according to Ozenfant described Jeanneret prior to their meeting as "un drôle d'oiseau, mais il vous intéressera."[6] If this did indeed occur in early 1918, we have virtually no clues to Jeanneret's activities in Paris in 1917--except for one item in Le Corbusier's library, a program booklet for the appearance of the Ballet Russes in Paris in May 1917.[7] On the page describing the performance of Stravinsky's "L'oiseau de feu," there are some notes and sketches of the scenery in Jeanneret's hand--thus suggesting that Jeanneret saw this performance and had moved to Paris by May 1917.[8] Of particular interest is the fact that this booklet contains Guillaume Apollinaire's brief essay "'Parade' et l'esprit nouveau," which praises Picasso's stage-sets and describes the "new spirit" of Cubism. Aside from the specific ideas in this essay which are of interest--such as Apollinaire's Provensalesque description of Cubism as leading art "à la hauteur des progrès scientifiques et industriels," his use of some terms which reappear later in _Après_

le cubisme,[9] and of course the use of the term "Esprit nouveau" it-
self--it is also significant simply that Jeanneret attended this
performance of the Ballets Russes and was thus presumably interested
in Cubism at this time, or at least in the avant-garde art scene in
general. For in his Mémoires, Ozenfant claims that when they met,
Jeanneret, though sharing his own admiration for "les chefs-d'oeuvre
de l'industrie moderne," was nevertheless still "tout à fait aveugle
devant le Cubisme, qui lui faisait hausser les épaules; je l'initiai
et il changea bientôt d'avis. . ."[10]

This question is of some interest, for it bears on whether or
not Ozenfant really made any significant contribution to Jeanneret's
development. The way Ozenfant describes it, Jeanneret had been virtually ignorant of and indifferent to the modern movement in art,
and especially painting, before they met. This is perhaps an exag-
geration--for as we saw, Jeanneret read Denis's Théories, and probably Meier-Graefe's book on Cézanne, before coming to Paris, and then
saw the Ballets Russes in May 1917.[11] Nevertheless, there is clearly
some truth in Ozenfant's claim. For one thing, Le Corbusier later
frankly admitted having begun painting only after meeting Ozenfant;[12]
and none of his sketchbooks from La Chaux-de-Fonds contains any drawings or notes revealing a particular interest in painting. All the
evidence suggests that Jeanneret simply was not very concerned with
painting before coming to Paris, and more specifically that Ozenfant
introduced him to Cubism.

Ozenfant, in fact, seems to have been a kind of mentor to

Jeannert in a number of ways, and even a psychologically stabilizing

figure at a time when Jeanneret was beset with anxiety and self-

doubt. For in a letter written to Ozenfant in June 1918, Jeanneret

is reported to have said:

> ...Tout est confusion en moi depuis que je me remets à des-
> siner. Des afflux de sang jettent mes doigts dans l'arbit-
> raire, mon esprit ne commande plus.
> ...J'ai la discipline dans mes affaires, je ne l'ai ni dans
> mon coeur, ni dans mes idées. J'ai trop laissé vivre en
> moi l'habitude de l'impulsion. Dans mon désarroi j'évoque
> votre tranquille, nerveuse, claire volonté. Il me semble
> qu'un gouffre d'âge nous différencie. Je me sens au seuil
> de l'étude, vous en êtes aux réalisations.
> Je vois derrière moi le papillotement de milliers d'inten-
> tions, de sensations violentes, successives, et toujours
> je me disais: un jour je batirai. Ces jours venus je
> suis un pauvre maçon au fond de la fouille, sans plan!...
> ...Vous êtes... celui qui me semble réaliser le plus
> clairement ce qui s'agite confusément en moi...[13]

The self-doubt expressed by Jeanneret here, concerning his dis-

cipline and readiness to create, is familiar to us; we saw it in his

1908 letter to L'Eplattenier, and there were suggestions that he had

experienced a similar emotional state in Vienna in 1907. It seems to

have been a recurring psychic event of Jeanneret's youth. It can

probably be seen as the typical anxieties of a young man with lofty

aspirations, in the case of Jeanneret intensified by his idealistic

view of the artist as an inspired prophet who must possess super-

human qualities and powers to be a true creator. His letter to

Ozenfant is also interesting for the fact that it comes so soon

after the two of them met (especially if they met in May 1918, just

a month earlier)--further suggesting Jeanneret's need for psycho-

logical support and encouragement at this time.

At this point, a brief summary ought to be made of Ozenfant's background.[14] Born in Northern France in 1886 (only one year before Jeanneret himself was born--which suggests the significance of Jeanneret's remark above that "un gouffre d'âge" seemed to separate them), Amedée Ozenfant was the son of the owner of a construction company who was associated with the pioneering structural engineer Hennebique --and it may well have been through this association that Ozenfant became interested in architecture and got to know Auguste Perret.[15] He went to Paris in 1905 to study painting and architecture, but in the following years seems to have become a kind of dilettante, interested in everything avant-garde but uncommitted to any particular art. He was fascinated with automobiles, and he and his brother even designed the body of a car--with an elegant low form unusual for this time--which was exhibited at the Salon de l'Automobile in 1911 and became known as the "Hispano-Ozenfant." He was also interested in the first airplanes; and this fascination for machines of transportation naturally suggests a connection with Futurism. Indeed, he must have been familiar with the Futurist ideas which were exposed in manifestoes in Paris around 1912; but judging from later remarks of his, he seems to have felt that the Futurists were mistaken in thinking they could capture the spirit of the modern machine age simply by painting or describing machines, rather than seeking out the underlying principles of the machine or of science.[16] This is an idea with which Jeanneret would have agreed also, and it appears in the Purist manifesto, Après le cubisme, which Jeanneret and Ozenfant were to

publish in October 1918. Yet the general Futurist faith in the beauty
and purity of the machine no doubt influenced Ozenfant's thinking, and
Jeanneret's too--and this will be discussed in a separate section below.

In 1915, during the War, Ozenfant founded (and edited, published,
wrote, and designed as well) a periodical entitled Élan, whose main
positions were an advocacy of Cubism and a patriotic attacking of
everything "boche" (the vulgar term for German.) Yet most of the
issues contained few if any articles, being devoted simply to vaguely
Cubistic drawings by Ozenfant and his friends, and to experiments in
avant-garde typography and page lay-out (e.g. Fig. 51) probably inspired by Apollinaire--some of which remind us of the freely-composed
pages in Le Corbusier's later books. Élan had folded by the time
Ozenfant and Jeanneret met; but Ozenfant presented Jeanneret with a
set of all the issues--which Le Corbusier kept wrapped up with a
string in his library. One of these issues was specially inscribed,
on the cover, "à mon ami / Jeanneret / bien cordialement / Ozenfant;"
and in this issue appears the major article Ozenfant wrote for Élan,
"Notes sur le cubisme."[17]

Ozenfant must have given this to Jeanneret as part of his introduction to him of Cubism, and of his own theories about modern
painting. This article is furthermore significant to us because it
reveals what ideas Ozenfant had before he met Jeanneret, and thus
helps us separate their individual contributions to Purism. Specific
points will be examined below; but in general, Ozenfant praised

Cubism for "cleansing the plastic language," as Mallarmé had done for poetry, and for emphasizing the abstract plastic value of visual elements (as the great art of the "assyriens, grecs, chinois, . . . [and] nègres" had also done); but he criticized Cubism for being too decorative and not appealing sufficiently to the "intelligence," for using too much pseudo-scientific jargon, and for being too elitist and ivory-towerish. Ozenfant also says that art should evoke "emotion," should not eschew "significance" or "representation," and should express the "lois organiques" of nature--and all of these ideas remind us of Maurice Denis's Théories, which we suspect must have influenced Ozenfant just as it did Jeanneret.

Most of these ideas in Élan were to reappear in Après le cubisme, with a few exceptions--notably Ozenfant's criticism that some Cubists had renounced "courbes vivantes" and relied excessively on dry geometric forms (ironic, since Purism was to become the most drily geometric Cubism of all.) It appears that Jeanneret's fervent devotion to geometry was one point on which he really altered Ozenfant's aesthetic position--a question which will be examined further below. In most other respects, Ozenfant's 1916 Élan article foreshadows Après le cubisme, even to the use of the term "Purisme" to designate the positive aspects of Cubism which Ozenfant wished to foster.[18]

Thus, when Ozenfant and Jeanneret met, Ozenfant was an established figure in the Parisian avant-garde, was thoroughly familiar with contemporary painting, had definite critical attitudes toward Cubism, and had already formed some of the basic doctrines of Purism.

Jeanneret on the other hand had shown no evidence--either in his notebooks, published writings, or even in his reading--of any special involvement in the contemporary aesthetic scene. This is surely the clue to Jeanneret's sudden attraction to Ozenfant. He saw in him a sophistication and knowledge of the avant-garde lacking in himself, despite the fact that they were the same age. This feeling is apparent in Jeanneret's letter quoted above; and after all, we must remember that he was already thirty-one years old in 1918, and part of his anxiety must have been due to his realization that if he was to be the prophet of a new art, he would have to move fast.

What did Jeanneret have to offer to Ozenfant in return? Mainly, it seems, his views on architecture. Ozenfant states frankly in his Mémoires that in their collaboration, both on Après le cubisme and then on the magazine Esprit nouveau, he himself handled painting while Jeanneret handled architecture.[19] Jeanneret's interest in reinforced concrete, and his Dom-Ino system researches, may have appeared to Ozenfant to be the architectural equivalent of his own theories about painting, and the necessary ingredient for turning his incipient "Purisme" into a total aesthetic doctrine. Jeanneret's idealistic attitudes toward architecture were similar to Ozenfant's ideas about painting--for example his view that painting should appeal to the "intelligence" and seek out the "lois organiques" underlying nature. It sounds like Provensal, and also like Jeanneret's attitude toward architecture. Jeanneret, in fact, may well have possessed a more clearly thought-out idealistic philosophy than Ozenfant (whose ideas in Élan are relatively crude and undeveloped), and may have clarified Ozenfant's own thinking--for example by insisting that geometry must be the key to art, a notion which as we saw Ozenfant had opposed, but which now was to become one of the main tenets of Purism.

Après le Cubisme

In October 1918, Ozenfant and Jeanneret published Après le cubisme, a sixty-page booklet of aesthetic theory which in effect was the manifesto of Purism.[20] Ozenfant says that he had originally shown his notes on Purism to Jeanneret, and that they had then formulated its doctrines and written this book, while at the same time painting the first Purist canvases--which they indeed then exhibited in December 1918.[21] If they did actually meet first in May 1918, this clearly is a great deal of activity in a short period of time. Ozenfant says that he himself wrote the parts of Après le cubisme devoted to painting, that Jeanneret himself wrote the parts on architecture, and that they both "tirions des leçons des belles choses de la technique industrielle. . ."[22] In general, these attributions seem to be accurate; but the book is not divided up that neatly, and only by examining its ideas in the light of our knowledge of Jeanneret's background can we really attempt to identify the respective contributions of its two authors--a task which hitherto has been impossible.[23]

The first chapter, "Où en est la peinture," does seem to be mainly the work of Ozenfant (except that the chapter-title itself was probably suggested by Jeanneret.[24]) It is largely a discussion of Cubism and modern painting in general, and reiterates many of the points of the 1916 article in Élan--although now Cubism is attacked more strongly and forthrightly. It is accused of being too decorative and hardly any different from the ornamental art of "les Mycéniens, les Orientaux et les nègres;" of fostering obscure theories and jargon; and of suppressing the third dimension in favor of an unsuccessful attempt to apply an abstract "fourth dimension" to painting. (pp. 15-17) Most basically, Cubism is accused of being too "traditional," of simply appealing to our superficial senses like Impressionism and all other recent art, instead of seeking out "les bases certaines," appealing to the "intellect," and thus creating "l'art pur" which will express "l'esprit moderne." (p. 20)

The second chapter, "Où en est la vie moderne," consists of several sections, the first of which--"L'esprit moderne"--we can identify as the work of Jeanneret. It argues that the new age of science, industrialism, and the machine will bring about a new art, and also a new society, in which workers will possess a "fierté collective" as a result of their contact with the "clarté," "puissance," and "perfection" of machines and machine-products; and that men will be led to "des idées plus générales" and to "la synthèse et. . . l'ordre." (p. 26) We recognize the ideas of Provensal and much of the rest of Jeanneret's early reading. The architecture of this new

age will be characterized by "rigueur," the application of laws,
order, and precision, and is said to have been heralded already
in certain work of engineers in "béton armé." (pp. 27-28) In fact,
reinforced concrete "permet pour la première fois la réalisation
rigoureuse du calcul; le Nombre, qui est la base de toute beauté,
peut trouver désormais son expression." (p. 28) This naturally
reminds us of Schuré's descriptions of Pythagorean numerology; and
it soon becomes clear that Jeanneret's attraction to machines, here,
is due to the mathematical and numerical perfection which he sees
in them:

> Déja les machines, à cause même de leur conditionnement par
> le nombre, avaient évolué plus rapidement, atteignant aujourd'-
> hui un épurement remarquable. (p. 28)

> On ne reste pas insensible devant l'intelligence qui régit cer-
> taines machines, devant la proportion de leurs organes rigour-
> eusement conditionnés par les calculs, devant la précision
> d'exécution de leurs éléments, devant la beauté probe de leurs
> matières, devant la securité de leurs mouvements; il y a là
> comme une projection des lois naturelles. . . (p. 28)

And Jeanneret concludes by saying that this new machine-art
will be able to attain "l'idéal de perfection" which even the Greeks,
in the Parthenon, attempted but were unable fully to achieve.

We can imagine Jeanneret writing virtually all of this section
before having met Ozenfant, so thoroughly do nearly all of its component ideas reflect thinking with which we know he was familiar since
his youth. And yet this is the first time that we find him drawing
it all together in essentially the same way--though not as clearly--
as he was able to do in his writings in the 1920's. The "machine" is
the one element here with which we are not totally familiar--except

for Jeanneret's references, in the Voyage d'Orient, to the Parthenon
as a "machine" (see Chapter III, p. 101). We might imagine that
Ozenfant, with his interest in automobiles and other machines, contributed to this enthusiasm. Yet Jeanneret's apotheosis of the
machine here is not related to the attraction of specific machines,
or even to the notion of speed or brute force as it was to the Futurists; rather, the concept "machine" had come to symbolize for him
that perfection, order, and numerical harmony which, as we have seen,
was the aim of all the idealistic philosophy to which Jeanneret was
exposed throughout his youth.

This four-page section--clearly the work of Jeanneret--is perhaps the most significant section of Après le cubisme. But many of
its ideas are elaborated in the rest of the manifesto, many parts of
which seem to have been composed jointly by Jeanneret and Ozenfant.
The remainder of the second chapter contains more criticisms of contemporary artists and their elitist pretentions (like Ozenfant's
remarks in his Élan article) and their misguided belief that by
painting modern machines ("des transatlantiques, des wagons") they
are capturing their spirit; criticism of the Fauves for having no
"conception," and of artists who artifically introduce "des formes
nègres" into their paintings without any of the "purity" which originally characterized these forms.(pp. 30-32) One section claims
that there is no incompatibility between art and science, since art
like science should be based on "laws," on "rigor," "precision,"
and the "purity" of science; and all of this reminds us of Provensal.

The frequency of the term "rigor," especially in the section by Jeanneret discussed above, is truly extraordinary, and is seen again in
the conclusion of this second chapter:

> Des faits rigoureux, des figurations rigoureuses, des archi-
> tectures rigoureuses, formelles, aussi purement et simple-
> ment que le sont les machines.
> Les lois ne sauraient être une contrainte; elles sont l'arm-
> ature fatale, mais inébranlable de toutes choses. Une arma-
> ture n'est pas une entrave. Assez de jeux. Nous aspirons
> à une rigueur grave. (p. 34)

This demand for strictness, seriousness, and unshakeable laws
seems definitely to be the contribution of Jeanneret. For in Ozenfant's Élan article there was a very different attitude: that much
of Cubism was too rigid and rigorous (especially too geometric) and
that the artist, while needing to understand certain "lois organiques,"
should nevertheless keep himself from being too bound to them. It is
a question of emphasis. For while both Ozenfant and Jeanneret recognized a need for formal "laws," Ozenfant's original tendency was to
stress freedom within these laws, whereas Jeanneret seems obsessed
with the necessity first of all of establishing them and of embodying
their "rigor." We have seen this in his earlier writings as well--
for example in the Voyage d'Orient where he associated the geometric
and formal precision of the Parthenon with moral notions of "austerity" and "rectitude." The same phenomenon occurs here in Après le
cubisme, where the "rigor" associated with machines and the new Purist
aesthetic, appears to refer as much to a spiritual or moral rigor as
to a formal rigor.

The third chapter of Après le cubisme, entitled simply "Les

lois," reiterates that the new art must "generalize," must discover
"les lois naturelles," and that both art and science "dependent du
nombre." (pp. 39-40) This type of art is "l'art pur," and its role
is to seek out "l'Invariant" which underlies reality. As in Maurice
Denis's Théories, Impressionism and Romanticism are criticized for
showing only the superficial world, the ostensibly chaotic face
which nature presents to us on the surface. (p. 14) But when properly understood, nature is to be seen as a perfect "machine," working according to geometric and mathematical principles:

> Les lois nous permettent de considérer que la nature agit
> à la manière d'une machine. Il sort de cette machine
> très compliquée un tissu très complexe, mais tissé sur
> trame géométrique. La géométrie physique et mathématique
> définissent les lois des forces qui sont comme des axes
> d'ordonnance.
> Cette machine agit suivant les lois si rigoureuses que,
> malgré son infinie complication, les plus rigoureuses
> mesures sont incapables de mettre en évidence la plus
> petite variation dans ses produits: INVARIABILITÉ.

This invariability is then related to "la loi des grand nom-
bres" (to which there is a footnote referring to Pythagoras), to the
laws of "ordre" and "harmonie," and to the "axes" underlying reality
--that same term which Le Corbusier later uses in his article "Architecture: pure création de l'esprit." We again recognize so many
elements from Provensal, Schuré, and Jeanneret's early reading in
general, that we have the impression that he alone must have composed
this section. The notion that the universe runs like a great weaving-
machine naturally reminds us of eighteenth-century Deism; but at the
same time, Jeanneret's corollary that Nature is ruled by "Invariability" is in effect a form of Calvinistic determinism--which we have

seen already in Jeanneret's writings, for example in his 1913 characterization of crystalline architecture as possessing "inexorability," and of the Parthenon as a "terrible machine" possessing a "fatalité extra-humaine."

Next, in <u>Après le cubisme</u>, comes a passage in which the artist is compared to a tuning-fork ("un résonnateur"), vibrating in accord with the underlying order of nature--exactly the same image which Bergson used to describe the artist, in Benoît-Lévy's book which Jeanneret read in about 1915. But here this tuning-fork analogy is made even more precise; for Jeanneret says that this aesthetic resonnance or vibration, like music, occurs in response to certain "numbers" or numerical proportions--about which he is vague, but which suggest visual proportions determined mathematically. (p. 44) And we are naturally reminded of Provensal's "certains rapports," as well as Pythagorean numerology, and of course Le Corbusier's own Modulor system.

Following this is a section in which a hierarchy of beauty is established, which ranks different types of subject-matter for painting, with inorganic forms at the bottom, landscape next, and at the top the human figure, which is eulogized as the most beautiful and worthy subject for the painter. (pp. 45-46) The irony here of course is that the Purist paintings which Jeanneret and Ozenfant actually executed, then and in the next several years (e.g. Fig. 52), are characterized by a complete absence of the human figure and a concentration on inanimate still-life objects. The only explanation

151

I can think of for this contradiction is that Ozenfant alone wrote

this section of Après le cubisme, and that it was Jeanneret--with

his passion for geometry and man-made forms--who turned the subject-

matter of Purism so thoroughly toward still-life objects. As we saw,

Ozenfant in his Élan article actually criticized the geometrizing

tendencies of Cubism; and indeed the human figure dominates the illus-

trations in Élan. Thus Ozenfant's natural preference was clearly

for the human figure; and our suspicion is reinforced that one of

Jeanneret's contributions to Purism was a demand for rigourous geo-

metric forms, and as a result a concentration in the paintings on

still-life objects such as bottles, glasses, and pipes.

Immediately following this section written by Ozenfant, how-

ever, the last three pages of the third chapter seem to have been

written by Jeanneret. The discussion returns to the artist's "re-

cherche des lois de l'harmonie" and to those mysterious "axes" under-

lying nature, through whose use the artist can "créer des construc-

tions cohérentes avec la nature, intelligibles et satisfaisantes."[25]

These universal "laws" are said to have been utilized by men like

Euclid, Pythagoras, and Archimedes, and also to have been the basis

of the geometric canons and "rapports numériques" used by the Egyp-

tians in the pyramids, the Assyrians in their palaces, the Greeks

in the Parthenon, the Persians in their "coupoles," the Gothics in

their cathedrals, and "renaissance" architects such as Blondel.[26]

We recognize here not only the familiar ideas from Provensal and

Schuré, but also Dieulafoy's researches into Persian architecture which we know Jeanneret had read in La Chaux-de-Fonds;[27] and further-more, Le Corbusier later repeated the notion that Blondel's architec-ture was based on a proportioning system similar to his own "tracés régulateurs;"[28] and his library reveals that he attempted to prove the same thing in regard to Egyptian architecture as well.[29] All in all, this section of Après le cubisme reveals how seriously Jeanneret was convinced that the most essential aim of architecture was its contact with a transcendent realm of perfection through the use of abstract laws of numerical and geometric proportioning. He, not Ozenfant, was clearly the author of this important aspect of Purist doctrine. It is worth pointing out that just as Le Corbusier con-tinued to be concerned with this issue throughout his life, Ozenfant shows no continuation of interest in it after his break with Le Cor-busier in 1925.[30]

The last chapter, entitled "Après le cubisme" like the book itself, summarizes all the points made earlier, and is presented as the actual manifesto of Purism. A couple of new ideas are presented, for example the notion that color, in Purist painting, is subordinate to form--hardly a surprising dictum in an aesthetic based on geometry, proportion, and formal purity. Other than that, Ozenfant's ideas-- such as the superiority of the human figure as subject-matter--are simply restated, side by side with Jeanneret's ideas--the need for invariable laws, geometry, generality, a basis in "numbers," and above all "la rigoureuse image d'une conception rigoureuse." (p. 57)

This rather detailed analysis of Après le cubisme, together

with our understanding of Jeanneret's earlier thinking based on our
knowledge of his reading and other activities, allows us to make
some basic conclusions about the respective contributions of Jeanneret
and Ozenfant to Purism. Ozenfant contributed, besides the term "Purism" itself, his intimate knowledge of contemporary painting and particularly Cubism, specific criticisms of Cubist theory and pretensions, and a general feeling that Cubism was guilty of the same "decorative" tendencies as Impressionism and ought to be "purified" and made
more expressive of ideal principles. Jeanneret agreed with this, but
went much further, emphasizing the need for a "rigorous" adherence to
underlying "laws" of numerical relationships and proportions, which
he clearly believed in much more literally and concretely than did
Ozenfant. As a result, Jeanneret imposed on Purism a reliance on
geometry and geometric forms which Ozenfant, hitherto, had actually
opposed.

Furthermore, of course, Jeanneret contributed his knowledge of
architecture; and despite the fact that Après le cubisme is principally
the manifesto of a movement in painting, the sections of it which we
recognize as Jeanneret's actually refer to architecture more than to
painting, and reveal that to him Purism was to be a total aesthetic
embracing all the plastic arts. The reference to a new "collective"
society, to industrial "taylorisation," (p. 26) and to the need for
"generalization," "synthesis," and similar philosophical notions,
can be recognized as ideas with which Jeanneret was familiar from his
reading; but it is possible that Ozenfant also was familiar with them,
and that these were points on which they agreed from the beginning.

As for the interesting references to "machines," we might
expect them to be inspired by Ozenfant's love of automobiles and
airplanes, and by Futurism; yet these references all occur in sections seemingly written by Jeanneret, and more importantly, they
do not suggest the passion for speed and power which characterized
Futurism or would naturally be associated with automobiles and airplanes. These "machines" are of a very different sort: an idealized kind of factory-machine or mechanism in general; and the emphasis is not on their power or brute force, but as we saw, on their
"perfection," "clarity," "rigorousness," "invariance," "order," and
on their supposed basis in "Number" and an underlying mathematical
truth. They are thus a kind of Pythagorean symbol of the underlying
structure of nature itself; and as we saw, one of the references
frankly uses the image of a weaving-machine as a metaphor for the
natural world. Furthermore, we have seen that this conception of
the "machine" had already been suggested by Jeanneret several years
earlier in the Voyage d'Orient, in his characterization of the Parthenon as a "machine" possessing the same kinds of rigor, rigidity,
rectitude, and fatalistic invariability as we find in Après le
cubisme--although these images which Jeanneret in 1911 had found
"cruel" and "terrifying," had shed these fearful connotations for
him by 1918. Thus the "machine" was an important personal image for
Jeanneret which he had been developing for some time, and does not
need to be explained by a contact with Futurism. Despite this, Jeanneret's relationship with Futurism cannot be dismissed so easily.

For he does seem to have had contact with Futurist thinking, and to have been influenced by certain Futurist ideas not specifically related to machines; and this question will be examined next.

Jeanneret and Futurism

Le Corbusier's library contains several early Futurist items; but there are no inscriptions, annotations, or markings in them by Jeanneret, so the problem is to know when he acquired them, and also of course what his attitude toward them was. The most interesting of these items are three manifestoes, or reprints of these manifestoes: Marinetti's original "Manifeste du futurisme," first published in Le Figaro in February 1909; Boccioni's "Manifeste technique de la sculpture futuriste," first published in 1912; and Marinetti's "Supplément au manifeste technique de la littérature futuriste," also of 1912.[31] At least two of these manifestoes are clearly reprints (the date on them being the date of their original publication elsewhere), and in fact all three of them may be reprints--although that of course does not rule out their being early reprints of the 1910's, in which case we can imagine Jeanneret acquiring them during his visits to Paris in 1912 or thereafter. But they were found all together in Le Corbusier's library, in the pages of a Futurist publication of 1924;[32] and they are all in good condition, which suggests that they were not picked up separately by Jeanneret, but perhaps were sent to him all at one time, maybe even in the 1920's when he was receiving Futurist periodicals like the one in which they were found. On the other hand, it is worth mentioning that in a later book on

Sant-Elia which Le Corbusier acquired in 1935, he wrote an inscription saying that "c'était une époque intense et de grandes découvertes, de courage, d'enthousiasme et de manifestes, 1910-1914"-- which implies that he was familiar with the Futurist manifestoes in this period 1910-1914.[33] All in all, it seems virtually impossible to determine just when Jeanneret became familiar with any specific manifesto, although it is reasonable to assume that he was aware of the Futurist movement in general from his trips to Paris in the 1910's.

Marinetti's "Manifeste du futurisme"--Jeanneret's copy of which was a reprint issued by the Futurist organ _Poesia_[34]--is well known and need not be examined carefully here. The significant point is that it calls for a dedication to speed, danger, anarchy, hatred of everything conventional, and all sorts of attendant ideals such as war, youth, and "contempt for women." It is individualistic, Romantic, and opposed to all systems of order--and therefore is basically the opposite of the Purism presented in _Après le cubisme_. There are, indeed, some superficial similarities between the two, for example a passionate faith in the modern age, and a fascination for machines. But Marinetti's machine-images are of hurtling locomotives, "adventurous steamships," airplanes greeted by the delirious roaring of a crowd, and gigantic, "violent" factories, consuming avariciously and belching out smoke--totally different in spirit from the precise, perfect, mathematically rigorous machines in _Après le cubisme_.[35] Thus, the "machine" has virtually opposite meaning for

Jeanneret and Marinetti: it symbolizes perfection, discipline and order for the one, brutishness and anarchy for the other.

It is interesting, however, to point out that some aspects of Marinetti's Futurist manifesto sound similar to the younger Jeanneret, for example around 1909 and 1910. A striking example of this is Jeanneret's romantic 1910 annotation in Cingria-Vaneyre's Entretiens about dedicating himself to "modernism" while on a mountain-peak, compared with the concluding'section of the Futurist manifesto:

> . . . Ils nous trouveront enfin, par une nuit d'hiver, en pleine campagne, sous un triste hangar pianoté par la pluie monotone. . . Debout sur la cime du monde, nous lançons encore une fois le défi aux étoiles! (Marinetti)

> Vive le modernisme. . . . une nuit même de pluie au sommet de la Jungfrau, je me la paierai et sacrificerai alors à notre brave siècle. (Jeanneret)

These two vows to proclaim the new art from a mountain-summit, at night, in the rain, seem too similar to be totally accidental;[36] and it is possible that Jeanneret had read the original publication of Marinetti's manifesto in Paris in February 1909, and the next year in Germany paraphrased this image. In more general terms, there are also similarities at about this time between Marinetti's manifesto and ideas which Jeanneret expressed in his letters--for example in his letter to L'Eplattenier, with its Romantic individualism, and its desire to destroy the past in order to create the future. Yet since this letter was written in 1908, the year before Marinetti published his manifesto, there is clearly no connection; and as pointed out earlier, these aspects in Jeanneret's letters probably came from Nietzsche's Zarathustra (which, in fact, undoubtedly was an influence on Marinetti himself.)

Interestingly enough, some of the other Futurist manifestoes in Le Corbusier's library are closer in spirit to Jeanneret's ideas than was Marinetti's manifesto. For example Boccioni's "Manifeste technique de la sculpture futuriste," dated 11 April 1912,[37] does not have Marinetti's emphasis on speed, brute power, and revolution, but rather speaks of a new sculpture which will possess "les merveilleux éléments mathématiques et géométriques des objets modernes," will employ a "compénétration des plans" as in Futurist painting, and will rely principally on the straight line--"la seule ligne correspondante à la simplicité intérieure de la synthèse que nous opposons à l'extériorité baroque de l'analyse." We recognize in this manifesto many terms and phrases from Jeanneret's reading and his own writings; but he absorbed most of them before he could have read this manifesto.

Marinetti's "Supplement au manifeste technique de la littérature futuriste," dated 11 August 1912,[38] may have had a more significant influence on Jeanneret--though only on his style of writing. Marinetti's theory about writing--that it should be "intuitive and unconscious" rather than "intellectual and voluntary" (he seems to have been cultivating a kind of stream-of-consciousness or automatic writing)--bears no relationship to Le Corbusier. But some of his specific suggestions may well have influenced Jeanneret, and appear as characteristics of Le Corbusier's writing-style in the 1920's-- which contrasts so strongly with his earlier writing-style. For example, Marinetti's suggestions of the use of unconventional typography and symbols, and especially of the attention-getting device of printing words and sentences in capital letters, were to become important aspects of Le Corbusier's polemical style of writing in his books. But Marinetti's principal demand is for the suppression of the adjective and adverb. And it is interesting that when we analyze the difference between Jeanneret's early writing-style (for example in the Voyage d'Orient), and that of his books of the 1920's --the first being so heavy, florid, and Romantic in feeling, and the second so sharp and aggressive--we realize that this difference is due primarily to a superabundance of adjectives in the one, and their near absence in the other.[39] Ozenfant's articles and typographic experiments in Élan also reveal these Futurist influences (as well as the influence of Apollinaire); and whether Jeanneret picked up this literary style from Ozenfant or directly from Marinetti's manifesto, it seems that the Futurist style of writing helped shape Jeanneret's own style. This is no small influence, when we consider how successful Le Corbusier's propaganda was, and how important his style of writing was to this success.

One other, later, Futurist item in Le Corbusier's library ought to be mentioned here: the 1 October 1922 issue of Le futurisme, devoted to a reprint of a 1916 manifesto by Marinetti entitled "La nouvelle religion-morale de la Vitesse."[41] One major idea appears here which is found in Le Corbusier's writings too--a contrasting of the chaos and passivity of nature (associated with the curved line) with the forthright aggressivenes of Man (associated with the straight line.) Marinetti describes machines as another aspect of this heroic domination of nature by Man, calling them Man's "army of slaves," and then contrasts curvilinear nature with rectilinear Man:

> Sentiers tortueux, grandes routes qui suivent l'indolence des fleuves, les dos des montagnes et leurs ventres inégaux, voici les vieilles lois de la terre. Jamais une ligne droite. Partout des arabesques et des zig-zags. La vitesse donne enfin à la vie humaine un des caractères de la divinité: la ligne droite.

This might remind us of the conviction in Après le cubism that art must discover the underlying geometry and order of nature, rather than presenting merely its superficial chaos; but actually it is very different, for Marinetti is suggesting that the "divine" straight line does not underlie nature, but is created only by Man. Thus it is significant that Le Corbusier, in his articles of the early 1920's, begins to express a very similar notion--for example in his well-known opening section of Urbanisme:

> L'homme marche droit parce qu'il a un but; il sait où il va. Il a décidé d'aller quelque part et il y marche droit. L'âne zigzague, muse un peu, cervelle brulée et distrait, zigzague pour éviter les gros cailloux, pour esquiver la pente, . . . (p. 5)

> La rue courbe est l'effet du bon plaisir, de la nonchalance, du relâchement, de la décontraction, de l'animalité. La droite est une réaction, une action, un agissement, l'effet d'une domination sur soi. Elle est saine et noble. (p. 11)

We are tempted to see in this a Futurist influence on Le Corbusier; but this section of Urbanisme was first published in the Esprit nouveau issue of June 1922, so Le Corbusier would have to have known Marinetti's original 1916 manifesto rather than simply the reprint. Whatever its source, this notion of a chaotic nature versus the order

which only Man can create, will become a favorite idea of Le Corbusier's and recur throughout his writings. It is, at least

ostensibly, incompatible with Jeanneret's other idea (with its

roots in Provensal and in idealistic philosophy in general) that

order underlies nature and needs only to be discovered by the

artist. Throughout his life, Le Corbusier was to express both

of these notions in his writing, often side by side; and we sense

that Le Corbusier himself may have been unable to resolve, in his

own mind, this basic philosophical question of whether order ulti-

mately resides outside Man or within him. But whatever the source

of the second of these views--whether Futurism, or perhaps Nie-

tzsche--it begins to appear in Le Corbusier's writings around 1921

and 1922.[42]

Finally, something should be said about the Futurist manifesto

on architecture, despite the fact that Le Corbusier's library does

not contain a copy of it--since Jeanneret still could have read it

when it appeared. It was published twice in 1914, in two somewhat

different forms but both over the name of Sant'Elia--although

Marinetti himself may have written parts of it.[43] A number of

Sant'Elia's specific ideas in this manifesto can indeed be related

to Jeanneret's thinking--for example his call for a totally new archi-

tecture, based on the spirit of science and technology, using new

materials like reinforced concrete, iron and glass, "like a gigantic

machine," and the ruthless destruction of old cities to make way for

the new (which were to have different levels for traffic, as in

Le Corbusier's urbanistic schemes of the 1920's.) Nevertheless, there
are more basic differences between the two of them. Sant'Elia's notion of the machine, like Marinetti's, is of something "extraordinarily
brutish," symbolizing speed and untamed power--quite the opposite of
Jeanneret's machines of precision and rigor. And Sant'Elia specifically rejects the traditional concern for "aesthetics" and "proportion"
(that most fundamental concern of Jeanneret's); and he also rejects
all that is "graceful and pleasing," as well as "Perpendicular and
horizontal lines, cubic and pyramidal forms, static, grave, oppressive
and absolutely foreign to our newest sensibilities." Like Marinetti's
ideas, Sant'Elia's were drastically more revolutionary and iconoclastic
than Le Corbusier's ever were to become. Indeed, Sant'Elia's architecture, like Marinetti's aesthetic in general, was meant to embody speed,
brute power, the agitated movement suggested by non-perpendicular lines,
and the rejection of all classical premises. If Jeanneret shared or
borrowed any of Sant'Elia's specific recommendations, he reshaped them
to fit into his totally different view of architecture as the embodiment of perfect forms, divine proportions, and universal "laws."

In conclusion, we have to admit that Jeanneret's relationship to
Futurism is difficult to characterize in a simple way. On the one hand,
it seems likely that Jeanneret was aware of the Futurist manifestoes
and ideas as early as the period around 1912, and perhaps even from
1909 when Marinetti's first manifesto appeared in Paris. Furthermore,
certain specific Futurist ideas and images do seem to have influenced
Jeanneret--for an example an interest in the machine as symbolizing

the new age; a sense of exhilaration and arrogance; a studied dis-
respect for the past; specific architectural ideas from Sant'Elia,
such as segregated traffic levels in cities; and also a style of
writing, lean and aggressive and polemical. Yet on the other hand
it is by no means true, as has been suggested, that Le Corbusier's
thinking was largely shaped by Futurist ideas.[44]   Indeed, Jeanneret's
basic attitudes toward art, for the most part, were diametrically
opposed to those of Futurism--typified by the significance which each
of them saw in the "machine," a symbol of brute power for the one,
but of perfect order for the other.

And even in the case of certain aspects of Le Corbusier's thinking which appear to derive from Futurism (such as the notion of the
artist as being uncommitted to any precedent or tradition, and of the
need to destroy ruthlessly the past in order to create the new order),
we have seen that they often come from other sources in Jeanneret's
reading (such as Nietzsche) and were part of his thinking before Futurism could have influenced him. But most significant is that, fundamentally,. there are more differences than similarities between the
attitudes of Le Corbusier and of Futurism. Futurism's ideals were
speed, violence, and individualism; Le Corbusier's were order, precision, and the adherence to those perfect, idealistic "laws" which
he believed the Artist must create (or discover) and then impose upon
the visible world.

Jeanneret's creation of Le Corbusier

After the publication of <u>Après le cubisme</u> in late 1918, there
are a couple of years before <u>L'esprit nouveau</u> was founded during which
Jeanneret's activities are rather vague. One of the few clues to this
period is one of Jeanneret's sketchbooks--the one labeled "A-3"[45]--
which is also inscribed "Paris, 1918-1919." It contains a number of
drawings and watercolours of landscapes and human figures, done in a
rather Expressionistic or Fauve-ish (but definitely not "Purist")
style; sketches of simple country farm-houses; and some studies suggesting further development of the Dom-Ino system. Furthermore, it
contains a sketch for a house which is very close to one of the first
houses which Le Corbusier was to design in Paris--the Vaucresson House
of 1922. If this sketch does indeed date from 1918-1919, it is probably the first design we know which exhibits the formal characteristics of Le Corbusier's first houses--which will be examined in the
next chapter.[46]

Jeanneret at this time is also reported to have been involved
in some way with a brick-factory near Paris.[47] His interest in structural and constructional problems is further suggested by his studies
for low-cost housing units in Troyes, and his "Monol" and "Citrohan"
systems of construction.[48] The "Citrohan" scheme, in particular, was
a significant step toward the formal synthesis which Jeanneret was
attempting to achieve at this time, and will be discussed in the following chapter. However, Jeanneret was not actually to build anything
until 1922;[49] and this lack of commissions must have been one of the

reasons Jeanneret decided to collaborate with Ozenfant in another literary venture. This time it was to be a much more ambitious venture--the founding of L'esprit nouveau, the revue in which, during the next five years, Jeanneret was to write the articles which would later be collected and form the two books, Vers une architecture and Urbanisme, which were to do more than anything else (even including his buildings) to spread his ideas and fame throughout the modern movement in the 1920's and later.

At this point, the major part of our study of Jeanneret's youthful intellectual development comes to a close. There are several reasons why this is an appropriate point in his career to stop and to draw conclusions from what we have examined. For one thing, with the founding of L'esprit nouveau Jeanneret became for the first time a really public personality. From this point on, his writings are well known and have been much more carefully studied than his earlier activities which this study has concentrated on. But more than this, Jeanneret's youthful development at this time really does come to a kind of halt. He seems finally to draw together the various aspects of his earlier thinking and self-education and to make a sort of synthesis of it all--a synthesis which will be analyzed in broad terms in the following, concluding chapter. As one result of this drawing-together and synthesizing, it seems that Jeanneret's reading, after about 1918, becomes less important for him; he no longer seems to be reading in search of "truth," as we saw earlier, for now in a sense he has the truth, and knows more or less what he wants to do. He still reads a great deal; but from now on it is principally in search of specific facts or information, generally to support or verify his own ideas.[50] Thus our study of Jeanneret's self-education, which was to such a large extent a search for knowledge and truth in the books he read, is appropriately concluded at this point when he formulates his attitudes toward architecture and his own role. It is perhaps not merely coincidence that at this very time Jeanneret also chooses a new name for himself--thus in a sense announcing symbolically this synthesis of thought, and the appearance of a new figure in the architectural world.

This pseudonym--"Le Corbusier"--deserves some comment itself, since it has been the source of a good deal of misunderstanding. It was adopted by Jeanneret in late 1920, when he and Ozenfant were putting together the first issue of L'esprit nouveau--which appeared in October of that year. Ozenfant also adopted a pseudonym at this time, "Saugnier" (which was his mother's name, just as "Le Corbusier" was a family-name of Jeanneret's); and these two names were assumed ostensibly to separate their articles on architecture from those on painting.[51] Probably there was also an intention simply to disguise the fact that Ozenfant and Jeanneret were writing most of the articles in L'esprit nouveau themselves. And in fact, soon they began fabricating even more pseudonyms; and this use of multiple pseudonyms naturally complicates the task of anlyzing the ideas in L'esprit nouveau--despite the fact that Ozenfant later recalled some of these secondary pseudonyms.[52]

But in spite of this somewhat comic multiplication of names, "Le Corbusier" clearly had a special significance for Jeanneret from

the beginning. For he chose it specifically to sign to articles on
architecture (leaving "Charles-Édouard Jeanneret" for articles on
painting), thus adopting it for his paramount role, that of prophet
of the new architecture. The situation however is complicated by
the fact that the important early articles on architecture (those
that were to form the bulk of Vers une architecture) are in L'esprit
nouveau actually signed "Le Corbusier-Saugnier." This clearly means
Jeanneret-Ozenfant; but this fact seems to have been misunderstood
by the public right from the beginning (and in fact still is misunderstood even by some Le Corbusier scholars).[53] Le Corbusier himself
seems to have gone to no special effort to disabuse people of this
misunderstanding (for in his library I found letters addressed to
him as "Monsieur Le Corbusier-Saugnier," some even from acquaintances
of his such as Walter Gropius);[54] and this may have been one of the
factors in the antipathy which developed between Jeanneret and Ozenfant and which led to their ultimate falling-out in 1925.[55]

Actually, it appears that these articles on architecture were
in fact written primarily by Jeanneret, despite the double signature
(we have seen for example that Jeanneret wrote the architectural sections of Après le cubisme); and thus when Vers une architecture was
published in 1923 under the name of Le Corbusier alone, no great injustice was being done to Ozenfant. The reason behind this double
signature seems to be that right at the beginning of their collaboration, in 1918, Jeanneret and Ozenfant made an agreement to publish
all of their writings on Purism under a common name, and to make no

distinction between their individual contributions.[56] It is worth
noting that in 1918 this sort of arrangement would have seemed to
Jeanneret to be definitely to his advantage; for as we saw, Ozenfant
at that time had the greater experience and knowledge of the avant-
garde, and Jeanneret himself recognized this (as revealed in his
letter of June 1918) and was plagued with doubts about his own ability and readiness to create. But by the early 1920's, Jeanneret must
have begun regretting this agreement, and looking for an opportunity
to separate his public identity from that of Ozenfant.

This period, from 1917 to about 1920, when Jeanneret was attempting to synthesize the elements of his education into a new architecture
(which we shall analyze in the concluding chapter), was thus in a sense
a period of psychological synthesis too--with Jeanneret attempting to
prove to himself that he was indeed worthy of the role of architectural
prophet which he had envisioned since his youth, and to overcome those
feelings of self-doubt and anxiety which we have observed at various
times, for example in his 1908 letter to L'Eplattenier and in his letter to Ozenfant. In the past, these periods of self-doubt had alter-
nated with Jeanneret's fantasies of grandeur and of his exalted destiny
--as for example in his identification of himself with the Christ, while
reading Renan's Vie de Jésus. Now, finally, Jeanneret was beginning
to fashion a more realistic image of his role and his career, as part
of the architectural synthesis he was also formulating. To be sure,
he was in a sense still under the spell of Schuré's notion of prophetic
"Initiates;" but now Jeanneret could feel that at last he was indeed an
Initiate, and was ready to announce himself to the world.

CHAPTER VI

LE CORBUSIER'S SYNTHESIS

With the founding of L'esprit nouveau in 1920 and the creation of
"Le Corbusier," Jeanneret in effect becomes a fully public personality.
Despite the temporary confusion of pseudonyms with Ozenfant, it becomes
possible from this point on to examine Le Corbusier's thought in the
prolific articles and other publications which he was to continue producing with amazing regularity throughout his career. And in the early
1920's he also designs and for the first time builds houses which can
be seen as expressions of his new synthesis. In the strictest sense,
perhaps it is incorrect to employ the term "synthesis" to describe Le
Corbusier's thinking and designing in these early years--since there are
so many diverse aspects of his thought, which in many cases are not
totally resolved or neatly subsumed under any overall system. Yet in a
looser sense, Le Corbusier is indeed producing a synthesis; for his
writing and designing reveal an attempt to draw together and resolve in
some way the two major forces which we have seen in his education--on
the one hand the idealism which so strongly shaped his youthful thought,
and on the other hand the rationalist attitudes and concerns represented
by Auguste Perret. We shall attempt here simply to suggest several different ways in which Le Corbusier synthesized these philosophies or
attitudes--and in particular how his fundamental idealism shaped and

interpreted specific architectural elements.

The geometric conception of form

First, we ought to review briefly the forms which Le Corbusier designed in this first phase of his mature career, in the early 1920's. These designs are characterized by a specific attitude toward form: a conviction that certain forms are inherently preferable to others, and that these preferred forms are those which are most easily conceptualized, such as cubes, cylinders, and spheres.[1] This is one of the most emphatic themes in Le Corbusier's Esprit nouveau articles, as well as his later writings; and it is of course an attitude whose development we have watched throughout our study of Jeanneret's early self-education.

Jeanneret's first architectural designs which truly express the "Le Corbusier" synthesis reveal the overwhelming importance to him of this geometric or "unified" view of form (Figs. 53-54). The "Troyes" project (dated 1919 by Le Corbusier), the "Citrohan" house project (apparently first designed in 1920), the "Monol" scheme (1920), and Le Corbusier's first executed houses in Paris, that at Vaucresson and the LaRoche-Jeanneret houses (1922)--as well as the first group of houses which Le Corbusier built for Frugès near Pessac, which may be as early as 1920[2]--all are in the form of the simplest cubic masses. The LaRoche-Jeanneret houses at first glance seem to be an exception to this, since the whole ensemble is composed essentially of two cubic volumes rather than just one; but this is merely because Le Corbusier first conceived this project as involving several houses, on both sides

and the end of the cul-de-sac street for which they were designed.[3]
Indeed, it is significant that the secondary volume of this ensemble,
the one which closes the end of the street, is actually only part of
the LaRoche house; and the fact that the rest of the LaRoche house and
the adjacent Jeanneret house are treated by Le Corbusier as one in-
divisible cubic form (it is even hard from the exterior to know where
one house ends and the other begins) reveals the extent to which Le
Corbusier felt that achieving one unified geometric form was paramount
to all other considerations, such as the expression of the individual
unit.

In the case of the Vaucresson house, this formal characteristic
is further revealed by Le Corbusier's own recollection that he had rejected his first design for the house, in which the stair-volume projected from the facade (thus creating two masses) and had replaced it
with one single mass, because: ". . . il apparut subitement que cette
cage d'escalier perpendiculaire était un rythme antagoniste brisant
l'unité de la composition. . . on sacrifie le détail piquant; on recherche l'unité."[4]

In two of the designs of this early period--the "Monol" system
and Ozenfant's studio--the roof is handled in a non-horizontal manner,
unlike all the other designs, which have flat roofs. And it is significant that these two experiments were never repeated in the immediately
following years (despite Le Corbusier's obvious delight at the interior
effects produced by the Ozenfant--studio skylights; and despite the fact
that many years later he was to return to the barrel-vaulted roof of the

"Monol" system in several designs.) The purity of the exterior form
mattered most to Le Corbusier, and it was thus the rigidly cubic
"Citrohan" house-type which was the starting-point for all of his
major design developments of his early career.

In many ways, the "Troyes" project seems to be the first expression by Jeanneret of this utter formal "unity." It is interesting that
one of the drawings for this project shows a prominent roof-overhang,
while another drawing completely suppresses any indication of roof or
cornice; and it is tempting to suggest that this was the point when
Jeanneret finally abandoned his earlier fascination for cornices (revealed so strongly in his notebooks around 1915 and 1916), and decided
that the formal integrity of the cubic whole demanded the elimination
of any projecting element from the roof. This suppression of the
cornice creates construction problems of course; and this no doubt was
one of the reasons that Le Corbusier became more and more attracted to
the roof-garden, which allowed a parapet-wall which could end perfectly
cleanly and disguise whatever water-drainage solution was used for the
flat roof. Window-lintels had to be suppressed for the same reasons of
formal unity--a fact which led to water problems on some of these early
houses, such as the LaRoche-Jeanneret houses. For Le Corbusier, practical construction techniques were secondary in importance to the
expression of a "pure" and "unified" form.

This purely formalistic desire by Le Corbusier to "unify" the
overall mass of every building is further revealed by an interesting
annotation by him, found in his library. In a brief article on

Perret's projected theatre for the 1925 Exposition, in an issue of
the _Bulletin de la vie artistique_ of 1924, Le Corbusier wrote in
the margin a criticism of Perret's design for having smaller volumes
appended to the main mass of the building ("les petites caisses
doivent être dedans"), and sketched the plan of the building as he
would have designed it--with all the functions subsumed under one
rectangular form (Fig. 55).[5] Perret's treatment of the box-offices
of this theatre as separate volumes seems to have been due at least
in part to considerations of circulation and accessibility, and also
to the odd-shaped site. But to Le Corbusier, these questions were
not nearly as important as the purity and "unity" of the form itself.
It is this formal preoccupation which characterized Le Corbusier's
own designs of this period.

As mentioned above, our study of Jeanneret's early years has
shown that this ideal of pure, geometric, and unified architectural
forms was a fundamental part of his thinking from the earliest stages
of his education. Furthermore we saw (for example in the _Voyage
d'Orient_) that for the young Jeanneret, this conception of pure,
geometric form had transcendant implications as well, and was related to ideals of moral rectitude, spiritual perfection, and the
Absolute itself. This identification seems to go back at least to
Jeanneret's reading of Provensal's _L'art de demain_, with its view of
pure, "cubic" forms as expressing the Platonic Idea underlying reality; and over the years of Jeanneret's youth these two aspects, the
formal and the metaphysical, seem to have become inextricably bound

up together for him. We shall now suggest several ways in which Le Corbusier interpreted specific architectural aspects in terms of his overall idealistic framework.

The idealization of structure

One of the principal components of Le Corbusier's architectural synthesis is a special attitude toward structure--an attitude which we have examined already in his "Dom-Ino" system around 1915. As we saw there, Jeanneret's principal concern in designing the Dom-Ino system seems to have been to create floor-slabs and columns that were "définitivement lisses," as he put it, that is, totally unencumbered by the usual ribs, column-splay, and other elements typical of concrete construction at that time. To achieve this, he had had to design a system which presented many technical problems; but this was less important to him than the abstract conception of the pure structural elements: a perfectly flat slab, and straight columns. We could see this as an example of form preceding technology--for Jeanneret had conceived the form before the technology at his disposal was ready for it, and it was only later that concrete technology caught up with this formal conception. But this would be only a partial description of the situation, since there could be many reasons for a form which precedes technology (for example a form invented for a new function); and the really distinguishing thing about the Dom-Ino system is the ideal purity and generality of each of its separate structural parts.

We find this same attitude toward structure throughout

Le Corbusier's designs and thinking in the early 1920's; specifically, this can be seen in his concept of "pilotis," his treatment of windows, of stairways, and in many other specific ways. For example Le Corbusier's "pilotis" or free-standing structural columns--which of course were to become one of the most chracteristic aspects of his architecture throughout his career--reveal a desire to isolate a structural element and to draw attention to it in its simplest and most generalized state. Le Corbusier later sometimes spoke justifyingly of the piloti as serving practical functions, such as providing more land in cities for circulation and other uses;[6] yet his earliest designs employing pilotis suggest strongly that the original motive was conceptual or aesthetic rather than pragmatic. In the "Citrohan" house design exhibited in 1922, and in the LaRoche house of the same year, large parts of the house are raised off the ground on rudimentary pilotis (some of round section, some of square section)-- for no apparent functional reasons, but rather to emphasize and isolate the structural column and its role. And even in Le Corbusier's later buildings such as the "Unités d'habitation," the spaces under the pilotis were not designed for specific uses--with the result that they are generally rather dismal areas avoided by the inhabitants.

Le Corbusier later said that when he first conceived pilotis he was creating "la maison en l'air;"[7] and this suggests to us the obvious fact that by isolating and emphasizing the supporting column, one also isolates and emphasizes that which is supported. So in fact, the use of pilotis in this manner heightens our awareness of the structural phenomenon of load and support, by presenting it in its purest, and also most dramatic, form. It also might be seen as heightening our awareness of the nature and potential of reinforced-concrete construction; but this is not actually done in these buildings, for as in the Dom-Ino system, Le Corbusier here shows very little interest in utilizing reinforced-concrete technology in the most efficient, or even in the most honest, manner.[8] Le Corbusier's attraction to pilotis seems to have been essentially intellectual and aesthetic; and it is appropriate that he listed them as one of the "5 points d'une architecture nouvelle"--thus making them a doctrine, rather than simply a practical solution to certain problems.

The rest of these "5 points" reveal a similar desire by Le Corbusier to separate the structural elements of architecture and to emphasis their most general and ideal natures.[9] One of these "points" is that only columns (and not walls) should be used for structural support, thus allowing greater freedom of floor-planning ("le plan libre") and allowing the exterior walls to be independent from the structure ("la façade libre"). This is advanced by Le Corbusier for its obvious advantages of flexibility; but again we can see that his real motive is deeper: the conceptual isolation and idealization of the elements of a building--or as he had expressed it as early as 1915, "la séparation des pouvoirs."[10] The bearing wall bothered Le Corbusier because it serves two functions (structure and enclosure), whereas idealistically, for him, a form ought to be the perfect fulfillment of one function alone. In practice, of course, it is often very convenient, or economical, or even necessary to employ bearing walls--as Le Corbusier's own use of them at this time reveals[11]--but philosophically they disturbed him, and thus their suppression became one of his doctrines.

Similar to this is Le Corbusier's devotion to the horizontal window ("la fenêtre en longueur"), another of the "5 points." A vertical window can be construed as being ambiguous: it is a space between structural elements, or just a hole in a wall? On the other hand, a horizontal window running the full length of the wall is conceptually unambiguous--and furthermore emphasizes the isolation of the other elements as well, the structure totally independent from the wall. Again, Le Corbusier does not explain his preference for the horizontal window this way; he talks about dark interiors (illustrating his argument, by the way, with diagrams of dubious validity.)[12] But in practical terms, one must recognize that in some cases long horizontal windows may be preferable, and in other cases small or vertical windows may be. This was recognized by Auguste Perret, the rationalist, and this issue was actually the source of an argument between him and Le Corbusier at this time, which led Le Corbusier to publish several bitter attacks on his former teacher's inability to comprehend the innate superiority of the "fenêtre en longueur."[13] For Le Corbusier, ideally there had to be one universally proper form for each element in architecture. It was these isolated and idealized forms (each corresponding to one conceptual function) which concerned him most, rather than their modifying interactions with each other, or with the specific conditions of the program, the clients, or the environment.

Many other specific aspects of Le Corbusier's designs in this early period around 1920 could be discussed in terms of this desire to purify and idealize the separate elements of architecture. One rather simple example is Le Corbusier's attraction to the ramp, as a replacement for the traditional stair. The ramp seems to be used first by Le Corbusier in 1922, in the LaRoche house (in which, incidentally, many of his important concepts were first realized--including pilotis and the roof-terrace.) It appears in the earliest projects for this house as a very long ramp with a gentle slope, but when finally built was reduced to a short reduced to a short ramp with an uncomfortably steep slope (one easily loses control on the way down)--a fact which points out the inherent disadvantage of a ramp in any building where space-limitations or economy does not permit the considerable length required to produce an acceptable slope. Nevertheless, Le Corbusier persisted in trying to design ramps for domestic projects in the 1920's--the best-known example being the great ramp around which the Villa Savoie is organized. It was clearly the abstract form itself of the ramp which appealed to Le Corbusier. And in a formal sense, the ramp is simply an idealized stair--a pure sloping plane, minus the cumbersome bumps of a real stair--just as the Dom-Ino system had presented idealized columns and slabs, unencumbered of the ribs and other appendages of real concrete construction.[14]

Of the many attitudes which an architect can have toward structure, Le Corbusier's was very distinctive. He obviously did not subscribe to the notion that the structure of a building should be the most efficient and economical and technically appropriate to its conditions. Nor to the idea that a building should "express" its structural realities in a thoroughly honest manner. Le Corbusier's attitude was one of conceptualizing, separately, each structural role in architecture, and then assigning to each a form which, in some dramatic or symbolic way, embodied it and raised it to a generalized and ideal level. Only someone with a background like Jeanneret's, so dominated by philosophical idealism, could have possessed this attitude as firmly and expressed it as clearly as did Le Corbusier.

The idealization of "standards"

Another important aspect of Le Corbusier's architectural synthesis in the early 1920's is one which is somewhat less easily characterized than that discussed above. For it involves a number of different attitudes and ideas--including Le Corbusier's notions of pre-fabrication and mass-production, his attitude toward the machine, and other diverse things such as many of his urbanistic concepts. But underlying all of these is an idea of "standards," a term which recurs throughout his early writings in his discussions of these various aspects. First we must try to understand what Le Corbusier meant by this term. This is rather complicated, for to Le Corbusier the idea "standards" clearly had several different meanings. On the one hand, he uses it to refer to forms which are simply the direct expression or embodiment of specific functions:

"L'architecture agit sur des standarts. Les standarts sont choses
de logique, d'analyse, de scrupuleuse étude. Les standarts s'établissent sur un problème bien posé."[15]   In several passages, Le Corbusier maintains that his attraction to airplanes, ships and automobiles is based on their rigid adherence to this form-follows-function notion of "standards:"

> L'établissement d'un standart procède de l'organisation
> d'éléments rationnels suivant une ligne de conduite rationnelle également. . . Les premières autos furent construites
> et carrossées à l'ancienne. C'était contraire aux modalités
> de déplacement et de pénétration rapide d'un corps. L'étude
> des lois de pénétration fixa le standart, un standart qui
> évolue entre deux fins différentes: vitesse, grosse masse
> en avant. . .[16]

Similarly, Le Corbusier maintains that these "standards" themselves have nothing to do with aesthetics or art, but are merely
problems of engineering:

> Le standart de la maison est d'ordre pratique, d'ordre constructif. . . . Le standart du mobilier est en pleine voie
> d'expérimentation . . . : besogne d'ingénieur. . . . une
> chaise n'est point une oeuvre d'art; une chaise n'a pas une
> âme; c'est un outil pour s'asseoir.[17]

Yet elsewhere, Le Corbusier reveals a somewhat different attitude, in which "standard" refers not only to the embodiment of a
specific function, but to any _formal_ type. Thus he writes that "Le
Parthénon est un produit de sélection appliquée à un standart établi.
Depuis un siècle déjà, le temple grec était organisé dans tous ses
éléments."[18]   Le Corbusier goes on to describe how this "standard"
was refined and perfected over time, finally "passing from construction to architecture."[19]   Yet the individual parts of a Greek temple,
unlike the parts of an airplane, do not relate rigorously to specific

functions (or if they had, at some early stage, they no longer did in Classical times.) Le Corbusier does not explain whether he would consider any form which has been established and refined over the years as qualifying as a "standard;" but our suspicion is that he would not--for example in the case of Baroque forms. If pressed for an explanation, he might have admitted that the Greek temple qualifies as a "standard" simply because its parts are aesthetically valid, or "pure," or "rigorous," whereas Baroque forms are not; so ultimately the question seems to be a formal one to him.

Furthermore, when we examine all of Le Corbusier's discussions of various types of "standards"--whether the Greek temple, the airplane and automobile, or prefabrication and mass-production in housing--we realize that underlying his whole notion of "standards" is the idea that by establishing them one does much more than simply fulfill a function; one creates order, harmony, and perfection--concepts which recur throughout his passages on "standards:"

> Le standart est une nécessité d'ordre apporté dans le travail humain.[20]

> En cette période de science, de lutte et de drame où l'individu est violemment secoué à chaque heure, le Parthénon nous apparaît comme une oeuvre vivante, remplie de grandes sonorités. La masse de ses éléments infaillibles donne la mesure de ce que l'homme absorbé dans un problème définitivement posé peut atteindre de perfection.[21]

Le Corbusier goes on to say that the only modern creations which evoke the same harmonies and perfection as does the Parthenon, are "those huge impressive machines with which we are familiar and which may be considered the most perfect results of our present-day activities"--a comparison which we recall from the Voyage d'Orient, and

which further suggests to us that Le Corbusier's attraction to the
"standard" represented by the Parthenon was basically the same as
his attraction to those represented by machines, and that function
was not the essential ingredient in either of these. Instead, the
motivating concept is that in a world of strife and confusion, a
great "standard" brings order and harmony into our life and our
mental processes; and this idea is found throughout Le Corbusier's
early writings. For example in his article on mass-produced housing ("Maisons en série"), he argues for "standardisation" in construction, not so much on the grounds of economy or inefficiency,
but because it will create an abstract kind of perfection and order.
"Natural" materials are to be replaced by "artificial" ones (presumably steel and concrete--versus materials like wood), because
"Le matériau fixe doit remplacer le matériau naturel, variable à
l'infini;"[22] and as a result of mass-production ". . . les villes
seront ordonnées au lieu d'être chaotiques."[23] Le Corbusier also
reveals in this article that to him, "mass-production" and "stand-
ardization" do not necessarily even have their normally-accepted
meaning (i.e. the factory production of identical, interchangeable
parts), but can simply represent a general notion of order and uniformity. For example he says that certain great urbanistic designs
of the past qualify as "maisons en série"--including the "Procura-
ties, rue de Rivoli, Place des Vosges, la Carrière, le chateau de
Versailles, etc."[24]

     This desire for the imposition of order and unity--for their

own aesthetic or psychological sake--is a basic theme in nearly all
of Le Corbusier's early writings, and especially in his urbanistic
writings. In fact, his book L'urbanisme (composed of articles on
city-planning which had appeared in L'esprit nouveau) opens with a
chapter on "Order"--in which Le Corbusier argues that Man should
rely on straight lines and right angles in his works and in laying
out his cities, because:

> Pour travailler, l'homme a besoin de constantes. Sans con-
> stantes, il ne pourrait même faire un pas devant l'autre.
> L'angle droite est, on peut le dire, l'outil nécessaire et
> suffisant pour agir puisqu'il sert à fixer l'espace avec
> une rigueur parfaite. L'angle droite est licite, plus, il
> fait partie de notre déterminisme, il est obligatoire.[25]

We recognize here many of the same attitudes which Jeanneret had
expressed earlier about "machines:" the attraction to them because of
their exactness, precision, absolutism, and their "determinism"--that
quality which he had described first in the Parthenon (in the Voyage
d'Orient) and then in machines (in Après le cubisme.) In Urbanisme,
Le Corbusier proceeds to reveal even more clearly his feeling that
architecture and urban-planning must create this abstract or spiritual
order precisely to counteract the chaos of the real (or of the visible)
world:

> Dans la nature chaotique, l'homme pour sa sécurité se crée une
> ambiance, une zone de protection. . . Ce qu'il fait, c'est une
> création et celle-ci contraste d'autant plus avec le milieu
> naturel que son but est plus près de la pensée et plus éloigné,
> plus détaché du corps. On peut dire que plus les oeuvres
> humaines s'éloignent de la préhension directe, plus elles
> tendent à la pure géométrie: un violon, une chaise qui tou-
> chent notre corps sont d'une géométrie amoindrie, mais la
> ville est de pure géométrie. Libre, l'homme tend à la pure
> géométrie. Il fait alors ce qu'on appelle de l'ordre.[26]

This is an extraordinary attitude toward urbanism and cities--
viewing them as "pure," "free" creations of Man's mind and spirit,
rather than as being shaped by a multitude of economic, social, psychological, and environmental forces. But we have observed it before,
in Benoît-Lévy's book on garden-cities which Jeanneret read in about
1915--with its view of city-planning as an expressive art, and of
the city-planner himself as Bergson's mystical artist "vibrating in
unison" with the Absolute.

But Le Corbusier makes of this a much more comprehensive theory
of urbanism; and more important, his urbanistic designs themselves
clearly express these conceptions of order. In his "Ville contemporaine" scheme of 1922, for example, there is a total suppression of
the winding roads of Jeanneret's earlier Dom-Ino site plans, and the
whole city is conceived as a vast geometric pattern, ruled by rigid
symmetries, axialities, and geometric repetitions which can be fully
comprehended only in the abstract terms of a plan. It is significant
that around the edges of this perfect, determined geometric creation
(and encroaching upon it at certain points), Le Corbusier emphasizes
the arbitrary meandering of natural landscape--streams, woodlands,
etc.--thus dramatically contrasting the two forces he writes about:
the "chaotic nature" in which Man finds himself, and the "pure geometry" which only his mind can impose on the world.[27] It is obviously
not possible here to examine Le Corbusier's urbanistic thinking
thoroughly; but we can suggest that just as Le Corbusier handled the
structural elements of his buildings in such a way as to symbolize

dramatically their ideal and generalized natures, so his urbanistic
schemes were conceived in such a way as to emphasize the contrast
which he saw between nature and Man. This conviction that the city
ought to embody an ideal order and perfection--rather than the Beaux-
Arts tradition which is sometimes offered as an explanation of the
formalistic aspects of his urbanistic plans--seems to be the underlying force in Le Corbusier's conception of urbanism. Cities, just
like individual buildings, were seen by Le Corbusier as opportunities
to embody in physical form the ideals of order, rigor, perfection,
and purity.

The idealization of proportion

Systems of architectural proportion are a basic part of Le Corbusier's thinking in the early 1920's--as they would continue to be
throughout his career. References have been made in earlier parts
of this study to these proportioning systems and to some of their
sources in Jeanneret's early reading; but some additional observations will be made here about the "tracés régulateurs," Le Corbusier's
first real attempt to create a "system" for determining architectural
proportions.

First, it is worth pointing out that whereas, in the case of
the other aspects of Le Corbusier's thought discussed above it was
sometimes unclear whether he considered them purely aesthetic aspects
or attempted to justify them as functional aspects, in the case of
the "tracés régulateurs" we are dealing with an aspect which for Le
Corbusier is completely aesthetic and, indeed, a fundamental

component of architectural beauty. In an article on "tracés régulateurs" in L'esprit nouveau, he introduces examples of the use of
regulating lines with the remark: "Voici des tracés régulateurs qui
ont servi à faire de très belles choses et qui sont cause que ces
choses sont très belles."[28] This belief in the direct relationship
between proportioning systems and architectural beauty is seen
throughout Le Corbusier's writings, and it is important to emphasize;
for there has been a tendency (especially among rationalist critics)
to assume that Le Corbusier's "tracés régulateurs," and later his
"Modulor" system, were peripheral or minor parts of his aesthetic,
rather than recognizing the central importance they had to Le Corbusier himself.

It is also important to point out that underlying Le Corbusier's
discussions of the "tracés régulateurs" we find the same concern for
order, harmony, and perfection which we found for example in his concept of "standards." He says that the "tracé régulateur" is "une
satisfaction d'ordre spirituel qui conduit à la recherche de rapports
ingénieux et de rapports harmonieux," and that it "apporte cette mathématique sensible donnant la perception bienfaisante de l'ordre."[29]
And in fact Le Corbusier opens his article on "tracés régulateurs"
with the familiar contrast of the chaos of nature with the security
represented by geometry:

> [Man] a pris des mesures, il a admis un module, il a réglé
> son travail, il a apporté l'ordre. Car, autour de lui, la
> forêt est en désordre. . . les axes, les cercles, les
> angles droits, ce sont les vérités de la géométrie et ce
> sont des effets que notre oeil mesure et reconnaît; alors
> qu'autrement ce serait hasard, anomalie, arbitraire.[30]

Here as elsewhere in Le Corbusier's writings, geometry and
mathematics clearly have psychological implications--providing
the certainty and security which Man needs to face the frighten-
ing disorder of nature. And it is this geometry, and particularly
the right angle, which is the basis of the "tracé régulateur"
system--as we can see in Le Corbusier's examples drawn from his
own designing and from buildings of the past (Figs. 56-58). Later
the "Modulor" system, which was to supersede these "tracés régulateurs," would be much more abstract and less related to any
visible geometry. But when we examine Le Corbusier's "tracé régulateur" drawings, we discover that they too are extremely abstract
--and that in many cases Le Corbusier's remark that they produce
"des effets que notre oeil mesure et reconnaît" is hardly accurate.

For example, when we look at the façade of the LaRoche--Jean-
neret houses which Le Corbusier ostensibly designed using "tracés
régulateurs" (Fig. 57), we discover that most of the regulating
geometry is only remotely related to anything which a real person
would see while standing in front of the real building. The largest
geometric figure (which Le Corbusier labels "A-1")--a right angle
laid diagonally across the major plane of the façade--really serves
only to determine an edge of the stair-tower which rises above the
roof-line in this elevation drawing (a correspondence which Le Corbusier emphasizes by extending this stair-tower edge as a dotted line
through the right angle.) Yet in actual visual terms of course, this
is quite meaningless, since this stair-tower is set way back from the

edge of the roof, so no one would ever see it in relationship to
the facade plane. Other examples of this sort could be described.
And even in the cases where the geometry of the "tracés régulateurs"
is kept in one plane, it is often highly doubtful that one would
really perceive it; for example in the drawing of Ozenfant's studio
(Fig. 58), the two sets of regulating angles determine such things
as the mid-points of windows and secondary mullions. The percept-
ibility of such relationships is rendered even more dubious when
we realize that the siting of these buildings requires the observer
always to view these facades obliquely rather than straight-on.

All in all, these are extremely abstract and non-visual geometric constructions, which in most cases can make sense only in
terms of the two-dimensional elevation drawing, or in the mind of
their creator. It is, in fact, their very abstraction, and complexity, which seems to have appealed to Le Corbusier. For of course it
would have been possible, if Le Corbusier had wished, to determine
the elements of a facade by geometry which really was visually apparent. Instead, he preferred these obscure relationships--which only
he, the architect (the Initiate) could fully understand or perceive.
Furthermore, as we shall see, he seems to have felt that by being
more abstract, these regulating lines became more "precise," more
"mathematical," and thus closer to the source of beauty; and we are
of course reminded of Le Corbusier's attraction to machines for their
precision, rigor, and mathematical perfection.

In this regard it is interesting to go back to the earliest

evidence we have of Jeanneret's interest in this sort of "tracé
régulateur," which is found in his notebooks of about 1915. On
a couple of pages in one of these notebooks Jeanneret copied out
two drawings from Marcel Dieulafoy's L'art antique de la Perse.[31]
Dieulafoy's drawings (Fig. 59) analyze the cross-sections of Achaemenian vaulted structures in a manner very similar to Le Corbusier's
later "tracés régulateurs," except that Dieulafoy employs circles
as well as the right triangles relied on by Le Corbusier. Le Corbusier later redrew these sketches from Dieulafoy and reproduced them
in his Esprit nouveau article on "tracés régulateurs," thus suggesting that they had impressed him greatly in 1915; and we sense this
impact in Jeanneret's original notebook sketches of them. Next to
his sketch of the simpler of Dieulafoy's diagrams, he jotted down
his observations, calling the diagram a "tracé modulaire," describing the various ways the right triangle was employed, and saying
that this geometry "serves to determine the elliptical vault"
(". . . sert à déterminer la voûte elliptique.") We notice Jeanneret's interest in "determining" something, of not leaving it to
chance or caprice--the same theme which runs throughout Le Corbusier's early writings and theory.[32]

And next to the second of Dieulafoy's diagrams, Jeanneret
wrote simply "le plus complexe, mais rigoureusement exact." The
geometric complexity of this drawing--so complex in fact that it
would render any real visual perception of it quite impossible--is
seen by Jeanneret as being "exact," and more specifically as "rigorously exact." We recognize "rigor" as that term which recurred

throughout Jeanneret's descriptions of machines, in <u>Après le cubisme</u>; and it is apparent that Jeanneret's attraction to Dieulafoy's diagrams (and Le Corbusier's attraction to the "tracés régulateurs" in general) is essentially the same as his attraction to machines: both are seen as embodiments of precision, exactness, mathematical perfection, and purity--in other words of the Absolute. And just as Jeanneret had characterized the Parthenon as the embodiment of "rectitude," that ambiguous term with moral as well as formal implications, so Jeanneret's original attraction to regulating lines seems based on its similarly ambiguous "rigor." Underlying Le Corbusier's interest in proportioning systems is the same assumption which we have seen throughout his early thought: that the right angle, mathematics, geometry, and the machine have moral and spiritual meaning, in their own right, and that an architecture which embodies their spirit will be able to rescue Man from the capricious uncertainties of nature and put him in touch with the determined certainty of the Absolute.

It should be pointed out here that a concern for architectural proportion, in itself, is of course not necessarily a manifestation of idealistic thinking. Only the most extremely anti-formalistic architects would be ready to deny that proportions and their psychological effects on the observer are a valid concern of the architect. Auguste Perret for example, whom we have presented in this study as a representative of architectural rationalism, fully recognized the importance of proportion in architecture. But the difference between

Perret's and Le Corbusier's attitudes toward proportion is very
significant. For Perret proportion was, on the one hand, simply
part of the Beaux-Arts tradition which had constituted his training, and which is expressed in his buildings throughout his career
--in the symmetrical and classically-proportioned forms which contrast so strongly with Le Corbusier's eccentric proportions and
unorthodox forms. But more fundamentally, architectural proportion for Perret--as for his teacher Julien Guadet--was essentially
the rational expression of the proper forms demanded by structural,
technical, and programmatic considerations--what Guadet called
"la vérité" in architecture. Thus, when Perret writes that

> C'est par la splendeur du vrai que l'édifice atteint à la
> beauté. Le vrai est dans tout ce qui a l'honneur et la
> peine de porter ou de protéger. Ce vrai, c'est la pro-
> portion qui le fera resplendir, et la proportion c'est
> l'homme même,[33]

he is clearly thinking in the same terms as did Guadet, who in
his Éléments et théories de l'architecture, had also defined "le beau"
as "la splendeur du vrai" (vol. I, p. 99), and who then, in his chapter on proportions, had explained what he meant by this definition--
saying that the rule underlying proportions is

> . . . tout simplement le vrai, le beau par le vrai. Et
> qu'entendons-nous donc ici par le vrai? L'architecture
> est la mise en oeuvre, pour satisfaire à des besoins
> matériels et moraux, des éléments de la construction.
> Sans construction, point d'architecture. Les lois de
> la construction sont les lois premières de l'architec-
> ture. . . . Pénétrez-vous profondément de cette vérité
> à la base de vos études, et vous serez tout étonnés de
> voir que les proportions naîtront pour vous de cette
> pensée dirigeante. (vol. I, pp. 174-75.)

Thus, for Guadet, proper proportions are virtually an automatic result of rational planning and construction. Perret clearly shared this conception, as he reveals in his few specific references to proportion, such as the one quoted above, and also when he wrote that "Harmony is what the Greeks obtained by perfectly adapting the laws of stability and waterproofing to optical laws; proportion is man himself."[34] There is, of course, an apparent contradiction, in the thinking of both Guadet and Perret, between their acceptance of the superiority of Classical forms and proportions on the one hand, and on the other their "rational" conviction that good planning and good construction will naturally produce good proportions. Guadet, at least, would probably have defended Classical forms as inherently the most rational (as proved by their continuous acceptance over the centuries); but whatever the validity of these positions, the significant point is that for both Guadet and Perret, architectural proportion was intimately linked to the rational expression of function and construction.

As we have seen, Le Corbusier had a very different view--in which proportions represented an abstract perfection, order, and purity, which when discovered by the architect and embodied in architectural form (not necessarily even visually apparent to the observer) could put Man in touch with universal and absolute forces. Just as Le Corbusier had taken Perret's structural system and had interpreted it idealistically, transforming each architectural element into an isolated, pure, and generalized ideal--so he transformed the rationalists' down-to-earth conception of proportion into a similarly pure

and generalized ideal. The fact that later in his career, Le Corbusier was to expend a great amount of energy devising another proportioning system even more abstract and intellectual than his "tracés
régulateurs," only emphasizes the seriousness with which he devoted
himself to these ideals.

Concluding remarks

It has been possible here to give only some suggestion of the
way in which Le Corbusier's early work and thought in the 1920's may
express the intellectual forces which we have examined in his youthful self-education. Obviously, to understand his early work fully
would require much more analysis and reference to many factors which
have not been examined in this study--such as Le Corbusier's contemporaries in his early career, and all the ideas and architectural experi-
mentation current at that time. The fact that this study has concentrated principally on the intellectual themes in Jeanneret's youthful
thinking, and particularly in his reading, is not meant to minimize
the importance of other forces which helped shape his work. But the
fact that so little has hitherto been known about Jeanneret's youthful development, or about the books he read, made this an especially
important area to explore--particularly since we discovered, in his
library, that during his youth he read in an extremely serious and
purposeful way, and that this reading can be shown to have formed his
philosophical attitudes in many ways. It is only natural that the
ideas which Jeanneret absorbed in his youth--whether or not themselves
directly concerned with architecture--would have shaped his ways of

thinking and inevitably influenced the formulation of his aesthetic views.

The major argument of this study--that Le Corbusier's attitudes toward architecture were fundamentally influenced by a way of think- ing which could be characterized as philosophically idealistic, rather than rationalist or pragmatic--naturally raises the larger question of the critical evaluation of his work. If Le Corbusier's architec- ture can indeed be shown to express specific philosophical assump- tions which we as individuals may or may not share, does this make it more or less valid or significant? To me, it seems that this ques- tion is unrelated to our personal preferences for idealism, or rationalism or materialism, or to our convictions about the ultimate truth of any philosophical system. If Le Corbusier had been a medi- ocre architect, this might be different; but his work is powerful, compelling, and (nearly all of us feel) beautiful in a very high sense. We feel this regardless of our personal philosophies. And yet, as I have suggested throughout this study, the power and beauty of Le Cor- busier's forms cannot be separated from the idealism of the mind which created them. We find these forms compelling, I believe, precisely because they embody so forcefully (and sincerely) a search for univer- sality, for timeless and absolute principles, and for a determined certainty with which Man can oppose himself to the vicissitudes and apparent chaos of the world. This search represents such a basic human desire (perhaps ultimately for security, and omnipotence), that we all respond to it.

But only Le Corbusier was capable of creating these forms, for this creation required an extraordinary sensitivity to these ideal- istic aspirations, and an uncompromising conviction that they could indeed be fulfilled. Le Corbusier did not possess this uncommon sensitivity without price, however; for his intensely idealistic convictions inevitably effected his reason and objectivity in certain areas--as we have seen in this study, for example in his proportion- ing systems which sometimes became so abstract as to be perceptually ineffective. But to describe this other side of the coin is in reality not to denigrate Le Corbusier's work, since it is an inti- mate and inevitable part of the intense idealism which alone makes his work possible. To analyze the excesses of Le Corbusier's ideal- ism is not to question the validity of his thinking, but rather to demonstrate the degree to which he was compelled by his ideals--which is the very key to the power of his work.·

Le Corbusier's buildings are among the most powerful architec- tural creations, I believe, because we sense in them a striving for absolute principles which--regardless of our own philosophical posi- tions--we all share.

NOTES

Introduction

[1] Charles-Édouard Jeanneret (1887-1965) first adopted the pseudonym
Le Corbusier in 1920. In this study, "Le Corbusier" will be used when
referring to his mature ideas and activities, and his real name when
referring to his youth.

[2] In its broadest sense, "idealism" in this study refers to a belief
in absolute principles or spiritual forces existing separate from matter
and the visible world, and is thus simply the opposite of "materialism"—
and obviously embraces countless religious and philosophical positions,
some of which will be shown to have influenced the young Jeanneret.
In a more specifically architectural sense, "idealism" will refer to
the attitude that beauty in architecture resides essentially in absolute
formal principles, in contrast to the "rationalist" assumption that
architectural form is shaped primarily by structural, constructional,
and programmatic forces. Attempts will be made throughout this study
to define these terms more clearly and in such a way as to clarify
the distinctive aspects of Le Corbusier's view of architecture.

[3] For example Peter Collins, in Changing Ideals in Modern Architecture (London, 1965), and Reyner Banham, in Theory and Design in the
First Machine Age (London, 1960).

[4] Most of this library came from Le Corbusier's apartment, Rue
Nungesser et Coli, and some also came from his Rue de Sèvres office
(both in Paris). I first made a catalogue of all the items published
before 1930—comprising about 260 books, about 20 exhibition catalogues,
and about 100 periodicals. A similar catalogue, but including only
those items published before 1920, is included in this study as
Appendix A.

[5] Le Corbusier treated his books very differently in various periods
of his life. After about 1920 he almost never signed or inscribed them,
but often annotated and marked passages in a bold hand. In his youth,
he often signed his books, but marked in them less often, generally in
a delicate, light hand. During his first stay in Paris in 1908-09, he
consistently dated his books as well as signing them, a practice which
he continued less consistently in the next decade. Furthermore, his
signature in these early years—"Ch.-E. Jeanneret"—changed markedly
almost from year to year; and by establishing its development from the
dated signatures, it became possible for me to date nearly all of the
books which are signed. My analysis of this development of Jeanneret's
early signature, with photo-copies of all the examples of it I found in

his books, is included in this study as <u>Appendix C</u>.

[6] From conversation with Maurice Besset, in Paris, December 1969.

Chapter I

[1] The major sources of information on Le Corbusier's youth are:
Maximilien Gauthier, <u>Le Corbusier</u> (Paris, 1944); Le Corbusier, <u>L'art
décoratif d'aujourd'hui</u> (Paris, 1925), pp. 197-218; Le Corbusier,
<u>L'atelier de la recherche patiente</u> (Hatje, Stuttgart, 1960); Le Corbusier
& Pierre Jeanneret, <u>Oeuvre complete 1910-1929</u> (Zürich, 1964); Stanislaus
Von Moos, <u>Le Corbusier</u> (Frauenfeld, 1968); and other material was
graciously made available to me by Mr. David Stewart. Gauthier's
biography is written in the third person, but it was clearly based on
interviews with Le Corbusier (especially the chapters on his youth),
and most of it can in effect be accepted as autobiographical (particularly
since Le Corbusier's library includes a copy of it which contains
favorable annotations by Le Corbusier, showing that in general he had
authorized its contents).

[2] Le Corbusier's father (as well as his grandfather) apparently
specialized in the enameling of watchcases, and owned an enameling
firm (Gauthier, <u>Le Corbusier</u>, p. 16; Le Corbusier, <u>L'atelier</u>, p. 19).

[3] Charles L'Eplattenier (1874-1946) was born in Neuchâtel, studied
painting and drawing, traveled extensively (Italy, Tunisia, Budapest,
London, Germany), studied briefly at the École des Beaux-Arts in Paris
(1893), became a drawing-teacher at the Art School in La Chaux-de-Fonds
in 1898, was named its director in 1903, and resigned in 1914 (David
Stewart; Von Moos, <u>Le Corbusier</u>, pp. 14-15).

[4] <u>Un mouvement d'art à La Chaux-de-Fonds</u> (La Chaux-de-Fonds, 1914),
p. 25; Gauthier, <u>Le Corbusier, p. 18f.</u>

[5] A number of these early drawings, and the watchcase, are reproduced
in Le Corbusier, <u>L'atelier</u>, p. 22f.

[6] <u>Art et décoration</u>, IX, January 1901, pp. 37-40. This and other
periodicals are listed in <u>Catalogue de la Bibliothèque, École d'Art de
La Chaux-de-Fonds</u> (La Chaux-de-Fonds, 1919), which was brought to my
attention by David Stewart.

[7] Gauthier, <u>Le Corbusier</u>, p. 26. Le Corbusier also mentions Rodin,
and two lesser-known figures whose work was not strictly art nouveau,
Rupert Carabin and Jean Carriès.

[8] Examples of this overlapping-planes style can be found around 1900
and 1901 in the interior decoration of Peter Behrens and others.
Magazines which illustrated this work, and to which the Art School
subscribed, include <u>Die Kunst</u>, <u>Deutsche Kunst und Dekoration</u>, and <u>The Studio</u>.

[9] _Die Kunst_, II, 1900, pp. 178-79.

[10] Le Corbusier, _L'art décoratif d'aujourd'hui_ (Paris, 1925), p. 198.

[11] _Ibid._, p. 198.

[12] The drawings for this house--the Fallet House--are reportedly dated 1906 (Étienne Chavanne & Michel Laville, "Les premières constructions de Le Corbusier," _Werk_, L, 1963, p. 483); but Le Corbusier said that he began his first house when he was seventeen-and-a-half years old, i.e. in Spring 1905 (_L'atelier de la recherche patiente_, p. 21). In any case, Jeanneret could not have had much technical training by this time; and he is said to have been assisted by a local architect, René Chapallaz, a friend of L'Eplattenier (Von Moos, _Le Corbusier_, p. 22).

[13] Gauthier, _Le Corbusier_, p. 19. In 1929 Le Corbusier also wrote of L'Eplattenier: ". . . c'est lui qui m'a ouvert les portes de l'art. Nous avons étudié avec lui les chefs-d'oeuvre de tous les temps et de tous les pays. Je me souviens de cette modeste bibliothèque, installé dans une simple armoire de notre salle de dessin et dans laquelle notre maître avait réuni tout ce qu'il considérait nécessaire à notre nourriture spirituelle." (_Oeuvre complète 1910-1929_, p. 8)

[14] _L'art décoratif d'aujourd'hui_, pp. 134-35. Other references to Grasset are found on pages 135 and 137 of this work, and in Gauthier, _Le Corbusier_, p. 27.

[15] _L'art décoratif d'aujourd'hui_, p. 135. In this passage, Le Corbusier seems to confuse the titles of Grasset's and Jones' works. Jones' _Grammar of Ornament_ is also mentioned by Le Corbusier in _L'atelier de la recherche patiente_, p. 24.

[16] Ruskin, _Lectures on Architecture and Painting_ (New York, 1856), p. 10. Le Corbusier's recollection of this rather innocuous passage is found in Gauthier, _Le Corbusier_, p. 19, and is a precise translation of it into French. Since the _Lectures_ apparently were not published in French before 1910, Le Corbusier either remembered the passage as L'Eplattenier had translated it, or later consulted a French edition.

[17] _L'art décoratif d'aujourd'hui_, p. 134. This is in a chapter describing the state of the arts in Le Corbusier's youth. It contains several other references to Ruskin, including a mention of _The Bible of Amiens_ (p. 135); the remark that "Ruskin, William Morris, Walter Crane, en Angleterre, fondaient une imprimerie pour y faire du beau livre (et Dieu sait si ce candide retour aux missels moyenageux nous est désagréable)" (p. 135); and the sentence "La voix douce de Ruskin: 'Voici les fleurs, les insectes et les bêtes du bon Dieu'" (p. 138). All of these passages were brought to my attention by Professor H. Allen Brooks, of the University of Toronto.

[18] See below, Chapter I, footnote 43, for a discussion of

the contradiction between this inscription date and the publication
date of the book).

[19] The Ruskin and the Taine were apparently bought by Jeanneret right
before he left La Chaux-de-Fonds in 1907, and used by him as guide-books
in Italy. They thus belong most appropriately to the next period of
Jeanneret's development, and will be discussed in Chapter II. The
Knackfuss is one of a number of German-language books in Le Corbusier's
library. Like many of his French-Swiss compatriots, Jeanneret was
apparently fluent in German since his early years.

[20] For example: Camille Flammarion, Astronomie populaire (Paris, 1880),
contains a decorative sketch by Jeanneret typical of this youthful period;
Eugène Fromentin, Les maîtres d'autrefois (Paris, 1902), has passages
marked in Jeanneret's typical early hand; and two popular-history books
by Gustave LeBon (La civilisation des arabes, Paris, 1884, and Les
premières civilisations, Paris, 1888?), simply make sense as books which
Jeanneret would have had as a child. But the lack of certainty in regard
to these books naturally complicates any analysis of their contents.

[21] The book is inscribed "à notre cher garçon," and dated "Noël 1902."
This work was first published in 1881.

[22] From the English edition (London, 1882), p. 1.

[23] On the inside front cover is a label inscribed "La Chaux-de-Fonds /
1903 / École Spéciale d'Art / Appliqué à l'Industrie / Classe de Modelage /
Prix de distinction / Louis Huguenin-Virchaux / décerné à / Charles-Édouard
Jeanneret."

[24] In the front of the book, Le Corbusier noted "couleurs expressives:
p. 281, 282, 285," and on these pages references to the use of color in
antiquity are circled boldly in heavy pencil. This is typical of Le
Corbusier's later markings in his books.

[25] Actually, this book contains three signatures of the young Jeanneret--
on the cover, on the half-title page, and on the title page. The first
two are typical of his early signature before he left La Chaux-de-Fonds
in 1907; and the third is typical of his signature in Paris in 1909 (for
analysis and photo-copies of these signatures, see Appendix C). Furthermore,
inside the front cover is a rubber-stamp impression (of which I found no
other example in Le Corbusier's library) reading "Ch. E. Jeanneret /
Rue Léopold-Robert 46." The Jeanneret family lived on this street when
Charles-Édouard and his brother Albert were boys (according to information
received through correspondence with Albert Jeanneret, Spring 1970), and
although their exact tenancy there has not yet been established, they
seem to have moved before 1907.
     Several passages in the text of this book are bracketed lightly in
pencil--a rather timid kind of marking typical of Jeanneret's earliest
books. There are no annotations. Perhaps it is also worth mentioning
that many pages in the book are spotted with colored specks of what appears

to be powder from pastel crayons, as if the book had been left open
on a table while Jeanneret was drawing next to it.

[26] Henri Provensal (born 1868) studied at the École des Beaux-Arts
from 1887 to 1892, was diplômé in 1896, and constructed various types
of buildings including a pavilion at the 1900 Paris Exposition. In the
1890's he exhibited at the salons such romantic projects as "l'Asyle du
Rêve," "Fontaine arabe et Minaret à Tunis," and "Tombeau du poète"--
as well as one in 1902 whose title, "Harmonies de l'espace," more closely
suggests the spirit of his ideas in L'art de demain. Besides this book
he also wrote L'habitation salubre et à bon marché, (Paris, Ch. Schmid,
1908). His interest in low-cost housing seems to have followed his
being awarded, in 1905, second prize in a workers'-housing design
competition sponsored by the Fondation Rothschild (designs published
in L'art et les artistes, December 1905). Later he was employed as
architect by the Fondation Rothschild. Both of his books bear the
English version of his Christian name, apparently an affectation. None
of his few published designs seem to reveal any of the cubism or other
advanced implications of his art theory in L'art de demain. References:
Thieme-Becker, Künstler Lexikon (Leipzig, 1933); E. Delaire, Les architectes, élèves de l'École des Beaux-Arts (Paris, 1907), p. 379; C.-E.
Curinier, Dictionnaire national des contemporains (Paris, 1905?), V, p. 206.

[27] Le Corbusier, Vers une architecture (Paris, 1923), p. 165.

[28] Page 9. Le Corbusier's writings also abound in references to
Man as a resolution of, or half-way point between, matter and spirit--
as for example when he opens the Ville radieuse with the statement that
"L'objectif et le subjectif sont les deux pôles entre lesquelles surgit
l'oeuvre humaine faite de matière et d'esprit" (La ville radieuse, Paris,
1933, frontispiece caption). The French word "esprit" can of course
mean either "spirit" or "mind;" but translators of Le Corbusier's works
have favored "mind" excessively. The evidence of Jeanneret's reading
shows that his own conception of the term would by no means have excluded
its religious and philosophical connotations. In Frederick Etchells'
standard translations of Vers une architecture and Urbanisme, the
suppression of the "spiritual" content of the term has probably had
an effect on the interpretation of Le Corbusier's thought in the English-
speaking world.

[29] Provensal attributes this theory to the German author Max Nordau
(1849-1923), whose major work was Biologie der Ethik.

[30] Page 88. Provensal uses the term "verbe" in the biblical sense
of a primeval creative force (for example see p. 8).

[31] Theory and Design, p. 18.

[32] Amedée Ozenfant & Ch.-É. Jeanneret, Après le cubisme (Paris, 1918),
p. 26. It is of course difficult to pin-point precisely which ideas in
this work were contributed by Ozenfant and which by Jeanneret; but with

the evidence of Jeanneret's early library, it is now possible to make reasonable suggestions about their respective contributions (see below, Chapter V).

33 Après le cubisme, pp. 18-19.

34 Page 145. Peter Collins has pointed out to me that Plato is not actually recorded as having made the statement attributed to him here, and that Provensal undoubtedly got this from Julien Guadet's Éléments et théorie de l'architecture (Paris, 1902), I, p. 99. For a discussion of the significance this phrase had for Guadet, see below, Chapter VI.

35 The well-known early uses of the words "cubes" and "cubique" in connection with the paintings of Braque occurred four years later, in 1908, and seem to have been unrelated to Provensal's ideas.

36 Page 162. Provensal may have got this idea from the philosophy of Friedrich von Schelling, for whom natural crystals revealed an underlying harmony which art strives also to attain. (M. C. Beardsley, Aesthetics from Classical Greece to the Present, New York, 1966, p. 232)

37 L'art et les artistes, XVIII, November 1913, p. 98. Ritter is speaking of the newly-completed "Völkerschlachtdenkmal" in Leipzig when he quotes Jeanneret. Incidentally, this is apparently the first reference to Jeanneret in a publication of note. For a suggestion of the reason Ritter mentioned Jeanneret in this article, see below, Chapter IV.

38 Vers une architecture, p. 16. This first appeared in the October 1920 issue of L'esprit nouveau.

39 Précisions sur un état présent de l'architecture et de l'urbanisme (Paris, 1930), p. 136.

40 Pages 318 and 312, respectively. As these quotes reveal, "drame plastique" was one of Provensal's favorite phrases. Peter Collins makes the interesting observation that Le Corbusier also uses both of these terms, but opposes them rather than linking them like Provensal, when he says (in Vers une architecture, p. 19) that the Gothic cathedral, because it is not based on geometric volumes, "n'est pas une oeuvre plastique; c'est un drame: la lutte contre la pesanteur, sensation d'ordre sentimental." Le Corbusier apparently saw a contradiction in Provensal's use of the term "drame" to describe the ordered harmony which ideal beauty is to embody.

41 Vers une architecture, p. 57. This first appeared in the February 1921 issue of L'esprit nouveau.

42 A whole section of Le Modulor (Boulogne-sur-Seine, 1948), pp. 193-205, is devoted to Le Corbusier's accounts of his lengthy and painstaking researches along this line, leading to discoveries that the precise dimensions of the "Modulor" system, often down to the fraction of a

centimeter, could be found in a certain mediaeval abbey-doorway, a
balustrade at Hagia Sophia, various dimensions in other Byzantine
churches, the basin of a fountain at Pompeii, etc. etc. This in spite
of the fact that elsewhere in the book he admits that the standard
human height on which the Modulor dimensions were all based, is obviously not the same for all places and times. There is, in fact, a deep
contradiction underlying the entire Modulor system, between Le Corbusier's
feeling that it should be a pragmatic device related to the actual
dimensions of real men, and his desire to discover that it is a perfect,
mystical system revealed universally and throughout history.

[43] Édouard Schuré, Les grands initiés (Paris, Perrin, 1908). Besides
having the same publisher, this book and Provensal's book both contain
labels showing they were bought at the same bookstore in La Chaux-de-
Fonds. The inscription reads "A mon cher élève Édouard Jeanneret /
Souvenir affectueux- / Ch. L'Eplattenier / sept. 07." This inscription
date is puzzling not only in relation to the stated publication date
of the book (which could, presumably, have been postdated), but also
because Jeanneret seems still to have been traveling in Italy in
September 1907. But in any case, Jeanneret was in possession of the
book when he settled in Paris the next Spring, for he added his own
inscription (see Appendix C), signing the book and noting his address
as 9 Rue des Écoles--where he stayed only briefly in 1908 before moving
to the Quai St. Michel.

[44] Édouard Schuré (1841-1929) was a French dramatist and critic who
was instrumental in familiarizing the French public with Wagner, and
wrote "mystical Wagnerian plays" as well as Les grands initiés (first
published in 1889), and another book, Précurseurs et révoltés, 1904.
(New Century Cyclopedia of Names)

[45] Page 363. This is in the small, neat hand typical of Jeanneret's
early annotations.

[46] This was "Tante Pauline," the elder sister of Jeanneret's father--
"profondément religieuse, qui vivait à leur foyer, et n'aima jamais rien
tant que se dévouer, incarnait les nobles traditions, maintenues alors,
à travers les siècles, encore intactes dans la haute vallée" (Gauthier,
Le Corbusier, p. 17).

[47] "A ce Jura dont la toile de fond est la forêt et la montagne, il
faut ajouter pour situer exactement Le Corbusier, le Languedoc des
'Parfaits' de provenance Cathare. Ces racines jurassiennes et méditerra-
néennes, Corbu en était fier, même s'il revendiquait peut-être plus
fortement les secondes" (Jean Petit, Le Corbusier parle, Paris, 1967, p. 12).

[48] Le Corbusier seems to have read everything he could find on these
mediaeval Catharists and their doctrines; and his annotations reveal
clearly that he considered himself to be descended from them and to have
inherited something of their mystical spirit. Whether or not this really
was true seems to be less significant than the fact that Le Corbusier

believed it to be true. Furthermore, there seems to have been a
traditional Jeanneret association between these Catharists and the
later Huguenots. In response to a question on this matter, Le Corbusier's
brother Albert Jeanneret spoke of ". . . les Jeanneret, classés comme
les habitants du Jura venus en France au moment des persécutions
religieuses huguenotes. Je pense que les huguenots eurent comme
ancêtres les cathares disciples de Manès vivants au sud-ouest de la
France et contre lesquels le pape déchaina la cruelle croisade des
albigeois" (from personal communication, February 1970). Albert
Jeanneret also said that his brother became interested in "la question
cathare" at the age of sixteen or seventeen, through his friend William
Ritter, who was also from this region of Switzerland. Actually,
Le Corbusier may not have met Ritter until several years later than
this (see below, Chapter IV); but in any case, it appears that the
Catharist legend was part of this region's culture, and that Jeanneret
was interested in it in his youth.

49 Page 437. This, and all subsequent page references, are to the
1960 Librairie Académique Perrin edition of the book, rather than to
Jeanneret's own copy.

50 Page 393. Also see p. 331. As important however as these superficial resemblances, is Le Corbusier's attitude toward the "Modulor" as
a transcendent mystical system. In a typical passage, the mathematics
underlying the Modulor system reveals "l'absolu et l'infini, le préhensible
et l'insaisissable. . . . une porte s'y trouve parfois; on l'ouvre, on
entre, on est en d'autres lieux, là où se trouvent les dieux, là où sont
les clefs des grands systèmes. Ces portes sont celles des miracles.
Passée l'une de ces portes, ce n'est plus l'homme qui opère: c'est l'univers
que celui-ci touche ici. . ." (Le Modulor, p. 73).

51 L'art décoratif, p. 201.

52 This was Viollet-le-duc's Dictionnaire raisonné de l'architecture
française (see below, Chapter II).

53 ". . . cet axe nous conduit à supposer une unité de gestion dans
l'univers, à admettre une volonté unique à l'origine" (Vers une architecture, pp. 165 and 170).

Chapter II

1 The main sources of information on this period of Jeanneret's
life are: Gauthier, Le Corbusier; Von Moos, Le Corbusier; and the last
chapter of Le Corbusier's L'art décoratif.

2 Von Moos, Le Corbusier, p. 25. Von Moos appears to have interviewed
Perrin.

3 L'art décoratif, p. 201.

[4] Gauthier, Le Corbusier, p. 21. As mentioned already (see Chapter I, note 1), Gauthier's remarks can in effect be accepted as Le Corbusier's own recollections.

[5] Gauthier (Le Corbusier, p. 21) names these towns except for Venice. Sophie Daria (Le Corbusier, Paris, 1964, p. 23) lists the same ones except for adding Venice and omitting Pisa. Although she may have interviewed Le Corbusier also, her book appears to be taken largely from Gauthier's.

[6] Précisions, pp. 91-92.

[7] Peter Serenyi, "Le Corbusier, Fourier, and the Monastery of Ema," The Art Bulletin, December 1967, p. 277ff.

[8] Le Corbusier, for example, suggests this himself by his inclusion of one of these drawings among his earliest sketches (L'atelier, p. 26). More important, however, is the evidence of the handwriting of the notes on these drawings (e.g. the drawing illustrated in Besset, Qui était Le Corbusier?, p. 13) which is the same as other samples of his hand known to date from 1907 and 1908.

[9] Among the works of Ruskin listed in the catalogue of the Art School's library were the French editions of The Seven Lamps, Mornings in Florence, Modern Painters, and The Stones of Venice.

[10] A number of people have recently been studying Jeanneret's early drawings.

[11] John Ruskin, Les matins à Florence, transl. E. Nypels (Paris, H. Laurens, 1906); Hippolyte Taine, Voyage en Italie, 2 vols. (Paris, 1907). The Taine was first published in 1866.

[12] Von Moos, Le Corbusier, p. 25. This contradicts Le Corbusier's later recollection that he went to Italy principally to see architecture (Gauthier, Le Corbusier, p. 22).

[13] Illustrated in Maurice Besset, Qui était Le Corbusier (Genève, 1968), pp. 12-13.

[14] John Ruskin, Mornings in Florence (Chicago, n.d.), p. 18. Subsequent page references are to this edition.

[15] Peter Blake, for example, presents this interpretation (in Le Corbusier, Baltimore, 1966, p. 76).

[16] From a letter to L'Eplattenier written from Paris in 1908 (see below).

[17] In very specific terms, this could be seen for example in the League of Nations competition for which Le Corbusier submitted drawings

which were not executed as prescribed by the competition-rules. But
in a broader sense, of course, it was the nature of Le Corbusier's
designs themselves which so often invited rejection.

[18] Both volumes of this work were signed by Jeanneret with his
typical signature of before 1908 (see Appendix C).

[19] Voyage en Italie (Paris, Julliard, 1965), vol. II, p. 61. Note:
this is not Le Corbusier's edition.

[20] Le Corbusier's edition, vol. I, p. 4.

[21] Taine's aesthetic theories were systematically presented in
Philosophie de l'art (1865f) and De l'idéal dans l'art (1867).

[22] Pierre Castex (in La critique d'art en France au XIXe siècle,
Paris, 1966) discusses this phenomenon in Taine's thinking, saying that
despite his desire to be consistent in his brand of "positivisme,"
Taine "demeurait, par tempérament, fidèle à l'idéalisme" (p. 116).

[23] Julliard edition, vol. I, p. 40. The rest of this passage which
Jeanneret marked expresses the idea that a beautiful and gentle environment such as that of Naples produces a people indisposed to work or to
monumental undertakings. This naturally is related to Taine's category
of "milieu" in his aesthetic theory.

[24] Julliard edition, vol. I, p. 36.

[25] Julliard edition, vol. I, p. 27.

[26] See for example Vers une architecture, p. 19. In fact Le Corbusier
has a very similar admiration for Roman architecture for its simplicity
and solidity, as can be seen for example in his article "La leçon de Rome"
(Vers une architecture, pp. 119-128).

[27] For example: Julliard edition, vol. I, pp. 32-33; vol. II, pp. 78 & 81.

[28] Julliard edition, vol. II, pp. 78 & 100, respectively.

[29] This is the only slip of paper found in this book. Le Corbusier
often marked pages of his books with slips of paper, sometimes with
notes written on them.

[30] Le Corbusier's edition, vol. I, p. 255.

[31] Julliard edition, vol. I, p. 31.

[32] For example: "L'architecture est un fait d'art, un phénomène
d'émotion, en dehors des questions de construction, au delà. La Construction, C'EST POUR FAIRE TENIR: l'Architecture, C'EST POUR ÉMOUVOIR"
(Vers une architecture, p. 9).

[33] Von Moos, Le Corbusier, p. 26f.

[34] Maurice Besset (Qui était Le Corbusier?, p. 198) claims this; and Sophie Daria (Le Corbusier, p. 24) actually maintains that Jeanneret worked for Hoffmann for six months. Both Besset and Daria seem to have had personal contact with Le Corbusier in his later years, and this suggests that Le Corbusier himself may have come to think that he actually worked for Hoffmann. Other confusions appear in his later recollections as well.

[35] Besset, Qui était Le Corbusier?, p. 198.

[36] The "Villa Jaquemet" and the "Villa Stotzer," illustrated in Chavanne & Laville, "Les premières constructions de Le Corbusier," pp. 484-85. Von Moos (Le Corbusier, p. 28) is certain that these two houses were designed in Vienna.

[37] Chavanne & Laville, "Les premières constructions," p. 484.

[38] November 1908 letter to L'Eplattenier (see below).

[39] Gauthier, Le Corbusier, p. 23.

[40] Von Moos, Le Corbusier, p. 30.

[41] Daria, Le Corbusier, p. 25; Gauthier, Le Corbusier, p. 26.

[42] Gauthier, Le Corbusier, p. 27. Le Corbusier also recalls a conversation with Grasset in Le voyage d'orient (Paris, 1966), p. 16.

[43] Auguste Perret (1874-1954) studied at the École des Beaux-Arts under Guadet, but before finishing his studies joined his father's construction company (with his brothers Gustave and Claude), which was among the first firms to experiment with reinforced concrete. His first important construction, the Rue Franklin apartment house, was built in 1903.

[44] Le Corbusier later said that upon seeing his drawings Perret had told him "Vous serez ma main droite" (Gauthier, Le Corbusier, p. 28). It is rather difficult to believe that Perret, for whom architecture was principally construction and structure, would have said this to a young man with as little technical background as Jeanneret; but Le Corbusier several times repeated this story and insisted it was true.

[45] For discussions of the term "rationalism" as applied to architecture, see the Introduction, note 2, and also the remarks on Guadet's and Perret's attitudes toward proportion, in Chapter VI.

[46] See below, Chapter VI, p.

[47] Letter written by Jeanneret to Charles L'Eplattenier, from 3 Quai

St. Michel, Paris, on 22 and 25 November 1908. It was published in
"La gazette littéraire" section of La Gazette de Lausanne, 4 September
1965, p. 13, and also, in a slightly different form (different punctua-
tion, capitalization, etc.) in Aujourd'hui, art et architecture, LI,
November 1965, pp. 10-11. The quotations in this study are taken from
the Gazette de Lausanne version, from which I suspect the other version
was taken. Throughout this letter as published in both versions, there
are occasional dotted breaks in the text which I interpret as being
original to Jeanneret's letter rather than edited omissions; and I am
therefore writing them here as unspaced dots (i.e. ...) to distinguish
them from the normal spaced dots signifying omissions.

[48] My impression--from Le Corbusier's own writings and from talking
with his friends and collaborators at the Fondation Le Corbusier-- is
that throughout his life Le Corbusier's knowledge of mathematics and
other technical subjects remained very minimal. He himself sometimes
admitted this frankly, as when he wrote that when he read Matila Ghyka's
books on proportion and the golden rectangle, he "n'était pas préparé
pour pouvoir y suivre pratiquement la démonstration mathématique (l'algèbre
des formules). . ." (Le Modulor, p. 29).

[49] L'art décoratif, p. 206. After recalling Perret's remark, Le
Corbusier adds that "Je fis des mathématiques qui, pratiquement, ne me
servirent jamais à rien dans la suite. Mais peut-être m'ont-elles
formé l'esprit."

[50] Among the buildings in Paris which Le Corbusier later recalled
as having impressed him at this time are: Franz Jourdain's Samaritaine
department store; two houses by Lecoeur in the Rue Cassini; and "la
maison d'acier et de verre de la rue Réaumur," which must be the
building at 124 rue Réaumur designed by Chédanne in 1900. (Oeuvre complète
1910-1929, pp. 9-10)

[51] Besset (Qui était Le Corbusier?, p. 199) claims that Jeanneret
visited Garnier in Lyon soon after coming to Paris. Le Corbusier himself
says that he met Garnier in Lyon "in about 1907" (Oeuvre complète 1910-
1929, p. 9); but of course it would have to have been 1908.

[52] Tony Garnier, Une cité industrielle: étude pour la construction
des villes (Paris, n.d., apparently 1917).

[53] Viollet-le-duc, Dictionnaire raisonné de l'architecture française
du XIe au XVIe siecle, 10 vols. (Paris, 1854f.) The price of the set
is inscribed at the end of the last volume as 190 Francs (which, as far
as I can discover, would have been at least one month's wages at that
time for someone in Jeanneret position).

[54] Peter Collins, Concrete, The Vision of a New Architecture (London,
1959), p. 155.

[55] This annotation was written on a slip of paper which was inserted

at page 66 of the first volume of the <u>Dictionnaire</u>.

⁵⁶ This comparison of architecture to the body of an animal was one of Perret's favorite notions. In his only published book on architecture, he wrote: "Les grands édifices d'aujourd'hui comportent une ossature, une charpente en acier ou en béton de ciment armé. L'ossature est à l'édifice ce que le squelette est à l'animal. De même que le squelette de l'animal, rythmé, équilibré, symétrique, contient et supporte les organes les plus divers et les plus diversement placés, de même la charpente de l'édifice doit être composée, rythmée, équilibrée, symétrique même" (<u>Contribution à une théorie de l'architecture</u>, Paris, 1952, pp. 35-39). Almost the same passage is also quoted by Peter Collins (in <u>Concrete</u>, p. 213) as coming from an article by Perret in <u>La construction moderne</u>, 19 April 1936, p. vi.

⁵⁷ <u>L'Iliade</u> (Paris, Garnier, n.d.); <u>L'Odyssée</u> (Paris, Flammarion, n.d.). See <u>Appendix C</u> for Jeanneret's signatures in all of these books. Jeanneret seems to have been particularly impressed by the works of Homer. His later writings include references to the Iliad (e.g. <u>Voyage d'orient</u>, p. 103); and in his later years Le Corbusier possessed another edition of Homer's works—which he filled with dozens of colored-pencil drawings more-or-less related to the text.

⁵⁸ Jean-Jacques Rousseau, <u>Les confessions</u>, 2 vols. (Paris, Flammarion, n.d.). Jeanneret marked several passages in both volumes, and there are post-cards and slips of paper stuck in them as well. One piece of paper has a drawing on it, by Jeanneret, of a rather Jugendstil-like building set in a park—which I have so far not identified.

⁵⁹ Charles Baudelaire, <u>Les fleurs du mal</u> (Paris, Calmann-Lévy, n.d.). Jeanneret seems to have taken this to Germany in 1910. There are several concert programs stuck in the pages, with notes by Jeanneret on them, one of which is dated by him "12 mars 1911."

⁶⁰ Gustave Flaubert, <u>Salammbô</u> (Paris, Charpentier, 1908).

⁶¹ Paul Claudel, <u>Connaissance de l'Est</u> (Paris, Mercure de France, 1907). A couple of passages in this book are underlined.

⁶² Jules Laforgue, <u>Moralités légendaires</u> (Paris, 1909).

⁶³ Frédéric Nietzsche, <u>Ainsi parlait Zarathoustra</u> (Paris, 1908). See below for discussion of this book.

⁶⁴ J.-K. Huysmans, <u>La cathédrale</u> (Paris, 1908). Jeanneret clearly read this book very carefully, for he wrote out brief notes on slips of paper which he stuck in the pages throughout the book. Most of these notes simply outline what Huysmans is talking about; but a couple of them contain remarks suggesting that Jeanneret was not impressed with Huysmans' approach (which concentrates mostly on the religious symbolism in the Gothic cathedral—especially in its sculpture and stained glass).

[65] For example: Dostoïevsky, L'idiot, 2 vols. (Paris, Plon, n.d.); and Lord Byron, Don Juan (French edition, Paris, 1904). There are no inscriptions or marks in either of these, but they are typical of the sort of book Jeanneret was reading in 1908-09.

[66] Ernest Renan, Vie de Jésus (Paris, n.d., 1906?). See below for discussion of this book.

[67] Louis Ménard, Histoire des anciens peuples de l'Orient (Paris, 1883). This book, a popular history of ancient civilizations, shows evidence of having been read by Le Corbusier at various times in his life—from 1909 when he inscribed and dated it (see Appendix C), up through the 1950's (judging for example from the post-marks on envelopes stuck in the pages, from underlined passages, and from a note to his secretary to have the book rebound). A number of the plates were marked for a printer to reproduce (I haven't checked yet to see which of Le Corbusier's books they appear in). The section on Zoroaster in the chapter on "Les Mèdes et les Perses" seems especially dog-eared and well-read—which is interesting in light of the fact that in 1909 Jeanneret was also reading Nietzsche's Zarathustra.

[68] Gustave LeBon, Les civilisations de l'Inde (Paris, 1887). This book is inscribed as having been given to Jeanneret by his Aunt Pauline on New-Year's Day 1909 (unlike all the other books discussed here, which were simply inscribed by Jeanneret himself). I suspect that this book—as well as the two other popular-history books by LeBon in this series (see Chapter I, note 20)—had been in the Jeanneret household for some time, and that when Jeanneret returned home for Christmas in 1908 (he speaks of doing this in his letter to L'Eplattenier), he asked his aunt for this book. It is consistent with his obvious interest at this time in history, religion, and especially oriental subjects.

[69] This is on the half-title page of the book (Jeanneret's original inscription is on the title-page). The fact that Le Corbusier himself says he read the book first in 1908 does not mean much in itself, since he often remembered details of his youth incorrectly in his later years.

[70] Page 26. Other examples appear on pp. 16 and 27.

[71] Erik Erikson, Young Man Luther (New York, 1958).

[72] For example: "Je veux continuer cette vie d'étude, de travail et de lutte encore longtemps,—vie heureuse, vie de jeune homme. . . . Je ne serai plus d'accord avec vous . . . Vous voulez, de jeunes hommes de 20 ans, faire des hommes épanouis, actifs, exécutants. . ." In another part of this letter, Jeanneret even develops an extended metaphor, of a tree which grows too quickly and as a result does not have a proper root-structure or foundation.

[73] Pages 14 and 11, respectively.

[74] L'art décoratif, p. xx.

[75] Une maison--un palais (Paris, n.d., 1928), p. 4.

[76] L'urbanisme (Paris, 1925), p. 6.

[77] 1908 seems most likely for a number of reasons--such as [J]eanneret's signature (see Appendix C), and the fact that by 1909 he was inscribing dates, as well as his signature, in all his books.

[78] This recalls Jeanneret's interest in monastic life (Ema, Mount Athos).

[79] In this regard,it is also interesting that one of the Gustave LeBon popular-history books which Jeanneret may well have had as a child--La civilisation des Arabes (see Chapter I, note 20)--contains many illustrations of Arabic architecture which emphasize its stark, cubic aspects.

[80] René Nelli, Le phénomène Cathare (Paris, 1964).

Chapter III

[1] Von Moos, Le Corbusier, p. 35.

[2] Oeuvre complète 1910-1929, p. 22.

[3] Two drawings of this project are reproduced in Oeuvre complète 1910-1929, p. 22. They are dated "24 janvier 1910" and "27/i/10."

[4] Ch.-E. Jeanneret, Étude sur le mouvement d'art décoratif en Allemagne (La Chaux-de-Fonds, Haefeli & Co., 1912).

[5] In a letter from L'Eplattenier (quoted in Étude, p. 5).

[6] It should be recalled here that Jeanneret seems to have spoken German fluently at this time (see Chapter I, note 19).

[7] Albert Jeanneret (born 1886) was a musician, and at this time was studying with Jacques Dalcroze, a Swiss composer who developed various theories about teaching "eurhythmic" music and dancing to children--an interest which Albert Jeanneret later pursued in Paris, in the 1920's, with a school of his own.

[8] Étude, p. 6.

[9] The next year, material from this city-planning exhibition was published in Werner Hegemann, Der Städtebau, vol. I (Berlin, 1911). Le Corbusier's library contains a copy of this book--as well as the second volume of it, published in 1913, which deals with a similar exhibition in Düsseldorf in 1912. Jeanneret must have acquired these books after

returning to La Chaux-de-Fonds (as he did the 1913 Werkbund Jahrbuch; see below). Jeanneret's markings in both of these volumes suggest that he studied them carefully.

[10] For example: L'art décoratif, p. 84.

[11] Étude, p. 43.

[12] Étude, p. 43. Jeanneret's specific reference to the machines in these buildings is interesting, for Le Corbusier's later recollections of his stay in Germany also mention these machines (e.g. L'art décoratif, p. 209), and they seem to have made a strong impression on him. Jeanneret's attitudes toward such machines will be examined later in this study.

[13] ". . . des petites villes toutes coquettes, . . conçues en un goût sobre, utilitaire et convenant" (p. 47).

[14] We also recall Henry Provensal's use of the term—though for him it had a more general philosophical meaning.

[15] Reyner Banham, Theory and Design, p. 73. This speech by Muthesius was reprinted in the 1912 Werkbund Jahrbuch.

[16] Banham, Theory and Design, p. 75.

[17] I have not yet been able to discover exactly when this Werkbund Congress took place in 1911. It is known, however, that Jeanneret left Germany in May 1911; but there is conflicting information about where he was just prior to his departure—Gauthier (p. 33) and Von Moos (p. 37) saying he was in Berlin, but Banham saying he was in Hellerau working for Tessenow. (See also Chapter II, note 59)

[18] Jahrbuch des deutschen Werkbundes, 1913 (Jena, 1913). The copy in Le Corbusier's library contains the impression of a rubber stamp, reading: "CH. E. JEANNERET / ARCHITECTE / LA CHAUX-DE-FONDS." I discovered no other example of this stamp in Le Corbusier's books; but it clearly dates from the period 1912-16. There are no annotations or other markings by Jeanneret in this book besides this stamp.

[19] Gropius's article, "Die Entwicklung moderner Industriebaukunst," was the first published writing of his. It has sometimes been claimed that Gropius, Mies van der Rohe, and Jeanneret all worked in Behrens' office at the same time; but Von Moos (p. 35) says that Jeanneret arrived there several months after Gropius had left to build the Fagus Factory with Adolf Meyer. However, neither Von Moos's nor any other account specifies exactly when Jeanneret began working for Behrens—so the question (for whatever it's worth) still seems unresolved to me. A couple of Jeanneret's book-inscriptions from this period (see Appendix C) reveal that he was in Behrens' office already by November 1910—earlier than most accounts have hitherto suggested.

[20] Vers une architecture, p. 175.

[21] These illustrations are inserted between pages 16 and 17 in the Werkbund Jahrbuch, and were reproduced by Le Corbusier on pages 17 and 18 of Vers une architecture. In addition, however, there are four other pictures of grain elevators in Vers une architecture (pp. 15, 16, 19, and 20) which do not come from the Werkbund Jahrbuch; and these must be the pictures which Amedée Ozenfant claims to have given to Jeanneret in 1920 (Ozenfant, Mémoires, Paris, 1968, pp. 111-113). Ozenfant quotes Walter Gropius as saying (in Aujourd'hui, Nov. 1965) that it was he who gave Jeanneret the Jahrbuch pictures—and accuses Gropius of lying. All of this simply illustrates the tangle of misunderstandings which so often surrounds the recollections of these figures.

[22] See Appendix B. One of these books, Catalog mathematischer Modeller. . ., is an illustrated catalogue of classroom scientific models, some of which are fascinating for their cubistic arrangement of volumes.

[23] Dante, La divine comédie (Paris, n.d.). Jeanneret's inscription includes "Neu-babelsberg, nov. 1910." Neu-babelsberg was a suburb of Berlin in which Peter Behrens had his architectural office.

[24] William Ritter (1867-1955) was originally from Neuchâtel, but lived in Germany and other countries at various times. He wrote articles for French and German art magazines; and as mentioned already (Chapter I, note 37), he referred to Jeanneret in one of these articles in 1913. It is unclear whether Jeanneret met Ritter in Germany, or had known him already in Switzerland (see Chapter I, note 48).

[25] Victor Cousin, Du vrai, du beau, et du bien (Paris, 1904). It was first published in 1836. The page-references here are to an English edition, Lectures on the True, the Beautiful, and the Good (New York, 1855).

[26] For example: Vers une architecture, p. 223.

[27] Alexandre Cingria-Vaneyre, Les entretiens de la Villa du Rouet (Genève, 1908). Jeanneret's copy is inscribed "Ch E Jeanneret / nov. 1910 à Neu-Babelsberg" (see Appendix C). Alexandre Cingria (born 1879 in Geneva) was primarily a painter, and lived in Paris, Constantinople, and for six years in Italy (Thieme-Becker, vol. 6, p. 607).

[28] The bill for the book, sent to Jeanneret from Geneva—and made out to "Monsieur Ch. E. Jeanneret, Architecte, Berlin" and dated "31.x.1910"—was left in the pages of the book. Perhaps it was William Ritter (or maybe L'Eplattenier?) who suggested to Jeanneret that he read the book.

[29] Page 68. Also p. 197. These notions are related by Cingria to various racial theories of art—especially those of Gobineau.

[30] Page 383. The first part of Jeanneret's annotation reads:
"Fini de lire le 23 nov 1910 à Neu-Babelsberg. Et pleinement d'accord
av. l'esprit général et génial. Les paradoxes d'ici n'en sont pas.
Je les souhaite /"1 jour"?_/ vérités vécues et vivantes. Pour moi. . ."

[31] Page 262. Cingria also feels that the simplicity of the Doric
order contrasts beautifully with this sort of mountainous landscape.

[32] Page 255. The topography and vegetation around Constantinople--
where Cingria himself had lived for a while--remind him even more
closely of the Suisse-romande than does Greece.

[33] Jeanneret had apparently climbed the Zugspitze, a mountain in
Southern Bavaria, three months earlier (see his other annotation-reference
to it, below)--that is, in August 1910. The second part of the annotation
suggests that he then had returned to his native Jura region for a visit.

[34] There are of course also similarities between these 1912 houses
and houses designed by Behrens and others in Germany. This will be
discussed in more detail in Chapter IV.

[35] Page 286. These are like the colors Le Corbusier was to use in
his early houses of the 1920's--for example in the LaRoche House
(where, incidentally, these original colors have been preserved).

[36] Page 30.

[37] Gauthier, Le Corbusier, p. 35. According to this account,
Perret asked Jeanneret to return to Paris to "collaborate" with him
on his largest commission so far, the Théâtre des Champs-Élysées.
Whether or not "collaboration" is an exaggeration of the role Perret
actually had in mind for Jeanneret, this was surely an outstanding
opportunity for Jeanneret to increase his experience and pursue his
studies of reinforced concrete construction.

[38] Gauthier (p. 34) says that this trip lasted seven months--that
is, until December 1911. August Klipstein later became an art-dealer
in Bern; and postcards and other correspondence discovered in Le
Corbusier's library show that they continued to maintain contact over
the years.

[39] Gauthier, p. 33; Von Moos, p. 37.

[40] Gauthier, p. 33.

[41] William Ritter, L'entêtement slovaque (Paris, 1910). On the
half-title page of this copy, Ritter inscribed: "A Monsieur Ch. Ed.
Jeanneret / bien amical souvenir du /"jour"?_/ de l'oeil sanglant /
William Ritter / 16.vii.1910." I have not yet been able to make sense
of this allusion.

[42] Le voyage d'Orient (Paris, Forces Vives, 1966). The history of

this work is not totally clear. In its preface, Le Corbusier says
that from the notes which he took during his trip he "extracted
articles," some of which were then published by La Feuille d'Avis,
a newspaper in La Chaux-de-Fonds. He says that he then "regrouped
and completed these texts to make a book of them—a book which, under
the title Voyage d'Orient, was to have been published by Gaspard
Valette in 1914 in the Mercure de France." He says the War prevented
that; but he kept the manuscript, and in July 1965 he "corrected it
and, with no recourse to any documents, wrote scrupulous footnotes"
(Le voyage d'Orient, p. 5). Thus the footnotes all date from 1965; but
other than that it is difficult to know which parts were his original
notes on the trip, which were written in La Chaux-de-Fonds between
1912 and 1914, and whether any of the 1965 "corrections" were substan-
tial or not (my impression is that they probably were not). Only an
examination of the manuscripts (if they still exist) and the original
newspaper articles could really clear this up.

43 Loos expressed this attitude in his article "Architektur"—but
not in his better-known "Ornament und Verbrechen" (of which Le Corbusier's library contains a copy, in its French version published in
Les cahiers d'aujourd'hui in June 1913, as "Ornement et crime"—which
was later reprinted in L'esprit nouveau in 1920).

44 Christopher Alexander, Notes on the Synthesis of Form (Cambridge,
Mass., 1964).

45 See Peter Collins' discussion of the differing attitudes toward
the Parthenon, in Concrete, pp. 194-98.

46 Von Moos (Le Corbusier, p. 43) says specifically four weeks,
but does not give his source.

47 For the bibliographical data of this publication see below, note
50. The only other item in Le Corbusier's library which seems to date
from this 1911 trip is a Baedeker tourist manual, Grèce (Leipzig &
Paris, 1910). A number of passages in it are marked or annotated by
Jeanneret—some of these being of considerable interest. For example
on a map of the sacred precinct at Eleusis (p. 109), Jeanneret drew a
section through the site, noting various features; and on a page
describing Delphi (p. 147) he drew the elevation of a wall, noting
its dimensions and writing "uni, cubique."

48 ". . . plus rien de la vie extérieure ne se manifestait ici"
(p. 159); and the height and form of the Acropolis "dérobent à la
perception tout vestige de vie moderne" (p. 160).

49 Vers une architecture, p. 165. It is important to note that Le
Corbusier clearly represents this "axis" as being of a divine, transcendent nature. It underlies the organization of "all the phenomena
and all the objects in nature," and even "the laws of physics follow
from this axis."

[50] Ernest Renan, Prière sur l'Acropole (Athènes, Eleftheroudakis
& Barth, Librairie Internationale, n.d.). This is simply a twelve-
page, unbound pamphlet. The essay was first published in 1899; but
I have found no reference to this Athens edition in the Bibliothèque
Nationale catalogues or anywhere else. It seems to have been printed
specially for sale to French tourists in Athens. Everything points
to Jeanneret's having bought it there in 1911. Furthermore, since he
had read La vie de Jésus only a couple of years earlier, it is natural
that he would have chosen to read this other work by Renan.

[51] Voyage d'Orient, p. 158, and Vers une architecture, pp. 170-71,
respectively.

[52] Vers une architecture, p. 166.

[53] Voyage d'Orient, p. 154. The French "fatalité" means "destiny,"
"determinism," or "fatalism." In connection with Jeanneret's association
here of machines with terror and related feelings, it is interesting to
note that later Le Corbusier was to recall a "machine abominable" which
he saw in Germany in 1910 (L'art décoratif, p. 209). The whole question
of Jeanneret's attitude toward machines will be examined in Chapter V.

[54] In a book in Le Corbusier's library--P. Gusman, La décoration
murale à Pompei (Paris, 1924)--I found a loose watercolor-drawing of
a Pompeiian room with decorated walls, on the back of which Le Corbusier
had later written: "Aquarelle de Corbu, faite sur place en 1910."
(For some reason, Le Corbusier in his later years tended to recollect
things from his youth as being one year earlier than they actually
had happened--see for example Chapter II, note 51). The drawing is
in a peculiar, rather expressionistic watercolor style.

[55] Actually, both of these references to himself are with the term
"constructeur" rather than "architecte" (pp. 138 and 163)--which probably
reflects the influence of Perret, who preferred to think of himself as
a "constructeur" (see Chapter VI). He also refers to himself once as
a "dessinateur" (p. 7), and once as a "peintre" (p. 19)--an odd reference in light of the accepted understanding that Jeanneret did not
think of himself as a painter until after 1917.

[56] Page 38. Yet in another passage--a rather obscure one--Jeanneret
seems to suggest that modernism can also be excessive and even danger-
ous (p. 124).

Chapter IV

[1] Gauthier's biography devotes only a couple of pages to this period.
Von Moos's study contains some important information, which he apparently
obtained from research and interviews. Other than this, and scattered
remarks in Le Corbusier's later writings, the main sources of information
are the pamphlet Un mouvement d'art (see below), and Jeanneret's own
notebooks of this period--which are described below.

[2] Some photographs of these houses were published in Perspecta, VI, 1960, pp. 28-33 (although with incorrect identifications and dating); and other photos and information are found in Chavanne & Laville's article "Les premières constructions de Le Corbusier," Werk, L, 1963, pp. 483-88.

[3] An article on the Schwob House appeared in L'esprit nouveau, March 1921, written by "Julien Caron"--which Amedée Ozenfant says was one of his pseudonyms (Mémoires, p. 126). Le Corbusier did not include it in the first volume of the Oeuvre complète, but later did in Le Corbusier, 1910-65 (Zürich, 1967).

[4] The failure was apparently due to lack of proper snow-drainage from the flat roof (information from David Stewart). Von Moos does not mention this reported structural failure.

[5] Chapallaz was the architect who had apparently helped Jeanneret in the design and execution of his first three houses. Von Moos (p. 47) also mentions another local architectural firm, "Curjel and Moser."

[6] It is not clear whether, or when, Jeanneret knew of the Wasmuth publications of Wright's work, which began in 1910. But Le Corbusier himself later recalled that "Un jour, en 1913, arriva un magasin apportant les oeuvres de Frank Lloyd Wright, ce précurseur, élève de Sullivan, plus grand précurseur encore" (Oeuvre complète 1910-29, p. 10). Von Moos (p. 52) says that this periodical was the Schweizerischen Bauzeitung, and that the year was 1912, not 1913; and he specifically mentions Wright's Thomas Hardy House in Racine as a possible influence on the Schwob House.

[7] Oeuvre complète 1910-1929, pp. 24 and 26. Jeanneret seems to have been particularly interested in designing cornices in this period. His sketchbooks contain many pages of drawings by him of cornices with different kinds of profiles--some of which seem to be based on cornice-profiles illustrated in Dieulafoy's L'art antique de de la Perse, which we know he studied at this time (see Chapter VI).

[8] Le Corbusier himself used the English word "sketchbook" to refer to these small notebooks (most of them spiral-bound pads of drawing paper) in which he drew and jotted down notes to himself. The Fondation Le Corbusier possesses dozens of these notebooks (I shall use the terms "sketchbook" and "notebook" interchangeably to refer to them), but nearly all of these date from the 1920's and later. I was able to find only two which seem to date from the 1912-16 period in La Chaux-de-Fonds; and I examined these carefully. They are labeled "A-1" and "A-2" on their covers (apparently written by Le Corbusier himself, later in his life). The one labeled "A-1" also has "Landeron, 1914" on its cover; but several of the drawings and pages in it are dated 1916--and my impression is that Jeanneret filled this notebook primarily in 1916. The book labeled "A-2" has "1915" written on its

cover, and contains dates in 1915 and 1916--so perhaps Jeanneret
filled this one before he filled "A-1," or else maybe he kept them
at the same time. There is also a sketchbook labeled "A-3," but it
seems to have been kept in 1918-19 after Jeanneret had moved to
Paris. None of these sketchbooks is paginated; but in studying them
I assigned consecutive numbers to the pages for purposes of keeping
my notes on them in order. Perhaps it is also worth mentioning that
these notebooks have book-store stamps on them showing that "A-1" was
purchased in La Chaux-de-Fonds, and "A-2" in Paris.

⁹ Oeuvre complète 1910-1929, p. 8. According to David Stewart,
it was not until 1916 that Ritter returned to Switzerland--settling
in Bienne, where Jeanneret is said to have visited him on Sundays.
But even while still in Germany, Ritter could have corresponded with
Jeanneret, given him introductions to his acquaintances, etc. In
fact, three books by Ritter were inscribed by him to Jeanneret during
these years--in 1913, 1914, and 1915 (see Appendix A). The 1915 inscription refers to a "carte postale" which Ritter had just received from
Jeanneret, apparently containing good news about Jeanneret's career
(perhaps his commission to design the Schwob House?) And Ritter's
1914 inscription, typical of his efforts to boost Jeanneret's ego, is:
"A Charles Édouard Jeanneret / l'aquarelliste, le dessinateur et
l'écrivain / si décidés et sommaires, l'architecte / si vivant, en tous
domaines l'artiste très / sincère qu'estiment tant ses vieux amis de
Munich / William Ritter / 27 janvier 1914."

¹⁰ L'art et les artistes, XVIII, 1913, p. 98. For the quotation
which Ritter attributed to Jeanneret in this article, see Chapter I, p. 21.

¹¹ Jeanneret's notes on this group are found in his notebook "A-2,"
on pages 121 to 125, and are dated by him "21 juin 1916."

¹² Le Corbusier, 1910-1965, p. 17. It was in studying his library,
however, that I became aware of the full extent of this desire of Le
Corbusier's to be accepted and respected by the intellectual establishment. Throughout his life, he read every article and book he could
find which mentioned him or discussed his work, circling or annotating
positive comments, and crossing out or angrily answering negative comments.
Special honors, such as his Cambridge degree, were carefully preserved
by him in special folders, along with pertinent correspondence, newspaper
accounts, accolades, etc.--and the manner in which he labeled and annotated
all this material clearly reveals the importance it had to him.

¹³ Jeanneret's salary is listed (in Un mouvement d'art ⌈see below⌉,
p. 9) as being 1320 Swiss Francs a year.

¹⁴ Von Moos, Le Corbusier, p. 45.

¹⁵ Un mouvement d'art à la Chaux-de-Fonds, à propos de la Nouvelle
Section de l'École d'Art (La Chaux-de-Fonds, Imprimerie Georges Dubois).
The concluding section of this pamphlet is signed by Charles L'Eplattenier,

Ch.-E. Jeanneret, Léon Perrin and Georges Aubert, and dated "11 avril 1914."

[16] Actually, I do not know for sure that Jeanneret knew Carabin (a relatively minor art-nouveau sculptor)--except to the extent that this may be suggested by the fact that Le Corbusier later listed him with well-known figures as being his favorite artists in his youth (see Chapter I, p. 5 , and note 7).

[17] Requête de MM. Le Corbusier et P. Jeanneret à M. le Président du Conseil de la Société des Nations (Paris, n.d., 1930?).

[18] Un mouvement d'art, p. 9.

[19] Each of these photographs has a typed label affixed, with "Nouvelle Section 1912-1913" or similar identification, and the name of the teacher whose projects these are. Most of these labels also include descriptions of the courses or the specific assignments represented in the photo. There are several prints of each of these photos-- and this fact suggests that perhaps they are the "photographies des travaux" which, according to Un mouvement d'art, were sent to Grasset and the others for their testimonials. If this is so, then Jeanneret's possession of these photographs is further evidence that he was behind the whole campaign to defend the Nouvelle Section.

[20] Von Moos, Le Corbusier, p. 46.

[21] Un mouvement d'art (p. 6) lists and describes some of these jobs.

[22] As discussed above in note 8, the two notebooks of this period-- "A-1" and "A-2"--are difficult to date precisely, but seem to have been kept in 1915 and 1916 primarily. Most of Jeanneret's "Ateliers d'art" sketches and notes are found in "A-1"--which, as pointed out above, seems to have been filled mainly in 1916.

[23] The only real evidence I found of this "art-lamp" enterprise is a printed publicity flyer, which Jeanneret left in the pages of a book he was reading at this time (Maurice Denis's Théories; see below).

[24] Maurice Besset, Qui était Le Corbusier?, p. 199. Besset says that these were watercolor drawings, and that Jeanneret exhibited them under the title "Langage de pierres," but doesn't give a source for this information. The fact that Besset also says that these drawings covered the period 1907-1913, and yet that this exhibition was in 1912, is typical of the factual inconsistencies and errors in this book.

[25] This is Choisy's Histoire de l'architecture (see below).

[26] Von Moos (p. 48) says simply that after the War began, Jeanneret visited Paris often, mainly to study old engraving in the Bibliothèque Nationale. David Stewart says more specifically that in the summer of 1915 Jeanneret studied urbanism in the B.N. Jeanneret's notebooks of

this period show evidence of his interest both in engravings and, to a much greater extent (see below) in urbanism. As for the buildings which Jeanneret noticed in Paris at this time, he seems to have been most impressed by several new apartment buildings which replaced the pitched roof with several stepped-back floors at the top. In notebook "A-2" (pp. 103-04) he described one of these buildings on the Champs de Mars across from the Eiffel Tower, and did a rough sketch of it.

27 Information from David Stewart.

28 See Appendix B.

29 These books are all signed by Jeanneret and dated "sept 1916," and many of them contain earlier signatures of members of the Soutter family (see Appendix C). The Soutters were related to Jeanneret on his mother's side. One of them, Louis Soutter, was a gifted musician and artist who went insane and spent his later life in an asylum; Le Corbusier took an interest in him, and tried to help him at various times by arranging exhibitions of his drawings.

30 These books which we know Jeanneret read, but which are not in his library, are listed separately in Appendix B. In a couple of cases, however, I have not been able to identify books which Jeanneret refers to in his notebooks; an example of this is a work on housing, whose author appears to be "Janet."

31 Jeanneret's references to this book in his notebooks will be discussed in Chapter VI in relation to the "tracés régulateurs."

32 Julius Meier-Graefe, Paul Cézanne (München, 1910). A book-shop label inside the front cover shows that Jeanneret bought this in La Chaux-de-Fonds. Jeanneret marked a passage lightly on page 16, but this is his only mark in the book (except for the fact that on the half-title page he pasted in a small reproduction of Cézanne's self-portrait, clipped from a German art magazine).

33 Maurice Denis, Théories, 1890-1910 (Paris, 1912). Jeanneret inscribed it "Ch E Jeanneret / Nov 1912 / la Chaux--" (see Appendix C). There are no marks or annotations in the book, but Jeanneret marked many pages with slips of paper and other things--such as a postcard (addressed to Jeanneret at the "Ateliers d'art réunis"); the publicity flyer for his "art-lamp" business, mentioned above; and a string-quartet program, in which his brother Albert Jeanneret was featured, dated 12 May 1915. One's impression is that Jeanneret read this book carefully during this period in La Chaux-de-Fonds.

34 This question of the beginnings of Jeanneret's serious interest in painting will be examined in the next chapter.

35 Pages 277, 272, and 277, respectively. These and all subsequent page-references to this work are to its 4th edition (1920) rather than to Jeanneret's 1912 edition.

36 Auguste Choisy, Histoire de l'architecture, 2 vols. (Paris, n.d.)
This work was first published in 1899. Oddly enough, it is the second
volume of Jeanneret's copy which contains his inscription ("Ch E
Jeanneret / Paris, Noël 1913"--see Appendix C); but both volumes
contain the same Paris book-shop label, and undoubtedly were bought
at the same time. A few of the pages of vol. I are not cut.

37 Reyner Banham, Theory and Design, Chapter II.

38 In both volumes of Jeanneret's copy of Choisy, many of the
illustrations are marked by him for the printer. Several of these
illustrations are found in Le Corbusier's publications of the 1920's,
but there seem to be a good many more of them marked by Le Corbusier
in his copy of Choisy.

39 Vol. I, p. 56.

40 It is also worth noting here that later in his life, Le Corbusier
was to slip a piece of paper in this first volume of Choisy, noting
the pages of the passages he had earlier marked, and adding the word
"Modulor."

41 See Chapter III, note 42.

42 The most important of these outlines--the one discussed here--
is found at the front of Notebook "A-2," which as mentioned above seems
to have been kept mainly in 1915. This outline, possibly, is what Von
Moos refers to (p. 48) when he says that Jeanneret worked on a "Studie
über Städtebau" during this period in La Chaux-de-Fonds. Indeed,
Jeanneret's notes in this outline refer to cities as much as to individual buildings. In this regard, it is also worth mentioning that Le
Corbusier later said that "En 1910, j'écris un livre, un peu idiot, sur
l'urbanisme, qui ne vit jamais le jour" (Le Corbusier Parle, Paris, 1967,
pp. 46-47). Whether Le Corbusier was really referring to a completed
book, or simply to an outline for a book, I was not able to find any
evidence of such a project dating from 1910 in Le Corbusier's effects.

43 Le Corbusier later tended to write the word as "Dom-ino," or
sometimes simply "Domino;" but in his original sketchbooks of this
period it is written "Dom-Ino."

44 The information on the Dom-Ino system which Le Corbusier later
published is found principally in: Oeuvre complète 1910-1929, pp. 23-
26; Vers une architecture, pp. 190-197; and Precisions sur un etat. . .,
pp. 93-95. Jeanneret's rough sketches and notes from around 1915 are
found in his Notebook "A-2."

45 Le Corbusier gives the dimension of each unit as 6 x 9 meters,
with a 1-meter cantilever (Précisions, p. 93). His descriptions of
the construction methods he envisaged are difficult to figure out in
complete detail, even with the help of his drawings of the system. The
columns were meant to be pre-cast, apparently; but for the slabs Jeanneret

devised a complicated system in which concrete was to be poured
around "un matérial de chantier spécial"--apparently pre-cast hollow
concrete blocks of some sort--which were to be held in place with a
"très simple échafaudage de poutrelles double T accrochées tempor-
airement à des colliers qui sont fixés au sommet de chaque poteau. . ."
(Oeuvre complète 1910-1929, p. 23). He doesn't specify how the stairs
were to be constructed, byt they probably would have to be normal
poured-in-place reinforced concrete construction. Thus, three totally
different types of concrete construction would be used on each unit--
a technical and economic problem in its own right. Jeanneret's
conception of the Dom-Ino system was clearly not based on simplicity
of construction.

46 The patent, found on page 89 of Notebook "A-2," is of considerable
interest, especially since it is a rough draft, in which Jeanneret was
searching for the right words with which to express his conception of
the important aspects of the Dom-Ino system:
Brevet
Système des constructions juxtaposables selon ~~toutes~~ ~~les~~ d'infinis
combinaisons de plans grace ~~aux~~ à un module sous-multiple uniforme
par ossatures de béton armé monolythes à plancher ~~massif~~ ~~monolythe~~
lisse. Séparation des pouvoirs   sur fondations de 6 poteaux
permettant par le genre de leur calcul (--de leur tache. . .) la
construction où n'importe quel point de cloisons de façades. . .
Particularités: les poteaux à l'intérieur n'apparaissent pas en
façade. distribution intérieure. à intervenir dans la suite, ad-
libitum par coulage automatique permettant l'érection et l'achève-
ment d'une maison dans un delai de 20 jours.
Autre brevet: cloisons isolantes moulées.

On page 39 of the same notebook, the Dom-Ino system is also described
by Jeanneret as "le système extensible par pièces. . ."

47 We know Jeanneret was thinking of the Garage Ponthieu at this
time, for his Notebook "A-2" contains a rough drawing of its façade
(on page 144).

48 See above, note 45.

49 Oeuvre complète 1910-1929, p. 23.

50 As can be seen above (note 46), the word "lisse" replaced the
crossed-out words "massif" and "monolythe."

51 For example, an English pre-fab concrete house system was
illustrated in Benoît-Lévy's Cité-jardin, vol. I, p. 101--which we
know Jeanneret read at this time (see below). Other similar experiments had been carried out in France.

52 This is the one labeled "A-2" (see above, note 8).

53 On the other hand, if Jeanneret had indeed written some sort of

study of urbanism in 1910, as he later recalled (see above, note 42), then he may have been interested in city-planning at an earlier time than this.

[54] See above, note 26.

[55] Georges Benoît-Lévy, La cité-jardin, 3 vols. (Paris, 1911). It is the third volume--sub-titled "Art et coöperation des cités-jardins"--which Jeanneret specifically refers to, in his notebook "A-2." He also wrote a number next to the name of the book, which looks like a Bibliothèque Nationale catalogue number (8º R. 24609), thus suggesting that he was reading it in Paris.

[56] Vol. III, p. 18. Stanley Davenport Adshead (1868-1946), trained as an architect, was the first Professor of Civic Design in the University of Liverpool, 1909-14 (the first town-planning chair in England), and was later Professor of Town Planning at the University of London. He was an active promoter of the garden-city movement, and wrote a number of books and articles on English town planning.(Information from The Town Planning Review, XIX, Summer 1947, pp. 120-22).

[57] Vol. III, p. 17.

[58] Vol. III, p. 21. On the next page, Benoît-Lévy claims that Bergson and Ruskin are the two greatest contemporary philosophers.

[59] Vol. III, pp. 18-19. This comes right after the long quote from Adshead which Jeanneret copied out into his notebook.

[60] In an interview with the newspaper La Patrie, published 21 June 1905, Perret is reported to have described his concept of "villes-tours," of twenty-storey buildings, all with roof-terraces, but spaced out rather than close together as in American cities (reported in Bernard Champigneulle, Perret, Paris, n.d., 1959?). Despite the fact that Perret never seems to have gone any further than to talk about these "villes-tours," Le Corbusier clearly recognized the fact that they were originally Perret's idea, by crediting them to him in an Esprit nouveau article ("Trois rappels. . .Le plan," Esprit nouveau, no. 3, 1921)--although when this article was republished in Vers une architecture in 1923, Perret's name was dropped, giving the impression that these "villes-tours" were Jeanneret's idea alone.

[61] There is some uncertainty in Le Corbusier's 1922 scheme about the extent to which the towers were meant to contain apartments or offices (a point about which Le Corbusier later became sensitive as a result of criticism, after which he claimed that he had never intended that the tallest buildings be used for housing). In the 1915 sketchbooks, however, these towers clearly seem to be residential--shown for example by the schools at their base.

[62] Champigneulle, Perret, pp. 97-98.

Chapter V

1 Von Moos (Le Corbusier, p. 53) says that Jeanneret moved in "early 1917," but gives no source for this; and none of Le Corbusier's accounts specify the date. A sketch in one of Jeanneret's notebooks ("A-3," p. 39) is inscribed "St. Nicolas--9 mai 1917;" but there are towns of that name both in Belgium (where Jeanneret might conceivably have gone in connection with his Dom-Ino schemes for rebuilding war-ravaged Flemish towns), and in eastern France near Nancy (where he might well have stopped on his way from La Chaux-de-Fonds to Paris). I was unable to find any other sketches dated 1917 in Jeanneret's notebooks. And in his library, there is only one book inscribed with that year (see Appendix C); but there is also a programme booklet for the Ballets Russes appearance in Paris in May 1917 which suggests that Jeanneret was there at that time (see below). Of course, as we have seen already, Jeanneret visited Paris often, before actually moving there, so the precise date of his move is perhaps not crucial.

2 Gauthier, Le Corbusier, p. 37; and L'art décoratif, p. 200. On the one hand, we are not totally convinced by Le Corbusier's claim that the painter L'Eplattenier tried to turn him away from architecture and toward decoration, since it had always been L'Eplattenier who encouraged his career as an architect, and since Jeanneret then went on to Paris and began painting for the first time. In another sense, however, it may be true that L'Eplattenier's view of architecture was that of decorated surfaces (in the tradition of Ruskin), and that this was at odds with Jeanneret's Provensalesque conception of architecture as volumes under light.

3 Gauthier, Le Corbusier, p. 37.

4 For example in notebook "A-2," in a list of notes to himself about the Dom-Ino patent and the setting-up of a Dom-Ino business enterprise, Jeanneret wrote: "Si ça marche, Jeanneret s'installe définitivement à Paris" (p. 44). On the next page, Jeanneret wrote out a schedule of dates when various phases of this business were to be accomplished-- including: "Brevet, sept.;" "dessins Brochures, sept octobre;" "impression, nov-décembre;" and "installation Paris, Janvier." The problem is to know what year this was. A later page in this sketchbook is dated 21 June 1916; but it is still hard to know whether Jeanneret wrote out this Dom-Ino schedule in 1915 or 1916. My guess is that it was 1916, and that the "installation Paris" was meant for January 1917.

5 Ozenfant (in Mémoires, p. 101) says May 1917; Gauthier (p. 40) says 1918, and that they were introduced by Perret at an "Art et liberté" meeting; Von Moos (p. 55) says the same thing and specifies May 1918; Besset (Qui était Le Corbusier?, p. 200) says 1917, at Perret's studio; and Le Corbusier (L'art décoratif, p. 217) says simply 1918. (Also see note 11, below).

6 Mémoires, p. 101.

[7] "Les Ballets Russes à Paris / Théâtre du Chatelet / Mai 1917 / . . . Artistes de Serge de Diaghilew. . ."

[8] Of course, since Jeanneret visited Paris often when still in La Chaux-de-Fonds, he could simply have been visiting there in May 1917; but I suspect he may have settled definitely in Paris by this time.

[9] For example, Apollinaire says of Picasso's stage-sets that "Il s'agit avant tout de traduire la réalité. Toutefois le motif n'est plus reproduit mais seulement représenté et plutôt que représenté, il voudrait être suggéré par une sorte d'analyse-synthèse embrassant tous ses éléments visibles et quelque chose de plus, si possible, une schématisation intégrale. . ." We seem to recognize a good deal of Maurice Denis's thinking here too.

[10] Mémoires, p. 102.

[11] On the other hand, if Ozenfant's claim that he and Jeanneret met in May 1917 is correct, then it could very well have been he who introduced Jeanneret to the Ballets Russes—especially since he states in his Mémoires (p. 92) that he saw the first performance of "Parade" and knew Eric Satie personally.

[12] For example, in L'atelier de la recherche patiente, p. 55, a painting of 1918 entitled "La cheminée" is referred to as Le Corbusier's "first picture." Sophia Daria (apparently based on interviews with Le Corbusier himself) says that "La cheminée" was painted in November 1918 and repeats that it was his first painting (Le Corbusier, p. 33). Ozenfant, in his Mémoires (p. 104), lists other occasions on which Le Corbusier acknowledged that he began painting at the instigation of Ozenfant.

[13] Ozenfant, Mémoires, p. 102. The dots (...) in this quotation are Ozenfant's, not mine. He says that this is only several lines from a "longue lettre" from Jeanneret, so of course he may have edited it to suit his own purposes; and thus it would be extremely interesting to see the original letter. The same passages quoted here were also reproduced in the special Le Corbusier issue of Aujourd'hui art et architecture, Nov. 1965, p. 14—but with a couple of changes of wording.

[14] This information comes primarily from his Mémoires, 1886-1962 (Paris, 1968).

[15] Mémoires, p. 96.

[16] Mémoires, p. 73.

[17] This was the tenth issue of Élan, dated December 1916—which incidentally was also the last issue.

[18] Ozenfant uses this term twice in this article: once, when he says that Cubism "a réalisé. . . son dessein puriste de nettoyer la langue

plastique des termes parasites. . .," and again in a section-heading, "LE CUBISME EST UN MOUVEMENT DE PURISME."

[19] Mémoires, p. 104f.

[20] Ozenfant et Jeanneret, Après le cubisme (Paris, Édition de Commentaires, 1918). At the end of the text is printed the date "15 octobre 1918." Furthermore, bound into the copies of this work which I have seen are catalogues of the exhibition of Purist paintings which Ozenfant and Jeanneret had in December 1918, "chez Thomas, 5, rue de Penthièvre, Paris."

[21] Mémoires, p. 104; also see last note.

[22] Mémoires, p. 104.

[23] For example, Robert L. Herbert, speaking of Ozenfant and Jeanneret's joint article "Le purisme," of 1920, says that ". . . even after a careful reading of their earlier and later individual writings, it is hard to pluck from the essay each man's independant contribution" (Modern Artists on Art, Englewood, N.J., 1964, p. 59).

[24] For in one of his La Chaux-de-Fonds sketchbooks ("A-2," on p. 59), Jeanneret had written out notes to himself about a booklet he was planning to write, of which either the title or the chapter-headings were to be "Où en est l'art francais" and "Où en est l'art allemand."

[25] Page 47. This term "axe" appears particularly in the sections clearly written by Jeanneret. It is about the only term which I cannot specifically trace to Jeanneret's earlier reading or writing; so it would be interesting to locate its source. It was later to be used by Le Corbusier in the same way throughout the article "Architecture: pure création de l'esprit"--for example: "Cette table d'harmonie qui vibre en nous est notre critérium de l'harmonie. Ce doit être cet axe sur lequel l'homme est organisé, en accord parfait avec la nature. . ." (Vers une architecture, p. 165).

[26] Page 48. In this list Jeanneret refers specifically to "triangles égyptiens"--which naturally reminds us of his later "tracé régulateur" system of proportioning which was based on triangles. Jeanneret had no doubt read about an Egyptian proportioning system based on triangles, but so far I have not located the source.

[27] See below, Chapter VI, p. 189.

[28] Vers une architecture, p. 49.

[29] Especially later in his life, Le Corbusier read and annotated a number of books on Egyptian architecture, religion, etc., which presented mystical or other unconventional theories of proportions in Egyptian art (for example: A. Fournier des Corats, La proportion égyptienne

et les rapports de divine harmonie (Paris, 1957); and R. A. Schwaller
de Lubicz, Le temple dans l'homme (Le Caire, 1949).

[30] Ozenfant's later writings on art, and also his paintings (as
illustrated for example in his book Journey through Life, New York,
1939), reveal little or no interest in geometry or proportioning
systems.

[31] All of these manifestoes have the same format: they are single
sheets of paper, about 12" by 17", folded over once, thus creating
four pages of text (although in the case of Marinetti's 1909 manifesto,
only two of these four pages are printed).

[32] This publication in which they were found is: Revista d'arte
futurista, Anno 1, N° Spec. (1924). Along with the manifestoes was
a copy of an article, Auguste Joly, "Le futurisme et la philosophie,"
reprinted from La Belgique artistique et littéraire, July 1912. In
this article Joly links Futurism to the philosophies of Plato, Bergson,
and Pythagoras, among others.

[33] Le Corbusier wrote this in Giulio Carlo Argan et al., Dopo
Sant' Elia (Milan, 1935). Jeanneret also wrote the date "9 juillet
1935" in this inscription, but there are no other notes by him in the
book.

[34] At the top of the first page of this reprint is the "Poesia"
seal, Marinetti's name and Milan address, and the heading "La Revue
Internationale 'Poesia' vient de fonder une nouvelle école littéraire
sous le nom de 'FUTURISME'." I have not yet tried to find out when
this particular reprint was published, but I imagine it could be done.

[35] Nevertheless, it must be pointed out that Le Corbusier later
did write with praise about steamships, airplanes, and automobiles--
most notably in his three articles entitled "Des yeux qui ne voient
pas" in L'esprit nouveau. It could hardly be denied that his interest
in these was related to Futurist thinking; yet the important thing is
that his admiration is for their precision, clarity, perfection, etc.,
rather than their speed or power.

[36] Of course, it should be noted that Jeanneret's annotation in
the Entretiens is related to a passage in which Cingria himself is
speaking of the beauty of a train passing through a mountain-valley
at night (see Chapter III, p. 89). But still, Jeanneret's remarks
are closer to Marinetti's images than to the passage he was annotating.

[37] The eleventh day of the month was a kind of canon to the Futurists,
and most of their maifestoes were dated with it. By the way, Jeanneret's copy of this particular manifesto looks as though it may be original
rather than a reprinting.

[38] This also might be the original manifesto and not a reprint.

[39] A hasty word-count taken of the first couple of pages of Le voyage d'Orient and of Vers une architecture revealed about twice as many adjectives and adverbs in the former than in the latter. Many passages elsewhere in these books show an even more drastic contrast in this regard.

[41] At the end of this reprint is this information: "Première édition de ce manifeste: le 11 mai 1916 / Édition augmentée: le 11 septembre 1922."

[42] The earliest example of this attitude which I can find in Le Corbusier's writings is in his article "Les tracés régulateurs" (first published in L'esprit nouveau, No. 5, 1921), in which he speaks of Man as having ". . . règle son travail /et 7 apporté l'ordre. Car, autour de lui, la forêt est en désordre avec ses lianes, ses ronces, ses troncs qui le gênent et paralysent ses efforts" (Vers une architecture, p. 54).

[43] Reyner Banham (Theory and Design, pp. 127-37) examines the question of Marinetti's possible contributions to it, as well as analysing its ideas in general. The quotations here are from Banham's reprinting of it (pp. 128-30), which presumably is his own translation. Unfortunately, I have not yet been able to discover whether the original 1914 publication of this manifesto was in French as well as in Italian.

[44] Reyner Banham, for example, suggests this in his chapters on Futurism and Le Corbusier in Theory and Design. In fact, he also makes the more general (and perhaps somewhat more valid) suggestion that ". . . the spirit of the times in the plastic arts was largely the creation of an interaction of Cubist forms and Futurist ideas" (p. 199).

[45] See Chapter IV, note 8.

[46] A word should be said here about the sketches for a "Villa au bord de la mer," which Le Corbusier dated as 1916 in the first volume of the Oeuvre complète (p. 28)--since if they did indeed date from 1916, they would be of great significance and a drastic contrast to his other designs of that period (for example his Dom-Ino house designs in his notebooks). Yet in Vers une architecture (p. 204) Le Corbusier dates this same design as 1921; and this is undoubtedly the correct date. This has been the source of considerable confusion; and Maurice Besset, for example, published these sketches as dating from 1916 (Qui était Le Corbusier?, p. 71).

[47] Von Moos writes that "Eine Reihe von Zufällen setzte ihn 1918 an die Spitze eines kleinen Geschäftes, der 'Société d'Études Industrielles et Techniques,' die auch eine Ziegelei in Fonteville, in der Banlieue von Paris, führte. Die 'Briqueterie' war ein eher improvisierte Einmannbetrieb. . ." (Le Corbusier, p. 55).

[48] See Chapter VI.

49 Philippe Boudon, in Pessac de Le Corbusier (Paris, 1969), claims
that Le Corbusier actually built several housing units for Frugès (the
industrialist who later built the Pessac complex) as early as 1920
(p. 7). This claim is apparently based on recollections of Henry Frugès
(which Boudon published in an article in the Bulletin de la Société des
Architectes Diplômés par le Gouvernement, No. 163, January 1968, p. 2).
If this is true, then these houses (which are illustrated both in
Boudon's article and in his book) are of considerable significance; but
there seems to be some question about whether they really are as early
as 1920.

50 An exception to this will be Le Corbusier's prolific reading in
politics and social theory in the 1930's--fields which he does not seem
to have been seriously concerned with before that time.

51 Ozenfant, Mémoires, p. 113.

52 Gauthier (Le Corbusier, p. 47) says that "Paul Boulard" was Le
Corbusier, that "Docteur Saint Quentin" was Ozenfant, and that articles
signed "Vauvrecy" and "Fayet" were written by either or both of them.
Ozenfant says that "Julien Caron " was also one of his own pseudonyms
(Mémoires, p. 126).

53 For example Maurice Besset (Qui était Le Corbusier?, p. 200).

54 This letter from Gropius was sent to Le Corbusier in 1924 along
with the new book Weimar-Bauten, Walter Gropius und Adolf Meyer.
Another book, Paul Klopfer's Von der Seele der Baukunst (Dessau, 1926?),
was also sent to Le Corbusier as "Le Corbusier-Saugnier." And as late
as 1965, in an article written by Lucien Schwob (a friend of Le Corbusier's
from La Chaux-de-Fonds), it is stated unequivocally that "Le Corbusier-
Saugnier" was Jeanneret's pseudonym alone--and even that it was the name
of "one of his distant French ancestors" (La Gazette de Lausanne, No. 206,
4 September 1965, p. 18 of the "Gazette littéraire" section).

55 Another source of antagonism between them seems to have been
disagreement over the dating of their early Purist paintings. In Le
Corbusier's library, a copy of the seventh issue of L'esprit nouveau,
which includes an article on Ozenfant and Jeanneret's paintings, contains extensive annotations by Le Corbusier in which he changes the
dates of the paintings and angrily accuses Ozenfant of lying in order
to make his paintings appear the earlier ones.

56 Ozenfant, Mémoires, p. 102.

Chapter VI

1 " . . . les cubes, les cônes, les sphères, les cylindres ou les
pyramides sont les grandes formes primaires que la lumière révèle bien;
l'image nous en est nette et tangible, sans ambiguïté" (Vers une architecture, p. 16).

[2] See Chapter V, note 49.

[3] This can be seen in Le Corbusier's early sketches for this project, reproduced in Oeuvre complète 1910-1929, pp. 60-61.

[4] Oeuvre complète, 1910-1929, p. 49.

[5] Le bulletin de la vie artistique, 15 septembre 1924, p. 419.

[6] For example: Oeuvre complète, 1910-1929, p. 45

[7] Oeuvre complète, 1910-1929, p. 45.

[8] This is seen in a number of ways in the LaRoche-Jeanneret houses. For example, the normal and efficient concrete floor-slab with ribs is employed here, but was left exposed by Le Corbusier only in the cellar where it would not be seen; elsewhere, it was either covered over, to appear perfectly smooth as in the Dom-Ino system, or else a different material altogether was used for spanning--as seems to be the case with the ceiling of the "galérie." Furthermore, many of the walls in this house (as in many of Le Corbusier's other buildings) are made of concrete block, but are plastered over and painted like all the other walls, with the result that everything looks like poured concrete. All in all, there is little real expression of the realities of reinforced-concrete construction in these houses.

[9] These "five points" seem to have been set forth by Le Corbusier first in Oeuvre complète, 1910-1929, pp. 128-29 (where they are included among the designs done in 1926, suggesting that he first formulated them in that year--although they had appeared, individually, in his work before then).

[10] See Chapter IV, p. 124, and note 46.

[11] For example in the LaRoche-Jeanneret houses.

[12] Oeuvre complète, 1910-1929, p. 129. These sketches purport to show that a room with two traditional windows is less than one-third as well lighted as a room with a narrow horizontal window of little more area than the two other windows together. This obviously does not make sense; and although the sketches are only diagrammatic and thus maybe could be excused for their inaccuracy, the point is that Le Corbusier is attempting to justify his preference rationally, and is not convincing.

[13] For example in Almanach d'architecture moderne (Paris, 1926?), pp. 95-97.

[14] Le Corbusier may have got the idea of using ramps in architecture from automobile ramps, either in garages, or in auto factories--such as that which he illustrated in Vers une architecture, p. 242.

15 *Vers une architecture*, p. 115. Subsequent page-references are also to this book, unless otherwise noted.

16 Page 109.

17 Pages 111-12.

18 Page 106.

19 Page 110.

20 Page 107.

21 Page 114.

22 Page 192.

23 Page 193.

24 Page 223.

25 *Urbanisme*, p. 21.

26 *Urbanisme*, pp. 21-22. Also see above, Chapter V, p. 160.

27 Incidentally, it is worth mentioning that later in his career, Le Corbusier was to make these two aspects interact in more dynamic ways--for example by having the arbitrary patterns of nature actually thread through, or under, the man-made urban geometry of his city-plans. But the symbolic meaning of these two aspects seems to have remained the same for Le Corbusier, and these later variations tend to heighten, if anything, the sense of contrast between the abstraction of Man's mind and the chaos of nature.

28 *Vers une architecture*, p. 57.

29 Page 57.

30 Page 54.

31 Marcel Dieulafoy, *L'art antique de la Perse* (Paris, 1885), vol. IV, p. 28. Jeanneret's sketches of these diagrams are in his notebook "A-2," on pages 77 and 79 (see Chapter IV, note 8).

32 Indeed, we are tempted to suggest that Jeanneret, with his rather weak background in the structural and technical areas of architecture, was especially attracted to the notion of an abstract or mystical system which could determine (or help to determine) structural forms themselves. This is later implied by Le Corbusier in his description of Dieulafoy's diagrams when he writes that "Once the conception of the cupola was established. . .in accordance with the static data of the constructive

principles applied to it, the regulating line comes in to rectify, correct, give point to and pull together. . ." (_Vers une architecture_, p. 58). To Le Corbusier, "tracés régulateurs" could even "correct" and "rectify" structural calculation—just as he later felt his Modulor system could (as for example in his use of Modulor dimensions for the floor-slab thicknesses in his Unités d'habitation—as Peter Collins pointed out in a review of _The Modulor_ in _The Architectural Review_, July 1954).

[33] Auguste Perret, _Contribution à une théorie de l'architecture_, pp. 47-49.

[34] Quoted in Peter Collins, _Concrete_, p. 200.

APPENDIX A

CATALOGUE OF JEANNERET'S LIBRARY UP TO 1920

This catalogue lists the books and other items in Le Corbusier's personal library--presently in the Fondation Le Corbusier--which were published before 1921. It is drawn from a larger catalogue which I compiled of the items published before 1930, which was mimeographed by the Fondation Le Corbusier in 1970.

Naturally, the publication-date of a book is not necessarily the same as the year Le Corbusier acquired it; so this catalogue represents only the rough beginning of my attempt to reconstruct Jeanneret's early reading. Some of these books are inscribed with the year Jeanneret acquired them (inscribed either by Jeanneret himself or by someone who gave him the book); and in these cases the inscription-date is noted in this catalogue between brackets, following the entry--e.g. /insc. 1912_7. Other ways in which I was able to determine the acquisition-dates of Le Corbusier's books are described in Appendix C and elsewhere in this dissertation. Furthermore, as I studied Le Corbusier's library, it became apparent that he almost always preferred to read new books; only occasionally did he acquire old books (one exception to this is a group of nineteenth-century books, all inscribed by Jeanneret "sept 1916," which were apparently given to him by a relative).

Several books in Le Corbusier's library have been omitted from this catalogue--including some books in Russian and Japanese, and some whose pages were never cut.

I. Books and Pamphlets, by Author

d'Annunzio, Gabriele, Le martyre de Saint Sébastien, Paris, 1911.

Apollinaire, Guillaume, Les mamelles de Tirésias; drame surréaliste, Paris, 1917.

     Le poète assassiné, Paris, 1916.

Arioste, Roland Furieux, Paris, 1844.

Baedeker, Grèce, Leipzig, 1910.

     Italie centrale; Rome, Leipzig, n.d.

     Italie des Alpes à Naples, Paris, 1909.

Balzac, Honoré de, Oeuvres illustrées de Balzac, vol. 4, Paris, 1852.

Barrès, Maurice, La colline inspirée, Paris, 1913. [insc. 1916]

Basin, J., Leçons de physique, Paris, 1901.

Baudelaire, Charles, Les fleurs du mal, Paris, n.d. [insc. 1909]

Baudot, Anatole de, L'architecture, le passé, le présent, Paris, 1916.

Bennett, Edward, Plan of Minneapolis, Minneapolis, 1917.

Boccioni, Umberto, Manifeste technique de la sculpture futuriste, Milan, 1912.

Boissonas, Fred., Athènes moderne, Genève, 1920.

     L'Épire, berceau des grecs, Genève, 1915.

     L'image de la Serbie, Genève, 1919.

     Salonique, Genève, 1919.

     Smyrne, Genève, 1919.

Bonnier, Gaston, L'enchaînement des organismes, Paris, n.d.

Breuil, Henri, et al., Peintures et gravures murales des cavernes paleolithiques, 2 vols., Monaco, 1910, 1912.

Byron, George Gordon Lord, Don Juan, Paris, 1904.

Cain, Georges, Le long des rues, Paris, 1913.

Cain, Georges, Promenades dans Paris, Paris, n.d. (1912?).

Casanova, Jacques, Mémoires, Paris, n.d.

Cendrars, Blaise, La fin du monde, Paris, 1919.

Cervantes, L'admirable Don Quichotte. . ., vol. 2, Paris, n.d. (1869?).

Chapuis, Albert, Histoire de la pendulerie neuchâteloise, Paris, 1917.

       La montre chinoise, Neuchatel, 1919. ⌐insc. 1919⌐

Chateaubriand, F.-R. de, René, Paris, 1917.

Choisy, Auguste, Histoire de l'architecture, 2 vols., Paris, n.d. ⌐insc. 191

Cingria-Vaneyre, Alexandre, Les entretiens de la Villa du Rouet, Genève,
    1908. ⌐insc. 1910⌐

Claudel, Paul, L'annonce faite à Marie, Paris, 1912.

       Connaissance de l'Est, Paris, 1907. ⌐insc. 1909⌐

Collignon, Maxime, Mythologie figurée de la Grèce, Paris, n.d. ⌐insc. 1903⌐

       Le Parthénon, Paris, n.d. (1912?).

Courrier, P.-L., Oeuvres de Courrier, Paris, 1848.

Cousin, Victor, Du vrai, du beau et du bien, Paris, 1904. ⌐insc. 1910⌐

Dante Alighieri, La divine comédie, Paris, n.d. (1908?). ⌐insc. 1910⌐

Denis, Maurice, Théories, 1890-1910, Paris, 1912. ⌐insc. 1912⌐

Dezobry & Bachelet, Dictionnaire général de biographie et d'histoire
    de mythologie, 2 vols., Paris, 1889.

Diderot, Denis, La religieuse, Paris, n.d. (1917?).

Dostöïevsky, L'idiot, 2 vols., Paris, n.d.

Flammarion, Camille, Astronomie populaire, Paris, 1880.

Flaubert, Gustave, Bouvard et Pécuchet, Paris, n.d.

       Salammbô, Paris, 1908. ⌐insc. 1909⌐

Fromentin, Eugène, Les maîtres d'autrefois, Paris, 1902.

Garnier, Tony, Une cité industrielle: étude pour la construction des
    villes, Paris, n.d. (1917).

Goethe, Le Faust, Lausanne, 1895. ⌐insc. 1916⌐

Hausenstein, Wilhelm, Der nackte Mensch in der Kunst, München, 1913.

Hegemann, Werner, Der Städtbau, nach den ergebnissen der allgemeinen Städtebau-Ausstellung in Berlin. . ., 2 vols., Berlin, 1911, 1913.

Homère, L'Iliade, Paris, n.d. (1909?).

　　　　L'Odyssée, Paris, n.d. ⌐insc. 1909⌐

Huysmans, J.-K., La cathédrale, Paris, 1908. ⌐insc. 1909⌐

Jeanneret, Charles-Édouard, Étude sur le mouvement d'art décoratif en Allemagne, La Chaux-de-Fonds, 1912.

Joly, Auguste, Le futurisme et la philosophie, reprinted article from La Belgique artistique et littéraire, July 1912.

Kipling, Rudyard, Le livre de la jungle, Paris, 1916. ⌐insc. 1917⌐

Knackfuss, H., Michelangelo, Leipzig, 1903.

Laforgue, Jules, Moralités légendaires, Paris, 1909. ⌐insc. 1909⌐

LeBon, Gustave, La civilisation des arabes, Paris, 1884.

　　　　Les civilisations de l'Inde, Paris, 1887. ⌐insc. 1909⌐

　　　　L'évolution de la matière, Paris, 1919.

　　　　Les premières civilisations, Paris, n.d. (1888?).

London, Jack, Le fils du loup, Paris, 1920.

Maillefer, Paul, Abrégé d'histoire général, Lausanne, 1914.

Mallarmé, Stéphane, Vers et prose, Paris, 1912. ⌐insc. 1914⌐

Marinetti, F. T., Manifeste du futurisme, Milan, n.d.

　　　　Supplément au manifeste technique de la littérature futuriste, Milan, 1912.

Meier-Graefe, Julius, Paul Cézanne, München, 1910.

Menard, Louis, Histoire des anciens peuples de l'Orient, Paris, 1883. ⌐insc. 1909⌐

Michelet, J., Jeanne d'Arc, Paris, 1899. ⌐insc. 1916⌐

Montaigne, <u>Essais de Montaigne</u>, vols. 3, 5, 6, 7, 9, London, 1754.

    <u>Les essais</u>, Paris, n.d.

Munier, Amedée, <u>Traité de lithographie</u>, Reims, 1898.

Müntz, Eugène, Raphaël, <u>sa vie, son oeuvre et son temps</u>, Paris, 1900.
    [insc. 1902]

Musset, Alfred de, <u>Premières poésies, 1829-1835</u>, Paris, 1867. [insc. 1916]

Nansen, Fridtjof, <u>Vers le pôle</u>, Paris, n. d. (1897?).

Nietzsche, Frédéric, <u>Ainsi parlait Zarathoustra</u>, Paris, 1908.

Ozenfant & Jeanneret, <u>Après le cubisme</u>, Paris, 1918.

Paris, Gaston, <u>François Villon</u>, Paris, 1901.

Paul, Bruno, <u>Typenmoebel für Stadt und Land</u>, München, n.d.

Perrochet, Ed., <u>Étude sur la Chronique des Chanoines de Neuchâtel</u>,
    Neuchâtel, 1914. [insc. 1914]

Plutarque, <u>Manuel moral des enfans, ou maximes</u>, Amsterdam, 1786. [insc. 1916]

Poincaré, H., <u>Science et méthode</u>, Paris, 1920. [insc. 1920]

Poe, Edgar, <u>Eureka</u>, Paris, 1887. [insc. 1916]

Praportchetovitch, L., <u>Baraquement pliant démontable "Stella"</u>, Paris, 1920.

Proust, Marcel, <u>A l'ombre des jeunes filles en fleurs</u>, Paris, 1919.

    <u>Du côté de chez Swann</u>, Paris, 1919.

Provensal, Henry, <u>L'art de demain</u>, Paris, 1904.

Reinach, Salomon, <u>Apollo: histoire générale des arts plastiques</u>, Paris,
    1907.

Renan, Ernest, <u>Prière sur l'Acropole</u>, Athènes, n.d.

    <u>Vie de Jésus</u>, Paris, n.d. (1906?).

Reutter, Louis, <u>Fragments d'architecture neuchâteloise, aux 16e-18e siècles</u>,
    Neuchâtel, 1914.

Richard & Quentin, <u>Nouveaux dialogues. . . français-anglais</u>, Paris, 1899.

Ritter, William, <u>Edmond de Pury</u>, Genève, 1913. [insc. 1914]

Ritter, William, L'entêtement slovaque, Paris, 1910. ⌐insc. 1910⌐

    Études d'art étranger, Paris, 1906. ⌐insc. 1915⌐

    Fillette slovaque, Paris, 1903. ⌐insc. 1913⌐

    Myrtis et Korinna, Paris, 1898.

Roller, Théophile, Les catacombes de Rome, 2 vols., Paris, n.d. (1881?).

Rousseau, J.-J., Les confessions, Paris, n.d. ⌐insc. 1909⌐

    Du contrat social, Paris, n.d.

    Oeuvres illustrées de Rousseau, Paris, 1851.

Ruskin, John, Les matins à Florence, Paris, 1906.

Sabatier, Paul, Vie de Saint François d'Assise, Paris, n.d.

Schilling, Martin, Catalog mathematischer Modelle. . ., Leipzig, 1911.

Schuré, Édouard, Les grands initiés, Paris, 1908. ⌐insc. 1907⌐

Shakespeare, William, The Sonnets, London, 1896.

Sloan, Maurice, The Concrete House & Its Construction, Philadelphia, 1912.

Sorel, Charles, Francion, Paris, 1909. ⌐insc. 1915⌐

Taine, Hippolyte, Voyage en Italie, 2 vols., Paris, 1907.

Taut, Bruno, Architektur-Schauspiel für symphonische Musik, Hagen, 1920.

    Die Auflösung der Städte, Hagen, 1920.

Töpffer, R., Le Docteur Festus, Paris, n.d.

Viollet-le-duc, Dictionnaire raisonné de l'architecture française du XIe au XVIe siècle, 10 vols., Paris, 1854 ff. ⌐ insc. 1908 ⌐

Vollard, Ambroise, Paul Cézanne, Paris, 1919.

Wordsworth, C., La Grèce, pittoresque et historique, Paris, 1841..⌐insc. 1916⌐

II. Exhibition Catalogues and Unauthored Books.

Anthologie des écrivains français du XVIe siècle: prose, Paris, n.d.

Architecture en Italie, 6 vols., Paris, n.d. (1907?).

Les Ballets Russes à Paris, (Theatre du Châtelet, Paris, mai 1917).

Catalogue des moulages en vente au palais du Louvre, Paris, 1908.

La Chaux-de-Fonds, La Chaux-de-Fonds, 1894.

Les chefs-d'oeuvre d'Ingres, Paris, n.d. /insc. 1914_7

Fontaine et Cie., Album de serrurerie décorative, Paris, n.d.

Jahrbuch des deutschen Werkbundes: die Kunst in Industrie und Handel, Jena, 1913.

Manuel d'algèbre et de trigonométrie, Tours, n.d.

Un mouvement d'art à La Chaux-de-Fonds, La Chaux-de-Fonds, 1914.

Plans de Paris. . ., Paris, 1908.

La sainte Bible, ("La Bible d'Ostervald"), Neuchâtel, 1744.

Salons d'architecture, Paris, 1913.

Schlussbericht über den internationalen Wettbewerb für einen Bebauungsplan der Stadt Zürich, Zürich, 1919.

III. Periodicals

Art et décoration, mars 1899, juin 1908, janvier 1914.

L'art et les artistes, mars 1914 (cover only).

Les arts français, No. 8, 1917.

Les cahiers d'aujourd'hui, juin 1913 (Adolf Loos's article only).

Deutsche Bauzeitung, Sonderabdruck, 1914.

Deutsche Kunst und Dekoration, Feb. 1906.

L'Élan, avril 1915 - décembre 1916.

L'Esprit nouveau, octobre 1920. ff.

Les Voix. . . La Chaux-de-Fonds, octobre 1919.

CHRONOLOGY OF JEANNERET'S READING UP TO 1920

This chronological breakdown attempts to list the books which
Jeanneret acquired and read in each of the important periods of his
youth: before 1908 (La Chaux-de-Fonds), 1908-09 (Paris), 1910-11 (Germany
and the Orient), 1912-16 (La Chaux-de-Fonds), and 1917-20 (Paris). For
each of these periods, there are three categories of books listed here:

a. Those books in Le Corbusier's library which contain clear
evidence of when they were acquired by Jeanneret. This evidence may be
either: the acquisition date itself inscribed in the book (noted here for
example "insc. 1908"); or Jeanneret's signature (noted here "sign.") when
this signature can be shown to belong to a specific period (see Appendix C);
or some other revealing inscription or annotation by Jeanneret (such as
the noting of one of his temporary addresses).

b. Those books in Le Corbusier's library which contain no specific
evidence of acquisition, but which can be assigned hypothetically to one
of these periods—either by a signature or annotation, or simply by the
publication-date itself (if it seems likely that Jeanneret acquired the
book in this period). In both of these categories—a. and b.—the books
are listed only by their short titles, since their full titles are given
in Appendix A.

c. Books which are not in Le Corbusier's library, but which we know
he read—either because he later mentioned having read them at a specific

time in his youth, or because they are mentioned in his youthful notebooks, or through some other evidence. For each of the books, this
evidence is described in parentheses after the bibliographical entry.

It hardly needs to be pointed out here that Jeanneret obviously also
read books of which we now have no knowledge; so this chronology makes no
pretensions to being a complete record of Jeanneret's early reading.

I. Before 1908

a. Known Acquisition-Date: Müntz, Raphaël, 1900 (insc. 1902); Collignon,
Mythologie, n.d. (insc. 1903); Schuré, Grands initiés, 1908 (insc. 1907--
see Chapter I, note 43, about this discrepancy); Knackfuss, Michelangelo,
1903 (sign.); Provensal, Art de demain, 1904 (sign.); Ruskin, Matins,
1906 (sign.); Taine, Voyage, 1907 (sign.).

⌈N.B. The date following the title is the publication-date of the book.

b. Hypothetical Acquisition-Date: Flammarion, Astronomie, 1880; LeBon,
Civilisations des arabes, 1884; LeBon, Premières civilisations, 1888?;
Nansen, Vers le pôle, 1897?; Munier, Lithographie, 1898; Richard,
Dialogues, 1899; Basin, Leçons de physique, 1901; Fromentin, Maîtres,
1902; Manuel d'algèbre, n.d. Also in this category can be listed
several old books which probably belonged to the Jeanneret family:
La sainte Bible, 1744; Montaigne, Essais, 1754; Arioste, Roland Furieux,
1844; Courrier, Oeuvres, 1848; Rousseau, Oeuvres, 1851; Balzac, Oeuvres,
1852; Cervantes, Don Quichotte, 1869?; Dezobry, Dictionnaire, 1889;
La Chaux-de-Fonds, 1894; Shakespeare, Sonnets, 1896.

c. Books not in Jeanneret's Library but which he is known to have read:
Eugène Grasset, Méthode de composition ornementale, Paris, 1905 (mentioned in Gautier, Le Corbusier, p. 27).

Owen Jones, A Grammar of Ornament (mentioned in Le Corbusier, Atelier de la recherche patiente, p. 24).

John Ruskin, Lectures on Architecture and Painting (see Chapt. I, Note 17).

Toepffer, Voyage en Zigzag (Von Moos, Le Corbusier, p. 13).

II. 1908-1909

a. Known Acquisition-Date: Viollet-le-duc, Dictionnaire, 1854 (insc. 1908); Baudelaire, Fleurs du mal, n.d. (insc. 1909); Claudel, Connaissance, 1907 (insc. 1909); Flaubert, Salammbô, 1908 (insc. 1909); Homère Odyssée, n.d. (insc. 1909); Huysmans, La cathédrale, 1908 (insc. 1909); Laforgue, Moralités, 1909 (insc. 1909); LeBon, Civilisations de l'Inde, 1887 (insc. 1909); Ménard, Histoire, 1883 (insc. 1909); Rousseau, Confessions, n.d. (insc. 1909); Nietzsche, Zarathoustra, 1908 (inscribed with Quai St. Michel address in Paris); Renan, Vie de Jésus, 1906 (inscribed with Quai St. Michel address in Paris).

b. Hypothetical Acquisition-Date: Homère, Iliade, 1909? (sign.); Dostoïevsky, L'idiot, n.d.; Byron, Don Juan, 1904; Catalogue des moulages. . .au Louvre, 1908.

c. Not in Jeanneret's library but which he is known to have read: Corroyer, Architecture Romane (see Chapt. II, p. 50).

III. 1910-1911

a. Known Acquisition-Date: Cingria-Vaneyre, Entretiens, 1908 (insc. 1910); Cousin, Du vrai, 1904 (insc. 1910); Dante, Divine comédie, 1908? (insc. 1910); Ritter, Entêtement, 1910 (insc. 1910).

b. Hypothetical Acquisition-Date: Baedeker, Grèce, 1910; Baedeker, Italie des Alpes, 1909; Meier-Graefe, Cézanne, 1910; Paul, Typenmoebel, n.d.;

Renan, Prière, n.d.; Schilling, Catalog mathematischer Modelle, 1911.

IV. 1912-1916

a. Known Acquisition-Date: Denis, Théories, 1912 (insc. 1912); Choisy, Histoire, n.d. (insc. 1913); Ritter, Fillette, 1903 (insc. 1913); Ritter, E. de Pury, 1913 (insc. 1914); Perrochet, Neuchâtel, 1914 (insc. 1914); Mallarmé, Vers, 1912 (insc. 1914); Chefs d'oeuvre d'Ingres, n.d. (insc. 1914); Sorel, Francion, 1909 (insc. 1915); Ritter, Études, 1906 (insc. 1915); Barrès, Colline, 1913 (insc. 1916); Huysmans, Ste. Lydwine, 1915, (insc. 1916); Jahrbuch. . .Werkbundes, 1913 (see Chapt. III, Note 18). Also, there are six books inscribed by Jeanneret "sept. 1916," which apparently came from the Soutter family (related to him on his mother's side): Goethe, Faust; Michelet, Jeanne d'Arc; Musset, Poésies, Plutarque, Manuel moral; Poe, Eureka; Wordsworth, Grèce.

b. Hypothetical Acquisition-Date: d'Annunzio, Martyre, 1911; Baedeker, Italie centrale, n.d.; Boccionni, Manifeste, 1912; Boissonas, L'Épire, 1915; Breuil, Peintures, 1910 & 1912; Cain, Le long, 1913; Cain, Promenades, 1912; Claudel, Annonce, 1912; Collignon, Parthenon, 1912?; Hausenstein, Nackte Mensch, 1913; Hegemann, Städtebau, 1911 & 1913; Joly, Futurisme, 1912; Marinetti, Manifeste, n.d.; Marinetti, Supplément, 1912; Reutter, Fragments, 1914; Ritter, Myrtis, 1898; Roller, Catacombes, 1881?; Sloan, Concrete, 1912; Architecture en Italie, 1907?; Salons d'architecture, 1913.

c. Not in Jeanneret's library but which he is known to have read: Georges Benoît-Lévy, La cité-jardin (mentioned in Jeanneret's Sketchbook "A-2;" see Chapt. IV, p.128).
Marcel Dieulafoy, L'art antique de la Perse (see Chapt. VI, Note 31.)

Chipiez & Perrot, <u>Histoire de l'art dans l'antiquité</u>, 1882 (mentioned
in Jeanneret's Sketchbook "A-2").

V. 1917-1920

a. Known Acquisition-Date: <u>BalletsRusses</u>, 1917 (see Chapt. V, p. 137);
Kipling, <u>Livre de la jungle</u>, 1916 (insc. 1917); Chapuis, <u>La montre</u>,
1919? (insc. 1919).

b. Hypothetical Acquisition-Date: Baudot, <u>Architecture</u>, 1916; Apollinaire,
<u>Poète assassiné</u>, 1916; Apollinaire, <u>Les mamelles</u>, 1917; Chateaubriand,
<u>René</u>, 1917; Chapuis, <u>Histoire</u>, 1917?; Diderot, <u>La religieuse</u>, 1917?;
Garnier, <u>Cité industrielle</u>, 1917; Boissonas, <u>Serbie</u>, 1919; **Boissonas**,
<u>Salonique</u>, 1919; Boissonas, <u>Smyrne</u>, 1919; Cendrars, <u>Fin du monde</u>, 1919;
LeBon, <u>Évolution</u>, 1919; Proust, <u>A l'ombre</u>, 1919; Proust, <u>Du côté</u>, 1919;
Vollard, <u>Cézanne</u>, 1919; <u>Schlussbericht. . .Stadt Zürich</u>, 1919; Boissonas,
<u>Athènes moderne</u>, 1920; Hildebrandt, <u>Wandmalerei</u>, 1920; London, <u>Fils</u>,
1920; Praportchetovitch, <u>Baraquement</u>, 1920; Taut, <u>Architektur-Schauspiel</u>,
1920; Taut, <u>Auflösung</u>, 1920.

JEANNERET'S SIGNATURES IN HIS BOOKS

As part of my attempt to determine the chronology of Jeanneret's reading, I examined the signatures which he inscribed in many of his books. Most of these inscriptions consist of a date as well as a signature; but several of the most interesting early books contain only the signature--so it seemed to me that by examining the evolution of Jeanneret's signature from the dated inscriptions, these undated ones perhaps could be dated. Furthermore, establishing the pattern of development of Jeanneret's early signature could prove useful in dating other material besides these books. I made tracings of as many of these book-signatures as I could find; and photocopies of these tracings are included in this appendix.

Several overall points were immediately apparent. First, Jeanneret's signature seems never to be inscribed in his books after about 1925. Before then, there are two clearly separate periods--the dividing line being around 1917 or 1918. After 1918, only a few of the books are signed; the signature seems always to be on the cover of the book, always in pencil, and never dated; and all the examples are either of a "Jt" monogram form, or simply the surname "Jeanneret" (see examples of these post-1918 signatures in Part III of this appendix).

The signatures which are of most interest to us are those before 1918. They are almost always in ink; and they are always in the form

"Ch. E. Jeanneret." Beyond that, there are few constants. But the variations, as it turns out, reveal patterns which allow us to describe the evolution of Jeanneret's signature in his early years. Twenty-seven of these signatures are dated; and three more include an address from Jeanneret's first stay in Paris and thus in effect are dated. These inscriptions are numbered 1 to 30 in this appendix, and are described in Part I. There are nine undated signatures in books published before 1918. They are lettered A to J, and discussed in Part II in terms of the conclusions of Part I.

I. The Dated Signatures (see tracings 1 to 30)

All of Jeanneret's dated inscriptions are dated before 1918; they are all in ink (except for the last one, 1917); and the signature is always in the form "Ch. E. Jeanneret." They are arranged here in chronological order--to the extent that this can be determined. Further- more, three inscriptions are included here which contain Paris addresses dating them to the period 1908-09. The inscription with the "rue des Écoles" address (see No. 1) must date from early 1908--since Jeanneret lived there only briefly, soon after arriving in Paris (Gauthier, Le Corbusier, p. 25). The two inscriptions with the "quai St. Michel" address cannot be pinpointed this closely (since Jeanneret lived there during much of 1908 and 1909), but have been tentatively placed on this list as Nos. 2 and 3, based on their formal relationships to the other signatures.

Examination of all of these dated signatures reveals that they fall clearly into two main groups--the first going up to 1910, and the second from 1910 to 1917. In the first of these periods (see Nos. 1 to about 13), the initials "Ch. E" are completely separate, whereas in the second period they become connected, developing into a kind of stylized succession of connected strokes which becomes progressively more abstract. As a result of this the dots after these initials are dropped, and the signature in general becomes much bolder and more cursive. Nos. 14 to 30 show the consistent development of this process. Indeed, No. 13 and No. 14, both dated "nov. 1910" and inscribed "Neu-Babelsberg" (the suburb of Berlin where Peter Behrens had his architectural office) seem to reveal the precise dividing-line of these two periods: No. 13 is thoroughly typical of the signatures before then; but No. 14 is a kind of transition to the new signature, with the initials joined, but not as boldly as thereafter, and with one of the dots retained.

Other characteristics of the second period include a completely different way of writing the "J," and can be seen by comparing the inscriptions before and after 1910. All in all, these two periods constitute completely different types of signatures; and it has turned out to be easy to place the undated signatures accordingly. As it is, all of them prove to be of the first period. This is perhaps not surprising when we notice another characteristic of the second-period inscriptions: all of them are dated in a standard way, with both the month and year-- whereas before 1910, sometimes the month is given, sometimes only the year, sometimes only an address. So it seems that by 1910, Jeanneret had adopted a standard way of inscribing his books, which included the date. Another aspect of this standard inscription after 1910 is that the signature is always inside the book rather than on the cover, as it sometimes is before 1910.

II. The Undated Signatures in Books Published Before 1918

There are nine of these undated signatures (see tracings A to J), although several of them appear in the same books (three in Provensal's book and two each in the Knackfuss and the Taine). They are arranged here in the order of the publication-dates of the books--although, as we shall see, this is not necessarily the chronological order of the signatures themselves.

A quick examination of these signatures reveals that, as mentioned above, they all clearly belong in the pre-1910 group. When we compare them more closely with the dated signatures, we see furthermore that two of them (E and J) can be associated specifically with the dated signatures of 1909 in Paris (compare them for example with Nos. 5 to 8). But the other six undated signatures are quite different in many respects from any of the dated signatures: they are in a smaller, neater, tighter hand, and certain letters are written differently--such as the "t," which is crossed in a more conventional way with two strokes, and the "h," which is written in an odd hooked way which is found only in a couple of the earliest of the dated signatures (Nos. 1, 2, and 4). All of these characteristics suggest that these six undated signatures (A to D and F to H) are earlier than any of the dated signatures, that is to say that they are before 1908. When we put these undated signatures before the Paris-period signatures, we see a clear development from the neat, small hand of an adolescent (just like Jeanneret's annotations in his earliest books) to a progressively larger, more simplified and bolder hand. And indeed, our conclusion that these six signatures are pre-1908 is verified by the fact

that three of them are also inscribed "La Chaux-de-Fonds"—since the
only other period Jeanneret spent in La Chaux-de-Fonds was 1912-17, while
as we have seen, these signatures are definitely pre-1910.

As suggested above, it is in fact reasonable that these undated
signatures should be earlier than the dated signatures, for as we saw,
Jeanneret in 1909 and 1910 adopted a more-or-less standard way of signing
his books, which included the date; but in his youth, in La Chaux-de-
Fonds, he had not yet begun dating his signatures. Furthermore, when
we look more closely at these undated signatures in terms of the development from a small, neat hand toward a bolder hand, those which seem
to be the earliest of all (B, C and D) have no address, whereas those
which seem to be later (A, F and H) are those accompanied by "La Chaux-
de-Fonds"—suggesting that even the inclusion of this address came
relatively late (perhaps around 1906 or 1907).

In conclusion, we can suggest when these books were signed by the
young Jeanneret. Provensal's L'art de demain contains three signatures:
two of these (C and D) seem to be among the earliest of all the signatures, and probably date from 1904 or 1905 (a suggestion which is supported by other evidence in this book; see Chapter I, note 25). But the
third signature (E) was added by Jeanneret in 1909 in Paris (which is
understandable since in 1909 he seems to have decided to sign all of his
books on the title page; see Nos. 5 to 11). Knackfuss's Michelangelo
contains two signatures: the one on the book jacket (B) looks very early,
perhaps around 1904; but the one on the title page of the book (A) is
later, prabably around 1906 or 1907. Taine's Voyage en Italie also
contains two signatures (G and H), and both of these look late, probably
about 1907 (consistent with the fact that the publication-date of the

book obviates their being any earlier). The signature in Ruskin's Les matins à Florence (F) is very similar to these last two, and is also probably about 1907. And the signature in Homer's Iliad (J), as mentioned above, is thoroughly consistent with Jeanneret's dated signatures of 1909 in Paris.

III. Signatures in Books Published After 1918

Jeanneret's signatures after about 1917 or 1918 are totally different from those before that time. First of all, they are not common: only about a half-dozen items of that period in Le Corbusier's library are signed at all; and by 1925, they seem to have disappeared altogether (perhaps part of the phasing-out of the "Jeanneret" side of Le Corbusier's personality). All of them are found on books and catalogues published from 1921 to 1924. All of them are in pencil; all of them are written on the cover; and none of them have a date or any other information. For all these reasons, they seem casual, almost more like doodles than the formal sort of inscriptions Jeanneret regularly put in his earlier books. There are two types of these late signatures (see the tracings):

Type I is a kind of monogram of the letters "Jt," presumably for "Jeanneret." It appears on the covers of: Maurice Raynal, Picasso (München, 1921); L. Kassak, Buch neuer Künstler (Wien, 1922); and three Hotel Drouot sales catalogues (30 May 1921, 17 Nov. 1921, and 4 July 1922).

Type II is simply the name "Jeanneret." It occurs on the covers of: Charles Lalo, La beauté et l'instinct sexuel (Paris, 1922); Jean Cocteau, Thomas l'imposteur (Paris, 1923); and Louis Aragon, Le libertinage (Paris, 1924).

I. Tracings of the Dated Signatures

1. Schuré, Les grands initiés (half-title page)

2. Renan, Vie de Jésus (title page)

3. Nietzsche, Zarathoustra (title page)

4. Ménard, Histoire des anciens... (half-title page)

5. Flaubert, Salammbô (title page)

6. Baudelaire, Fleurs du mal (title page)

Signature	Reference
Ch. E. Jeanneret *Paris* *aout 1909* *3 quai St Michel*	7. Rousseau, Les confessions (title page)
Ch. E. Jeanneret *3 quai St. Michel* *Paris 1909* *Sept. —*	8. Claudel, Connaissance. . . (title page)
Ch E. Jeanneret *Paris 1909 —*	9. Homère, L'Odyssée (title page)
Ch. E. Jeanneret *3 quai St Michel* *Paris* *oct 1909*	10. Laforgue, Moralités. . . (title page)
Ch. E. Jeanneret *Paris* *décembre 1909*	11. Huysmans, La cathédrale (title page)
Ch. E. Jeanneret *münich mai* *1910*	12. Cousin, Du vrai, . . . (title page)

Ch. E. Jeanneret

nov. 1910 à Neu-Babelsberg

13. Cingria-Vaneyre,
Entretiens
(half-title page)

Ch. E. Jeanneret

Neu-Babelsberg 1910
Novembre

14. Dante, La
divine comédie
(half-title page)

Ch. E. Jeanneret

nov 1912

la Chaux —

15. Denis,
Théories
(half-title page)

Ch. E. Jeanneret

Paris noël 1913

16. Choisy,
Histoire...
(half-title page)

Ch. E. Jeanneret

janvᵉʳ 1914

la Chaux-de-Fonds

17. Ritter, Edmond
de Pury
(title page)

Ch. E. Jeanneret

la Chaux-de-Fonds

juillet 1914

18. Perrochet,
Étude...
(inside front
cover)

Cst Jeanneret
oct 1914
la Chaux....

19. Mallarmé,
Vers et Prose
(half-title page)

Cw Jeanneret
oct 1914

20. Les chefs-d'oeuvre
d'Ingres
(half-title page)

(-1)E Jeanneret
La Chaux, décembre 1915

21. Sorel, Francion
(half-title page)

CwE Jeanneret
La Chaux, mar 1916

22. Barrès, La
colline inspirée
(title page)

La Chaux, mar 1916 CwE Jeanneret

23. Huysmans,
Sainte Lydwine
(title page)

CwE Jeanneret
sept 1916

24. Goethe, Faust

(25-29 are the same:
Michelet, Jeanne d'Arc;
de Musset, Poésies;
Plutarque, Manuel moral;
Poe, Eureka; Wordsworth,
Grèce. These came from
the Soutter family).

CiE Jeanneret
août 7917

30. Kipling, Livre
de la jungle
(half-title page)

II. The Undated Signatures (in books published before 1918)

Ch. E. Jeanneret. *La Chaux-de-Fonds.*	A. Knackfuss, Michelangelo, 1903 (title page)
Ch. E. Jeanneret.	B. Knackfuss, Michelangelo, 1903 (book jacket)
Ch. E. Jeanneret	C. Provensal, L'art de demain, 1904 (cover of book)
Ch. E. Jeanneret	D. Provensal, L'art de demain, 1904 (half-title page)
Ch. E. Jeanneret	E. Provensal, L'art de demain, 1904 (title page)

Ch. E. Jeanneret
La Chaux-de-Fonds.

F. Ruskin, Les matins
à Florence, 1906
(half-title page)

Ch. E. Jeanner....

G. Taine, Voyage en
Italie, 1907
(cover of vol. I)

Ch. E. Jeanneret
La Chaux-de-Fonds.

H. Taine, Voyage en
Italie, 1907
(half-title page
of vol. II)

Ch. E. Jeanneret

J. Homère, L'Iliade,
n.d., 1909?
(title page)

III. Signatures in Books Published After 1918

$J\llcorner$

$J\llcorner$

$J\pm$

Jeannoret

Jeamerel

SELECTED BIBLIOGRAPHY

Note: This bibliography does not include books in Le Corbusier's own library which are listed here in Appendix A.

Autret, Jean, Ruskin and the French, before Proust, Geneva, 1965.

Banham, Reyner, Theory and Design in the First Machine Age, London, 1960.

Beardsley, M. C., Aesthetics from Classical Greece to the Present, New York, 1966.

Benoît-Lévy, Georges, La cité-jardin, 3 vols., Paris, 1911.

Besset, Maurice, Qui était Le Corbusier?, Geneva, 1968.

Blake, Peter, Le Corbusier, Baltimore, 1966.

Boudon, Philippe, Pessac de Le Corbusier, Paris, 1969.

Castex, Pierre, La critique d'art en France au XIXe siècle, Paris, 1966.

Catalogue de la Bibliothèque, École d'Art de La Chaux-de-Fonds, La Chaux-de-Fonds, 1919.

Champigneulle, Bernard, Perret, Paris, 1959.

Chavanne, Étienne & Michel Laville, "Les premières constructions de Le Corbusier," Werk, L, 1963, pp. 483-88.

Chipiez, Charles & Georges Perrot, Histoire de l'art dans l'Antiquité, Paris, 1882.

Choay, Françoise, Le Corbusier, New York, 1960.

Collins, Peter, Changing Ideals in Modern Architecture, London, 1965.

          Concrete, The Vision of a New Architecture, London, 1959.

Daria, Sophie, Le Corbusier, sociologue de l'urbanisme, Paris, 1964.

Dieulafoy, Marcel, L'Art antique de la Perse, vol. IV, Paris, 1885.

Erikson, Erik, Young Man Luther, New York, 1958.

Gauthier, Maximilien, Le Corbusier, ou l'architecture au service de l'homme, Paris, 1944.

Guadet, Julien, Éléments et théorie de l'architecture, Paris, 1902.

Herbert, Robert L., Modern Artists on Art, Englewood New Jersey, 1964.

Jeanneret, Charles-Édouard, Étude sur le mouvement d'art décoratif en Allemagne, La Chaux-de-Fonds, 1912.

Jones, Owen, The Grammar of Ornament, London, 1856.

Kaufmann, Walter A., Nietzsche: Philosopher, Psychologist, Antichrist, Princeton, 1950.

Le Corbusier, Almanach de l'architecture moderne, Paris, 1926.

        L'Art décoratif d'aujourd'hui, Paris, 1925.

        L'Atelier de la recherche patiente, Hatje, Stuttgart, 1960.

        Une Maison, un palais, Paris, 1928.

        Le Modulor, Boulogne-sur-Seine, 1948.

        Précisions sur un état présent de l'architecture et de l'urbanisme, Paris, 1930.

        L'Urbanisme, Paris, 1925.

        Vers une architecture, Paris, 1923.

        La Ville radieuse, Paris, 1933.

        Le Voyage d'Orient, Paris, 1966.

Le Corbusier & Pierre Jeanneret, Oeuvre complète, 1910-1929, Erlenbach, 1929.

McNeill, John T., The History and Character of Calvinism, New York, 1957.

Un Mouvement d'art à La Chaux-de-Fonds, La Chaux-de-Fonds, 1914.

Neff, Emery, The Poetry of History, New York, 1947 (chapter on Renan).

Nelli, René, Le phénomène cathare, Paris, 1964.

Ozenfant, Amedée, Mémoires, 1886-1962, Paris, 1968.

Ozenfant, Amedée & Ch.-É. Jeanneret, Après le cubisme, Paris, 1918.

Pawlowski, Christophe, Tony Garnier et les débuts de l'urbanisme fonctionnel en France, Paris, 1967.

Perret, Auguste, Contribution à une théorie de l'architecture, Paris, 1952.

Petit, Jean, Le Corbusier parle, Paris, 1967.

Rowe, Colin, "Chicago Frame," Architectural Design, Dec. 1970, pp. 641-47.

Ruskin, John, Lectures on Architecture and Painting, New York, 1856.

Serenyi, Peter, "Le Corbusier, Fourier, and the Monastery of Ema," The Art Bulletin, Dec. 1967, p. 277f.

Stewart, David, "Le Corbusier's Architectural Theory and L'Esprit Nouveau," (dissertation in preparation).

Tessenow, Heinrich, Hausbau und der gleichen, Baden-Baden, 1916(?).

          Der Wohnhausbau, Munich, 1909.

Von Moos, Stanislaus, Le Corbusier, Elemente einer Synthese, Frauenfeld, 1968.

Viollet-le-duc, Emmanuel, Entretiens sur l'architecture, Paris, 1863.

"The Work of Charles-Edouard Jeanneret," Perspecta, No. 6, 1960, pp. 28-33.

Zahar, Marcel, D'une doctrine d'architecture--Auguste Perret, Paris, 1959.

LIST OF ILLUSTRATIONS

1. Charles-Édouard Jeanneret, Engraved watch-case, ca. 1902.
   (Le Corbusier, L'atelier de la recherche patiente, Stuttgart, Gerd Hatje, 1960, p. 23)

2. René Lalique, Watch-cases, illustrated in Art et décoration, 1901.
   (Art et décoration, IX, 1901, p. 39)

3. Peter Behrens, Door, illustrated in The Studio, 1901.
   (The Studio, XXIV, 1901, p. 26)

4. Hermann Obrist, "Gewölbepfeiler," illustrated in Die Kunst, 1900.
   (Die Kunst, II, 1900, p. 178)

5. Jeanneret, Fallet House, La Chaux-de-Fonds, 1906.
   (Étienne Chavanne & Michel Laville, "Les premières constructions de Le Corbusier," Werk, L, December 1963, p. 483)

6. Owen Jones, The Grammar of Ornament, Plate IX.
   (London, 1856)

7. Jeanneret, Drawings, ca. 1902-06.
   (L'atelier de la recherche patiente, p. 24)

8. Jeanneret, Drawing, ca. 1902-06.
   (Maurice Besset, Qui était Le Corbusier?, Geneva, Skira, 1968, p. 14)

9. Illustration in Collignon's Mythologie figurée de la Grèce.
   (Maxime Collignon, Mythologie figurée de la Grèce, Paris, n.d., p. 13)

10. Jeanneret, Sketch left in his copy of Collignon's Mythologie.
    (La Fondation Le Corbusier)

11. Jeanneret, Drawing, ca. 1902-06.
    (L'atelier de la recherche patiente, p. 22)

12. Fallet House, Detail of bracket.
    (Chavanne & Laville, p. 483)

13. Inscription by L'Eplattenier to Jeanneret, in Schuré's Les grands initiés.
    (La Fondation Le Corbusier)

14. The "Monastery of Ema," near Florence.
    (Stanislaus Von Moos, Le Corbusier, Elemente einer Synthese, Frauenfeld, Huber, 1968, pl. 4)

15. Jeanneret, Drawing of the Baptistery, Siena.
(L'atelier de la recherche patiente, p. 26)

16. John Ruskin, Drawing of San Michele, Lucca, illustrated in The Stones of Venice.
(The Stones of Venice, London, 1858, vol. I, pl. XXI)

17. Jeanneret, Drawings of the Campo Santo, Pisa.
(Boesinger/Girsberger, Le Corbusier, 1910-1965, Zurich, Artemis, 1967, p. 20)

18. Jeanneret, Sketch of Santa Croce, Florence.
(Besset, p. 12)

19. Jeanneret, Jaquemet House, La Chaux-de-Fonds, 1907-08.
(Chavanne & Laville, p. 484)

20. Jeanneret, Stotzer House, La Chaux-de-Fonds, 1907-08.
(Chavanne & Laville, p. 485)

21. Perret's office, 25 bis rue Franklin, Paris.
(Siegfried Giedion, Space, Time & Architecture, Cambridge, Harvard, 1967, p. 330)

22. Page from Jeanneret's 1908 notebook on Corroyer's Architecture romane.
(La Fondation Le Corbusier)

23. Annotation by Jeanneret in his copy of Viollet-le-duc's Dictionnaire, vol.I, p. 66.
(La Fondation Le Corbusier)

24. Inscription by Jeanneret on first page of Viollet-le-duc's Dictionnaire.
(La Fondation Le Corbusier)

25. Le Corbusier, Sketch for "la main ouverte" monument, Chandigarh, 1950s.
(Boesinger/Girsberger, Le Corbusier, 1910-1965, p. 229)

26. Jeanneret, Design for "Ateliers d'art," 1910.
(Le Corbusier & Pierre Jeanneret, Oeuvre complète, 1910-1929, Zurich, Artemis, 1964, p. 22)

27. Fallet House bracket (Fig. 12), rotated.

28. Peter Behrens, A.E.G. Turbine Factory, Berlin, 1909.
(P.J. Cremers, Peter Behrens, Essen, G.D. Baedeker, 1928, pl. 27)

29. Heinrich Tessenow, Houses in Hellerau, 1909.
(Richard Hamann & Jost Hermand, Stilkunst um 1900, Berlin, Akademie Verlag, 1967, p. 201)

30. American grain elevators illustrated in 1913 Werkbund Jahrbuch.

31. Illustration in Vers une architecture.
(Le Corbusier, Vers une architecture, Paris, Vincent-Fréal, 1923, p. 17)

32. Annotation by Jeanneret in Cingria-Vaneyre's Entretiens.
(La Fondation Le Corbusier)

33. Jeanneret, Sketch of Turkish house, 1911.
(L'atelier de la recherche patiente, p. 31)

34. Jeanneret, Sketch of the Acropolis, Athens.
(Besset, p. 21)

35. Jeanneret, Jeanneret House, La Chaux-de-Fonds, 1912.
(Perspecta: Yale Architectural Journal, VI, 1960, p. 30)

36. Jeanneret, Favre-Jacot House, Le Locle, 1912.
(Perspecta, VI, 1960, p. 29)

37. Jeanneret, Schwob House, La Chaux-de-Fonds, 1916.
(Perspecta, VI, 1960, p. 33)

38. Jeanneret, Cinéma Scala, La Chaux-de-Fonds, 1916.
(Perspecta, VI, 1960, p. 31)

39. Schwob House, Plan of ground floor.
(Von Moos, fig. 7)

40. Jeanneret, "Dom-Ino" house design.
(Oeuvre complète, 1910-1929, p. 24)

41. Jeanneret, "Dom-Ino" structural system.
(Oeuvre complète, 1910-1929, p. 23)

42. Section through "Dom-Ino" system.
(Oeuvre complète, 1910-1929, p. 23)

43. Perret's Garage Ponthieu, Paris, during demolition, 1969.
(Author)

44. Jeanneret, Design for linkage of "Dom-Ino" houses.
(Oeuvre complète, 1910-1929, p. 24)

45. Hennebique system of reinforced concrete construction.
(Paul Christophe, Le béton armé et ses applications, Paris & Liège, 1902

46. Robert Maillard, Warehouse, Zurich, 1910.
(Giedion, p. 453)

47. Jeanneret, "Dom-Ino" site plan.
(Oeuvre complète, 1910-1929, p. 26)

48. "Dom-Ino" site plan.
(Oeuvre complète, 1910-1929, p. 25)

49. Garden-city plan illustrated in Benoît-Lévy's La cité-jardin.
(Georges Benoît-Lévy, La cité-jardin, Paris, 1911, vol. II, p. 14)

50. Site-plan by Raymond Unwin, illustrated in Benoît-Lévy's La cité-jardin.
(Vol. I, p. 73)

51. Typical page lay-out in Ozenfant's magazine Élan, 1915.

52. Jeanneret, Purist painting, 1920.
(L'atelier de la recherche patiente, p. 57)

53. Le Corbusier, "Citrohan" design, ca. 1920.
(Oeuvre complète, 1910-1929, p. 31)

54. Le Corbusier, LaRoche-Jeanneret Houses, Paris, 1922.
(Oeuvre complète, 1910-1929, p. 63)

55. Le Corbusier's correction of design by Perret in Bulletin de la vie artistique, 1924.
(La Fondation Le Corbusier)

56. Le Corbusier's application of "tracés régulateurs" to photograph of the Petit Trianon.
(Vers une architecture, p. 61)

57. Le Corbusier, Elevation of LaRoche-Jeanneret Houses.
(Vers une architecture, p. 64)

58. Le Corbusier, Elevation of Ozenfant Studio.
(Vers une architecture, p. 62)

59. Geometric analysis of Achaemenian structures in Dieulafoy's L'art antique de la Perse, 1885.
(Marcel Dieulafoy, L'art antique de la Perse, Paris, 1885, vol. IV, p. 28)

1. Jeanneret, Engraved watch-
   case, ca 1902.

2. René Lalique, Watch-cases, illustrated
in <u>Art et Décoration</u>, 1901.

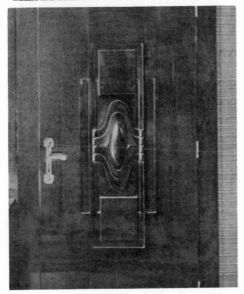

3. Peter Behrens, Door, illustrated
in <u>The Studio</u>, 1901.

4. Hermann Obrist, "Gewölbepfeiler,"
   illustrated in <u>Die Kunst</u>, 1900.

5. Jeanneret, Fallet House,
   La Chaux-de-Fonds, 1906.

6. Owen Jones, _The Grammar of Ornament_,
   Plate IX.

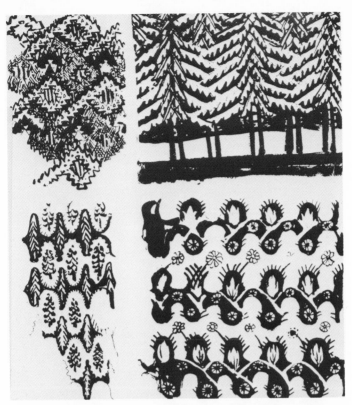

7. Jeanneret, Drawings, ca 1902-06.

8. Jeanneret, Drawing, ca 1902-06.

qui avait un ca-
Si plus tard ces
urent étroitement
'Hermès, c'est par
e de langage, qui
nom de ces bor-
:lui du dieu. Cette
ument, qui n'est
ble avec une exé-
bignée de la tête
nermès, s'est con-

FIG. 2.

IDOLE PRIMITIVE

HABILLÉE.

9. Illustration in Collignon's
   Mythologie figurée de la Grèce.

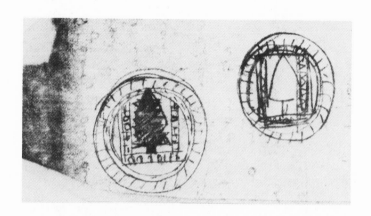

10. Jeanneret, Sketch left in his
    copy of Collignon's Mythologie.

11. Jeanneret, Drawing, ca 1902-06.

12. Fallet House, Detail of bracket.

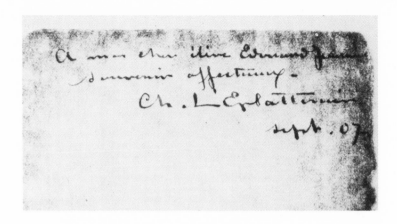

13. Inscription by L'Eplattenier to Jeanneret,
in Schuré's <u>Les grands initiés</u>.

14. The "Monastery of Ema," near Florence.

15. Jeanneret,
    Drawing of the
    Baptistery,
    Siena.

16. John Ruskin,
    Drawing of San
    Michele, Lucca
    (fr The Stones
    of Venice)

17. Jeanneret, Sketches of the Campo Santo, Pisa.

18. Jeanneret, Sketch of Santa Croce, Florence.

19. Jeanneret, Jaquemet House, La Chaux-de-Fonds, 1907-08.

20. Jeanneret, Stotzer House, La Chaux-de-Fonds, 1907-08.

21. Perret's office, 25 bis rue Franklin, Paris.

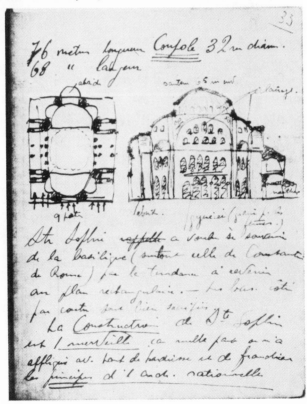

22. Jeanneret, Page from notebook, 1908.

23. Annotation by Jeanneret in his copy of Viollet-le-duc's <u>Dictionnaire</u>.

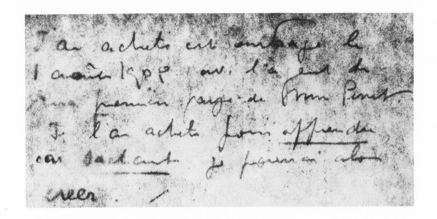

24. Inscription by Jeanneret on first page of
Viollet-le-duc's <u>Dictionnaire</u>.

25. Le Corbusier, Sketch for "la main ouverte"
monument, Chandigarh, 1950s.

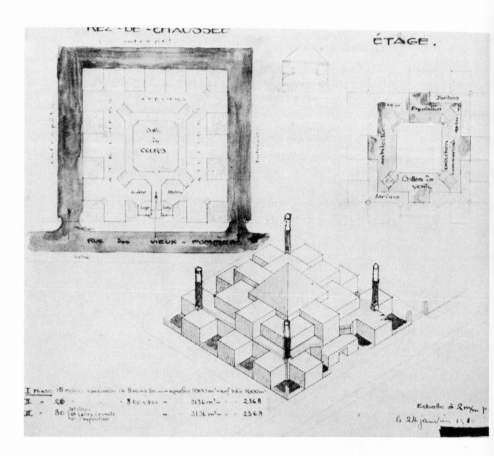

26. Jeanneret, Design for "Ateliers d'art," 1910.

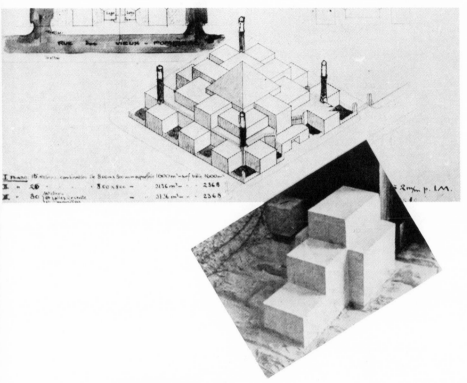

27. Rotated view of
    Fallet Hse bracket
    (Fig. 12), compared
    with "Ateliers d'art"
    design.

28. Peter Behrens, A.E.G. Factory, Berlin, 1909.

29. Heinrich Tessenow, Houses in Hellerau, 1909.

30. American grain elevators illustrated in 1913 Werkbund <u>Jahrbuch</u>.

31. Illustration in <u>Vers une architecture</u>, p 17.

GAUDENS. — Tandis que quelque belle esclave de couleur, les reins entourés d'un pagne rose, apporte le vin dans une amphore rouge, ornée de palmettes blanches, et que Constance, sur un tapis de Perse, surveille le bain de ses enfants en compagnie de Lygée et de quelques autres femmes circassiennes qui feraient des danses en rond pour les amuser.

CONSTANCE. — Non, pourtant pas, Gaudens, et ne me faites pas non plus immoler ce bélier aux faux dieux, que l'on reprocha tant à Ronsard... Car je suis encore chrétien et monogame, malgré tous mes goûts pour l'antiquité. Et puis, *soyons sérieux*, comme l'on dit à Genève, car, avec ces plaisanteries, vous allez faire croire que tout ce que nous avons dit ne sont que des mystifications pour indigner nos journalistes, et je ne veux rien avoir à dédire des préceptes de discipline que j'ai formulés pour le bien de ma patrie, des vrais patriotes et des gens sensibles.

GAUDENS. — Quitte à vous attendre à des désillusions, si vous pensez voir mettre vos principes à exécution chez nos Suisses français.

CONSTANCE. — Peut-être bien, mais qu'importe en somme, puisque d'avoir créé cette renaissance idéale, c'est déjà avoir réagi contre les courants germanisateurs et contre le sentimentalisme. Et, maintenant, vous avez obtenu ce que vous vouliez de moi, Clothaire, vous m'avez fait prononcer une profession de foi; que ces paroles demeurent; elles risqueront d'agir dans le temps par leur vertu intime, et n'en parlons plus.

La Belotte,
Florence, 1905-1907.

32. Annotation by Jeanneret in
Cingria-Vaneyres's **Entretiens**.

33. Jeanneret, Sketch of Turkish house, 1911.

34. Jeanneret, Sketch of the Acropolis, Athens.

35. Jeanneret, Jeanneret House,
La Chaux-de-Fonds, 1912.

36. Jeanneret, Favre-Jacot House, Le Locle, 1912.

37. Jeanneret, Schwob House, La Chaux-de-Fonds, 1916.

38. Jeanneret, Cinéma Scala, La Chaux-de-Fonds, 1916.

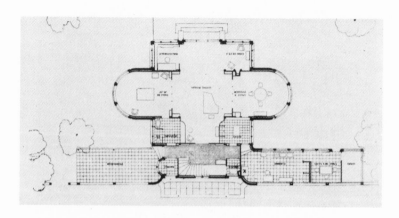

39. Schwob House, plan of ground floor.

40. Jeanneret, "Dom-Ino" house design.

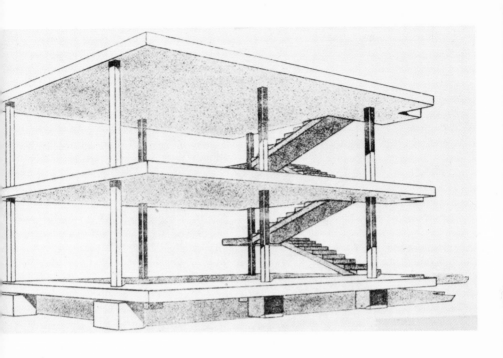

Jeanneret, "Dom-Ino" structural system.

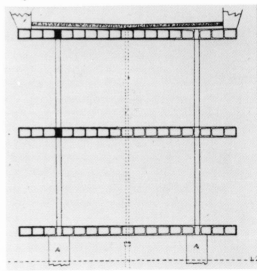

42. Section through
   "Dom-Ino" system.

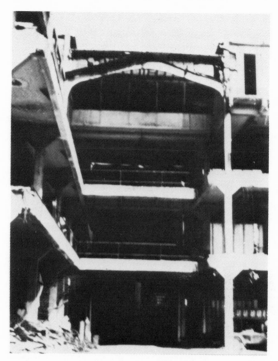

43. Perret's Garage Ponthieu, Paris,
during demolition, 1969.

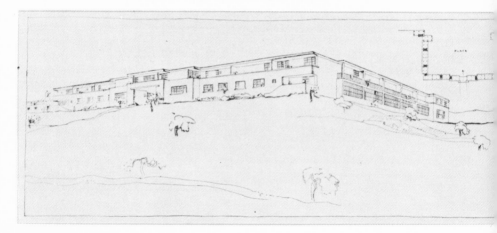

44. Jeanneret, Design for linkage of "Dom-Ino" houses.

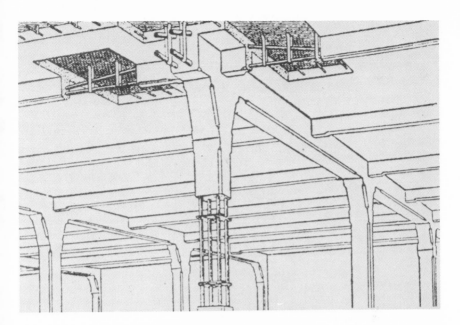

45. Hennebique system of reinforced concrete construction.

46. Robert Maillard, Warehouse, Zurich, 1910.

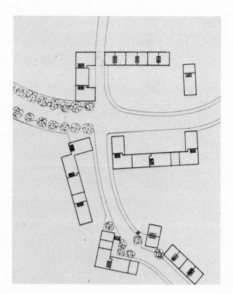

47. Jeanneret, "Dom-Ino" site plan.

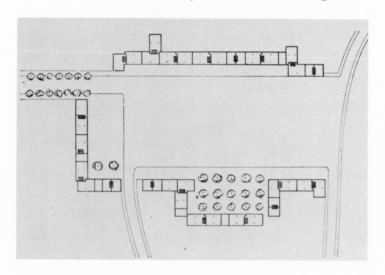

48. Jeanneret, "Dom-Ino" site plan.

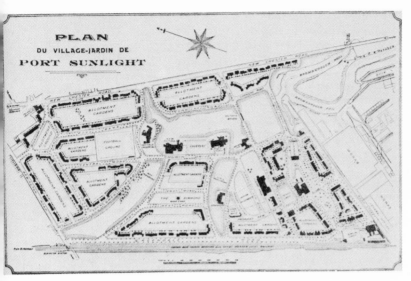

49. Garden-city plan illustrated in Benoit-Lévy's
La cité-jardin, 1911.

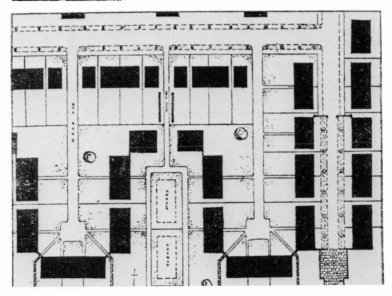

0. Site-plan by Raymond Unwin, illustrated in Benoit-Lévy.

*   a   u   x   c   a   m   a   r   a

LE CUBISME EST PEINTURE BOCHE
Voilà l'injure où descendent ses adversaires.

TELUM IMBELLE   •   •   •

En rétablissant construction & infusant synthèse, le Cubisme ouvrait chantier
de sensibilité. Car il n'est de sensibilité que RATIONNELLE, rien ne pouvant
se greffer à l'inconsistance.
Et c'est par la sensibilité rationnelle que se caractérisent à la fois le Cubisme
& le « CLAIR GÉNIE DE NOTRE RACE ».
A moins que n'apparaisse mieux imprégnée de ce génie la phrase suivante :

« Hier encore le Cubisme, végétation monstrueuse, décorait dignement la boutonnière de nos
snobs. La rose malodorante était toute l'originalité dont nous nous piquions. »

(EMILE BAYARD.)

LE CUBISME SERAIT BOCHE

Simple question :
— « Lui connaîtriez-vous un précurseur allemand ? »
— « Non_____MAIS

DÈS qu'apparut le Cubisme les Allemands se mirent

à l'imiter »   (CAMILLE MAUCLAIR)

?   ?   ?

?

Ajoutons, à titre surérogatoire, que l'Allemagne ne fournit pas plus d'imita-
teurs que de précurseurs :

« Berlin méprisait les Welches tombés dans l'aberration cubiste. »

(CAMILLE MAUCLAIR)

*   *
*

51. Typical page lay-out in <u>Élan</u>, 1915.

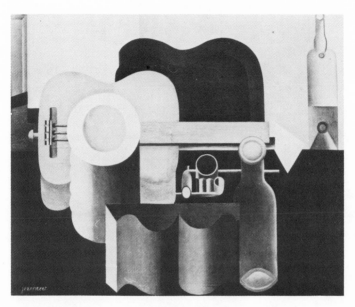

52. Jeanneret, Purist painting, 1920.

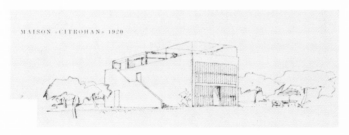

MAISON «CITROHAN» 1920

53. Le Corbusier, "Citrohan" design, ca 1920.

54. Le Corbusier, LaRoche-Jeanneret Houses, Paris, 1922.

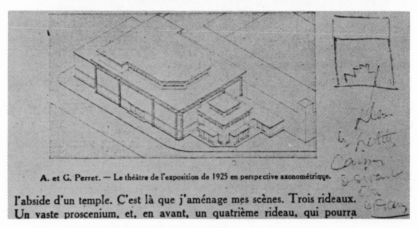

A. et G. Perret. — Le théâtre de l'exposition de 1925 en perspective axonométrique.

l'abside d'un temple. C'est là que j'aménage mes scènes. Trois rideaux. Un vaste proscenium, et, en avant, un quatrième rideau, qui pourra

55. Le Corbusier's correction of design by Perret in Bulletin de la vie artistique, 1924.

56. Le Corbusier's application of "tracés régulateurs"
to photograph of the Petit Trianon.

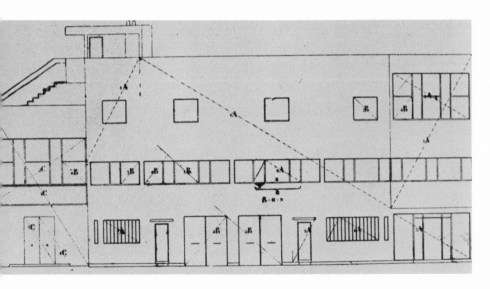

Le Corbusier, Elevation of LaRoche-Jeanneret houses.

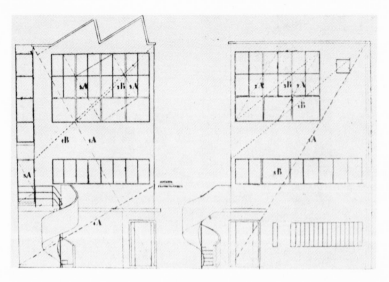

58. Le Corbusier, Elevation of Ozenfant Studio.

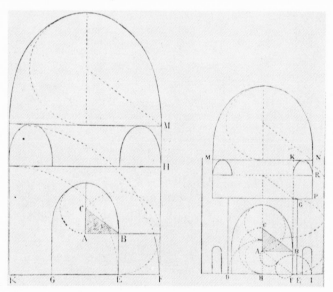

59. Geometric analysis of Achaemenian structures in Dieulafoy's <u>L'art antique de la Perse</u>.